APPLIED LINGUISTICS IN THE REAL WORLD

Applied Linguistics in the Real World introduces readers to situations in which applied linguistics can be and is used. Presenting a panoramic view of the interdisciplinary area of applied linguistics and highlighting the diverse range of twenty-first century occupations that have linguistics at their center, this book:

- Describes, discusses, and furthers the idea that linguistic knowledge is useful everywhere—from forensic investigations to diplomatic talks; from disability studies to creative writing; and from translation studies to machine learning;
- Breaks new ground, expanding beyond well-established areas of applied-linguistic interest in its inclusion of disability studies, peace studies, and the new literature;
- Provides readers with original research questions and practical applications for them to expand their own research portfolios.

Written in an accessible, direct style, *Applied Linguistics in the Real World* will be essential reading for all students of applied linguistics and is an important addition to the library of anyone who feels passionate and inspired by language matters.

Patricia Friedrich is a Professor of Rhetoric and Composition/Linguistics at Arizona State University, USA, where she also serves as Associate Dean at the New College of Interdisciplinary Arts and Sciences.

APPLIED LINGUISTICS IN THE REAL WORLD

Patricia Friedrich

Routledge
Taylor & Francis Group
LONDON AND NEW YORK

First published 2019
by Routledge
2 Park Square, Milton Park, Abingdon, Oxon OX14 4RN

and by Routledge
52 Vanderbilt Avenue, New York, NY 10017

Routledge is an imprint of the Taylor & Francis Group, an informa business

British Library Cataloguing-in-Publication Data
A catalogue record for this book is available from the British Library

Library of Congress Cataloging-in-Publication Data
Names: Friedrich, Patricia, author.
Title: Applied linguistics in the real world/Patricia Friedrich.
Description: London; New York, NY: Routledge, 2019. | Includes bibliographical references and index.
Identifiers: LCCN 2018045829 | ISBN 9781138630321 (hardback) | ISBN 9781138630338 (pbk.) | ISBN 9780429032219 (e-book)
Subjects: LCSH: Applied linguistics.
Classification: LCC P129 .F75 2019 | DDC 418–dc23
LC record available at https://lccn.loc.gov/2018045829

ISBN: 978-1-138-63032-1 (hbk)
ISBN: 978-1-138-63033-8 (pbk)
ISBN: 978-0-429-03221-9 (ebk)

Typeset in Bembo
by Deanta Global Publishing Services, Chennai, India

For Akua Duku Anokye, a most wonderful scholar and role model

CONTENTS

PREFACE

For the last several years, I have invested my time in expanding the reach of my linguistic investigations any way I can and conducting research that is transdisciplinary in nature and thus addresses real questions in the world. In that spirit, I set out to write *Applied Linguistics in the Real World.* I wanted it to be pragmatic, accessible, and useful for a variety of people interested in language and its relationship to practices in the world around us.

The advanced undergraduate, graduate student, and (to an extent) early-career professor interested in linguistics can find a number of intermediate- and advanced-level books in sociolinguistics, applied linguistics, and language studies. Many of these books dwell on the intersection of theory and practice, and on the relationship between linguistics, education, and language acquisition. These are all important aspects of linguistics to cover, and students/researchers are lucky to be able to refer to these publications and use them as an integral part of their instruction. However, in browsing through these books, and using a few of them to teach, I noticed that while essential, many of these books do not spend much time, if any, on the new areas of action and on the doors that linguistic knowledge can open for the students and readers in terms of concrete ideas for research and practice.

I am referring specifically to real-word, many times outside-of-academia areas in which linguistic knowledge plays a central role, whether by itself or integrated with other multidisciplinary knowledge. *Applied Linguistics in the Real World* proposes to present readers with a broad survey of areas, some of them quite new and others well established, where learners and scholars of linguistics can apply their knowledge. They range from aiding police investigations through forensic linguistics to improving translation techniques; from working with computer programming experts interested in artificial languages to designing speech-therapy courses; from training medical personnel on issues pertaining to the language of disability to working toward peace. *Applied Linguistics in the Real World* presents a panoramic view of these expanding fields and of the new occupations of the twenty-first century that have linguistics at their center. Given the broad scope, each chapter offers commentary on a few aspects of these inter- and transdisciplinary efforts while showing other areas to be addressed through possible, suggested research questions and a list of suggested readings.

Applied Linguistics in the Real World can work as a course book (or supplemental material) for independent studies at the undergraduate level, 400/500-level courses (US or equivalent) in applied linguistics (both of these if the students are advanced), sociolinguistics, linguistics electives, and one-to-one mentoring of graduate students. It can also be used as a self-development tool by early career faculty, especially those who come to linguistics from related areas or through interdisciplinary pursuits, for the identification of possible research projects, and/or for collaboration with graduate students.

Because of the scope of the book, I envision that it could be used in a variety of courses rather than a specific one. Likewise, the scope is certainly global rather than local. Though I focus on English(es), it is not difficult to extrapolate the language dynamics discussed here to other languages. I also expect it can be a book that one reads on their own and that they can keep for future reference when they try to think through new projects.

There is an increased flow of ideas and of work between academia and professional areas. It is not uncommon for students to pursue graduate studies before working in the private sector or in non-profit organizations, where they have to apply their linguistic knowledge to an ever-broadening number of fields. However, even within applied areas, there can be a tendency to leave a gap between knowing that linguistic knowledge could have practical applications and delineating what those practical applications are in concrete terms and examples. *Applying Linguistics in the Real World* proposes to be one of the venues to bridging that gap.

The book is intended for students with a more advanced knowledge of linguistics and early professionals/academics in language studies who are making decisions about areas of research and activity. It provides ideas for topics of investigation and areas for action. While I am indeed casting a wide net, I believe that provided a reader has at least an intermediate knowledge of linguistics, they could still benefit from the book, and the more advanced reader (an Assistant Professor, for example) might know quite a bit about Second Language Writing (SLA) but be new to forensic linguistics. Therefore, both an Honors student who needs to develop a graduating thesis or applied project and a more advanced researcher aiming for interdisciplinarity or embarking on a project in a new subfield of linguistics can make use of the text.

Each of the chapters can be read in isolation or as part of the whole book. Some information is referenced across chapters, showing just how transdisciplinary linguistics research can really be.

ACKNOWLEDGMENTS

I am very pleased to present to readers this work, which received the title of *Applied Linguistics in the Real World*. In it, I have tried to share thoughts and ideas about the application of linguistic knowledge to several areas of action and practice. While some of them are more traditional areas of overlap with applied linguistics (e.g., language education, TESOL, world Englishes), others are less often written about (e.g., forensics, peace, computer science, and disability studies). I hope there will be ideas here to help graduate students, early-career scholars, other scholars interested in linguistic matters, and all those who have an appreciation for language to forge their own research agendas.

In my attempt to cover such a large territory, I was lucky enough to count on the expertise of colleagues and friends who were so generously willing to entertain my questions, provide me with informal commentary, and listen to my creative (I hope) interpretations of real-world phenomena. I would like to thank Julie Amparano Garcia, who is always willing to talk to me about creative writing and share her experience with the written word. Thank you to Cristian Go, for all the conversations about computer science and technology.

Francisco Cardoso Gomes de Matos has, for a significant length of time now, been my mentor on issues of peace and diplomacy, and I am forever grateful for his complete dedication to a peace achieved through language and for the wisdom he shares so selflessly with colleagues like me.

To my linguist friends and colleagues, in particular Aya Matsuda, Matthew Prior, Jeff MacSwan, and Eduardo Henrique Diniz de Figueiredo, thank you for always being willing to have a lively (often virtual) conversation regarding any aspect of linguistics. I would also like to acknowledge Kendra Beeley who agreed to contribute and write with me the chapter on the intersection of applied linguistics and speech pathology, thus furthering my own creative work on that important intersection.

To my academic unit, the New College of Interdisciplinary Arts and Sciences at ASU, I owe thanks for the support I have received for the last 15 years and for an interdisciplinary vision that allows me to do what I do. I am grateful that Arizona State University is a place for innovation, creative ideas, interdisciplinary undertakings, diversity, and access.

To my family, I speak directly: I am forever grateful for the enthusiasm with which you greet all the things I set out to do and for being supportive of me in all spheres of life.

And thank you to Routledge for once again believing in my work and my writing.

Patricia Friedrich
Peoria, Arizona
August 26, 2018

1

UNDERSTANDING APPLIED LINGUISTICS

THIS CHAPTER WILL DO THE FOLLOWING

1. Discuss the meaning(s) of applied linguistics.
2. Summarize important elements of the history of applied linguistics.
3. Present ideas regarding the relationship between theoretical and applied linguistics and different branches of linguistics.
4. Present aspects of applied linguistics in the real world.
5. Describe what the book contains in its subsequent chapters.
6. Provide ideas for students and scholars who would like to start work in applied linguistics.

Introduction

There are two quotes that encompass the mood with which I set out to write this book. The first, by Thomas Friedman (2016), is recent and speaks directly of the historical moment we are living:

> Anyone who falls back in tried-and-true formulae or dogmatisms in a world changing this fast is asking for trouble. Indeed, as the world becomes more interdependent and complex, it becomes more vital than ever to widen your aperture and to synthesize more perspectives.

What better way to set out to widen the scope of applied linguistics than to "synthesize more perspectives" in a world of increasing velocity?

The other, one of my favorites about language, for it speaks of everything applied linguists and sociolinguists in their effort to be descriptive tend to believe in, is by Emerson (1883, p. 147) and goes, "Language is a city to the building of which every human being brought a stone."

The first decades of the twenty-first century have been marked by very quick changes in social and linguistic dynamics, fueled by our growing reliance on digital modes of communication, arguably at a speed not seen before in modern history. Friedman above has claimed that the year 2007, the time of the release of the iPhone, coinciding with the advent of widespread use of social media such as Facebook, created an exponential change in the role and scope of technology use in our lives, one that our cognition is striving to accompany, sometimes with less than perfect results. In that sense, Friedman argues, we are in a constant state of catching up, trying to cope with a complex reality of lives in flux both within and without our computer and phone screens. I wonder if it becomes hard to bring a stone to build a city, as Emerson proposes in the second quote, if we hardly have the energy to move forward.

Part of our cognitive stress is related to the amount of information we are exposed to every day, the many decisions we have to make about their relevance, and the sheer amount of stimulation that processing such information results in. Bohn and Short (2012, p. 980) estimate that

> in 2008, Americans consumed about 1.3 trillion hours of information outside of work, an average of almost 12 hours per person per day. Media consumption totaled 3.6 zettabytes and 1,080 trillion words, corresponding to 100,500 words and 34 gigabytes for the average person on an average day.

Notice that these numbers, already several years behind us, come from a time when, compared to today, the average American was being exposed to a lot less information, and yet the figures are already staggering. It is not hard to hypothesize that more recent numbers would show even greater cognitive stress and impact on behaviors, including linguistic ones.

While taxing and challenging, these changes—one could argue—have made for a democratization of communication. After all, the advent and multiplication of blogs, personal and professional websites, self-published books and e-books, as well as the possibility of posting for a large number of followers and friends on Twitter and Facebook could potentially allow everyone to have "a voice," one unregulated by the alleged gatekeepers of other times, a truly democratic building of a linguistic city.

However—one could also argue—the downside of this widespread exchange of information and opinion is that oftentimes factual knowledge and the very idea of truth can become lost in the noise created by so many conflicting expressions, which reveal very different levels of understanding of the phenomena they seek to explore. Additionally, while the globalization of information at first created access to diverse voices, cultures, and expressions, it now seems to be the case that speech communities have formed among those who share values and beliefs to the point of stark opposition between groups.

A search for endorsement of views sponsored within those groups has created political, cultural, and linguistic divides that go beyond the divides we found before our lives went digital. In many contexts, it has become hard to distinguish between fact and opinion, informed expert testimony and confabulation. It is no wonder that the *Oxford English Dictionary*'s Word of the Year 2016 was "post-truth," whose definition is "relating to or denoting circumstances in which objective facts are less influential in shaping public opinion than appeals to emotion and personal belief."[1] In the tension between appeals to logos, pathos, and ethos, a closer look at Internet media would likely indicate that the two latter appeals are taking over a lot of space that once belonged to the former, and although many of us might have already realized this shift has consequences, its full implications will likely be felt for years to come.

In bringing up these factors, I am not preparing myself to defend some idea of absolute, irrefutable truth and to place it in opposition to the notion of relative knowledge embedded in cultural, affective, and contextual understandings. Quite the opposite. Never before were diverse, sensible voices more needed in a global debate often marked, seemingly paradoxically, by superficiality and extreme views. Nevertheless, the democratization of knowledge should not be an excuse for an "everything goes" approach to sharing information and to learning (be that learning informal or formal), where opinions replace expertise and where five-minute Internet searches are considered enough background research for a particular view to be then advanced.

Indeed, we are in more need of experts than ever. As opinions get polarized, it is not uncommon for people to seek out only those media containing views that reinforce what they already believe in, and this in turn helps the proliferation of misinformation and antagonism. In the end, it is not unusual for discussions to not resonate with reality anymore. In a post-truth world, it is much harder to tell fact from fiction.

In this climate, education itself is at a crossroads: when so many are the sources of (mis)information that compete for a viewer's or reader's attention, it is often hard to convince learners, and other stakeholders, to reexamine beliefs, points of views, and standpoints—however necessary such examination is for learning. Education runs the risk of serving only to support particular views, and newer findings, especially those which might contradict long-held or now-cherished beliefs, are in greater danger of being ignored or chastised.

What has this social reality got to do with applied linguistics? It turns out, quite a lot. First of all, half-truths, post-truths, and lies are conveyed through language. Rhetorical devices are often replaced with logical fallacies, and content analysis oftentimes reveals inconsistencies that can go unnoticed by laypersons. Flame wars erupt, trolling becomes common, and long-standing principles of politeness and courtesy can fall by the wayside. These dynamics are facilitated (or hampered) by use and misuse of language. Note that when I write of misuse of language I do not mean prescriptive ideas about split infinitives or sentences that end in prepositions. These are common and linguistically justifiable usage matters. What I am referring to is the misuse of language to exclude, disrespect, or silence others. Those are the ones applied linguistics should really be concerned about.

Furthermore, our digital selves have come to rely on many different kinds of text and forms of linguistic expression to try and stay relevant and participate in our speech communities, communities of practice, and increasingly complex linguistic networks. Because we, as digital selves, interact locally, regionally, and globally, often across varieties and linguistic borders (however porous those are), new ways of communication as well as new genres have had to be forged. Living language has always been in flux and susceptible to changes, but the speed and the reach of these changes have increased, arguably like never before, and at present they show no signs of slowing down. A 2017 study by global tech company Asurion revealed that on average Americans check their phones 80 times a day, with millennials checking on average 150 times a day.[2] These are for the most part linguistic or partially-linguistic interactions in social media which have come to require our attention every 12 minutes.

Digital communications have direct impact on our language use but also many indirect ramifications. For example, forensic linguistics as a science has accelerated greatly with the study of digital texts, Internet searches, and the incorporation of large data sets that make corpus studies possible. In fact, corpus studies facilitated by our sharp technological tools can now cut across pretty much every area of applied linguistics, from studies in English as a Lingua Franca (ELF) to content and discourse analysis of literary and journalistic texts.

In that context, language experts, capable of transferring knowledge to influence the key elements of social development of our time have a central role to play in making connections between theoretical knowledge, practical application, and linguistic problems in the real world. That is where the title and the premise of this book come from. As the reader will see in this introduction, my aspiration is to place this work at the intersection of linguistic theory, what became known as applied linguistics (practice), and a further realm where that application goes beyond areas such as Teaching English to Speakers of Other Languages (TESOL), writing instruction, and language acquisition to eventually populate, influence, and solve pressing problems in areas as diverse as forensics and engineering. In this intersection, mixed methodologies and partnerships with experts from other fields are not only desirable but *sine qua non* elements of success. While heavily linguistic, those realms are not *exclusively* linguistic, and whereas social problems can have a linguistic component to them, more often than not, they will not be exclusively linguistic.

Although some intellectual enterprises require that the scope be narrowed for the sake of depth, what I attempt to do in this book requires a lot of breadth. Whereas I do not believe these efforts have to be at odds, the kind of flexibility that the latter requires is sometimes confounded with lack of rigor. It is not difficult to be faced with the fear that to cover a lot of ground one is necessarily losing complexity. What needs to be considered, in this case, is that application of linguistic knowledge to very different areas still depends on a common thread of linguistic expertise and understanding of language dynamics that transcend disciplinary boundaries. Applied linguistics knowledge that is solid and sound will necessarily have to stand the test of application to many areas of human interaction. Applied linguistics does not stop being applied linguistics because participants in observable linguistic exchanges are in a speech-therapy environment instead of in a classroom, or because the data being studied by a forensic linguist comes from a fiction book rather than an authentic dialogue or a second-language learning textbook. In sum, the dynamics of language remain across the most different environments of language use, and it is the job of an applied linguist to not only identify all these realms of use but also to study and try to understand them.

In the chapters that follow, I will attempt to argue for an applied linguistics that goes everywhere and forges alliance with many disciplines in its search for expansion and further meaning. Besides a discussion on the elements of these partnerships, each chapter brings ideas for research for people who are passionate about language and want to ask an ever-widening set of questions, whether their primary affiliation is with linguistics or with related disciplines.

What applied linguistics is: Conceptual elements and historical antecedents

Simpson (2011b, p. 1) defines applied linguistics as "the academic field which connects knowledge about language to decision-making in the real world." In this book, I am choosing that definition over others, some of which are more well known and widely used, because of its focus on action, on making decisions informed by linguistic knowledge. I am also privileging the idea of "decision making" grounded on sound linguistic knowledge and the "real-world" reference, which also appears in the title of the book. I am giving applied linguistics great latitude in terms of scope and greater flexibility in terms of influential theories, which come not only from linguistics and language studies but also sociology, anthropology, business management, and cultural studies, among others.

Linguists often use the launch of the *Journal of Language Learning: A Journal of Applied Linguistics* in the late 1940s as the starting point of the discipline (Davis, 1999; Kaplan, 2002; Grabe, 2010). At that stage, applied linguistics was framed as "applied directly to second language teaching and also in some cases to first language literacy and language arts issues as well" (Grabe, 2010, p. 1).

As I will argue and demonstrate throughout this book, now, in the twenty-first century, the roles and the uses of applied linguistics have expanded much beyond its original sphere, which is not to say that those do not continue to be important realms of application. In fact, they were always there: what changed was our willingness to journey to those realms. Language learning, second-language acquisition (SLA), pedagogy, and first- and second-language writing not only continue to advance as independent disciplines and as areas of applied linguistics interest and action, but they also help provide ideas and insights that can then be reapplied to the new additions to applied linguistics realms of action and influence. For example, understanding of language acquisition can be used in forensic investigations and knowledge of both sociolinguistics and language acquisition (alongside syntax, semantics, etc.) is necessary for the development of artificial intelligence. Disability studies projects often make reference to analysis of texts, especially discourse and content analysis. World Englishes is a whole field of English studies that relies heavily on applied linguistics knowledge. Fully understanding translation principles requires a certain knowledge of sociolinguistics, cross-cultural communication, and applied linguistics.

Grabe (2010, p. 2) calls applied linguistics a "language-centered problem-solving enterprise." Its potential started to be further realized by the addition of areas of performance such as rethinking assessment, addressing the challenges of multilingualism, and influencing language planning. The idea of solving real-world problems has been a constant presence in applied linguistic formulations since the 1970s. However, at first, the notion of "applying" linguistics to address real-life issues was geared toward improving language teaching more specifically.

That mission was so important that Cook (2005), for example, divides the history of applied linguistics into three periods: 1950–1984, when language-teaching application was the focus; 1984–mid 1990s, after Widdowson's challenge to that notion led to the expansion of applied linguistics and its parallel positioning to other branches such as historical linguistics; and the mid 1990s–present, when "the theoretical and empirical investigation of real-world problems in which language is a central issue" (Brumfit, 1995, p. 27, cited in Cook, 2005) gained momentum.

Grabe (2010, p. 3) contends that it was in the 1980s that applied linguistics expanded to systematically include issues beyond language teaching and its ramifications, such as lexicography, language and technology, and corpus linguistics, for example. It is intuitive to imagine that once linguistic knowledge makes it to the classroom, it cannot stop there. Those in the classroom will have questions about and new insight regarding the place of language in their lives beyond the classroom: they will remember a time when their intention did not match their language production and the results were not what they expected, or, on the other hand, they will note that one particular speech or utterance was very well received and will try to abstract the reasons why, so that they can reapply such knowledge when similar situations arise. That is when other lines of applied linguistics research become necessary.

The real shift that made possible the kind of research and practice I outline in this book came in the 1990s. Referencing van Lier (1997), Grabe (2010) explains:

> For applied linguistics research, the shift to discourse analysis, descriptive data analysis, and interpretation of language data in their social/cultural

settings all indicate a shift in valuing observable language data over theoretical assumptions about what should count as data.

The breadth of linguistic data that qualifies as such in this vision of applied linguistics is what makes possible that at present many more areas of human action and interaction participate as data-generating environments for linguistic enquiry, from forensics to diplomacy, from computer technology to speech therapy.

Applied linguistics within the realm of linguistics

The existence of an applied discipline is often taken for granted as a counterpart to a theoretical one, as if the separation of the two were a natural rather than an academic proposition. Thus, over the years, it has become common to contrast theoretical linguistics and applied linguistics as if they were two sides of the same coin, sides that never really meet. However, the coin analogy fails to convey an awareness of the bilateral movement that allows one branch to feed information to the other and vice-versa and to many times work in tandem rather than in opposition or competition. In that sense, language-theory knowledge should ideally inform practices in the real world, and insight gained through those practices should be used to revisit and revise theory.

Unfortunately, there is a greater tendency for theoretical linguistics to inform applied linguistics than the other way around. This binary—theory and practice—is, however, not the only possible way to systematize linguistics, nor necessarily the most productive. Common too is the opposition of prescriptive and descriptive linguistics, where the former supposes extrinsic linguistic laws that must be observed for language to "count," as I mentioned earlier. These can include rules of grammar and syntax (e.g., "Don't split your infinitives," "Don't end a sentence with a preposition"). The latter is more concerned about describing language as it is used and about understanding the intrinsic rules that help define such use (e.g., "users of variety X tend to use double negatives in the context of Y and that means Z"). In terms of applied linguistics, researchers with a background in pragmatics, sociolinguistics—and other disciplines that focus on users and uses of language in context—tend to privilege descriptive views over prescriptive ones, though prescriptive views themselves can become the object of their study (i.e., how they occur, who supports them, who is left out, what kind of status they represent).

Other configurations are also in circulation, for example, that in which theoretical, descriptive, applied, and experimental linguistics are presented as complementary. Within this framework, disciplines such as syntax and semantics are considered theoretical; historical linguistics and sociolinguistics are considered descriptive; computational and forensic are areas within applied linguistics; and experimental linguistics overlaps with psycholinguistics and quantitative linguistics (Hemforth, 2013) in that they often engage quantitative methods.

I find the inclusion of experimental linguistics as parallel to the other three branches problematic because its description seems to point more at methodological decisions (which in truth, are available to many of the other areas) rather than to a realm/research focus or a set of beliefs and values regarding language. If we were to bring together descriptive and applied areas and posit that they often use experimental, qualitative, quantitative, and mixed methods to arrive and descriptions and approaches to solving linguistic problems in the world, then the remark by Prideaux et al. (1980, p. 18) would largely apply: "Although experimental linguistics was prompted by developments in linguistic theory, the direction of influence has been largely one-way (cf. Kess 1976)." I will speak of the need for multidirectionality in linguistics a little later in this introduction.

Citing Widdowson (2000, p. 5), Davies and Elder (2004b, p. 9) discuss the distinction and the tension between applied linguistics and linguistics applied, in which the former represents the expert view on the application of linguistic theory to correct a problem and the latter the application of linguistics that "uses language data to develop our linguistic knowledge about language" (2005, p. 11). In that sense, one represents an outward movement that expands expert knowledge into the world whereas the second moves inward to ultimately change linguistic theory itself. I see both dynamics at work in this book and in the kind of proposal it makes for the engagement of linguistic knowledge.

Dineen (1995, pp. 11–12) writes of a three-way partition that includes 1. Theoretical; 2. Applied; and 3. Comparative, historical, and descriptive linguistics, thus giving the impression that the first two are in categories of their own and that the latter three are grouped together in that the methodology used would help define the realm one is in. This is a challenging partition because applied linguistics can engage, for example, in comparative pursuits and theoretical linguistics can use historical data as a springboard to theory building. Either one can engage in description of linguistic phenomena too.

It is hard to say that any of these frameworks is "incorrect." Rather, depending on the goals behind each taxonomy, a particular one might be more useful than the others. In general, I will avoid unnecessary "problematizations" in this book. Often times, academic discourse is peppered with lengthy discussions on the inadequacy of terms, the impossibility of frameworks, and the difficulty of the research endeavor itself. It would be incompatible with the message of this book, which proposes to motivate students and scholars to go solve problems in the world, to dedicate too much space and energy to digressing into the ontology of research. That is, I would like to avoid too much "deconstructing" to engage more productively with building up. While it is important to maintain scientific rigor, it is also paramount to find creative solutions to challenges and to spend most of the time working on the challenges themselves rather than on the limitations of language and taxonomies. For the sake of simplicity and functionality, I have chosen to use the traditional partition between theoretical and applied linguistics in this book, with four important provisos:

1. The framework that includes theoretical and applied linguistics will also reflect an appreciation for the descriptive nature of some of its endeavors, including studies in sociolinguistics, discourse analysis, and historical linguistics.

2. A further, interdisciplinary group of areas of action will reflect the impetus toward the application of linguistic knowledge to very diverse aspects of human experience, from forensic investigations to diplomatic training. These, in turn, can inform and provide insights into the nature of language itself.
3. It is understood that the reflections, suggestions, and descriptions in this book presuppose multidirectional movement and flux of ideas across the three constitutive parts. In that sense, what we know about phonetics and phonology informs practices, methods, and conclusions in forensic analysis; knowledge of world Englishes impacts how diplomats are educated; but at the same time, what we learn while implementing language policy should cause us to revisit sociolinguistic knowledge; and as we program computers to translate from one language to another, we might want to reconsider tenets of syntax. An additional implication of this view of the world is that there is no hierarchy of value where theoretical linguistics is above applied linguistics, nor is one, in itself, more rigorous than the other.
4. The real-world realms represented in the third column below (only a sample), are not exclusively linguistic. Successful performance and problem-solving in those areas will often require knowledge beyond linguistics, and therefore might depend on successful partnerships across and between the humanities, social sciences, and mathematical/natural sciences. That is the reason they are in the third column in the first place. For example, to do forensic linguistics, one might come to rely on sociolinguistics, phonetics and phonology, computer science, and statistics but also knowledge of the law. To do medical humanities, one might want to align biomedical expertise, discourse analysis, semantics, and historical linguistics. To investigate within digital domains, a researcher might rely on sociology, linguistics, anthropology, and other disciplines, including computer science and coding, performed by self or others. Below is a representation of these dimensions in context. I acknowledge that this representation is as subjective as any other I might have come up with and I offer it not to problematize other configurations but to facilitate access to the reasoning behind the book.

Table 1.1 lays out some examples from the ways of seeing linguistics that I privilege in this book. Areas often considered descriptive and applied are combined because they all concern themselves with what happens when human beings use language (and not how they should use language for example through notions of ideal language users). These stand in complementarity to the mental models that make communication and language use possible and that are major foci for the disciplines on the left. In turn, the rightmost column does not stand in opposition to the middle or (or even in opposition to theoretical linguistics) but rather indicates that application is being pushed even further.

As for the challenges faced by applied linguistics, one of the most prominent is the misbelief to which I alluded above, still held by some, that application is second to theory and to abstraction, which would mean that applied knowledge is of a

TABLE 1.1 The Many Faces of Linguistics

Theoretical Linguistics	*Applied and Descriptive Linguistics*	*Applied Linguistics in the Real World*
Syntax	Discourse analysis	Medical Humanities/Disability Studies Education
Morphology	Second Language Education/Writing	Forensic Investigations
Semantics	Sociolinguistics	Translation and Transcreation
Language Acquisition	Corpus Linguistics	Language Policy Implementation
Phonetics & Phonology	Peace Linguistics	Language for Diplomacy Training
Pragmatics	World Englishes (Studies in Languages of Wider Communication)	Editorial and Literary Work Work on the New Literature
Semiotics	Sociolinguistics	Speech Training/Education
Psycholinguistics	Mathematical Linguistics	Language Programming and Linguistic Engineering
Theoretical Lexicography	Applied Lexicography (Hans Heinrich Meier)	Environmental/Ecolinguistics

lesser order than theoretical knowledge. Additional challenges include the view that mixed-methodologies and appeals to sister disciplines create chaos and disorganization (and/or the idea that there are areas where linguistics cannot go). These views, often covertly held and subscribed to, disregard several important points:

1. Applied linguists tend to be very educated on language theory. They do not take that for granted. Rather, they build bridges between that knowledge and real-life applications they feel strongly about and they deem important to understand better.
2. When those with the expertise to effect positive change and to better the life conditions of others do not do it, chances are less prepared individuals will attempt to do it, often enough with the best of intentions, but with results that might not be the same or as successful. One case in point is the importance of applied linguists being consulted in matters of language policy and planning or educational policy.
3. In an effort to strive for the "purity" of disciplines, we may miss out on opportunities to creatively address problems in the real world by combining their knowledge base, their methods, and their approaches. If we start with

> that goal instead of with a notion of what areas and methodologies can and cannot be combined (see Kramsch, 2015, cited in Chapter 2), we run less of a risk of abstracting for the sake of abstraction.

Because of the increasingly varied and large scope of application of applied linguistics, methods can be equality varied, ranging from those originally borrowed from anthropology and sociology such as ethnographic and sociolinguistic analysis to statistical analysis of corpora, design of surveys and interview, methods in literary criticism, and discourse/content analysis.

One central goal in this book is to motivate researchers, new to solving language problems, as well as those more seasoned and trained in traditional language-related disciplines, to make more daring moves toward the application of linguistic knowledge and to leap increasingly further when it comes to asking questions about real uses of linguistics (attention to the original disciplines that brought them into this endeavor notwithstanding).

Providing answers to questions about how language is both a catalyst of change and a solution to problems in the real world is part of that mission. The state of applied linguistics is such that we are ready to make these enquiries and to be bold to the point of proposing further partnerships with disciplines and fields of knowledge as diverse as engineering, medicine, and computer science. Some of these alliances are already in place and have been for years, but it is time they received greater visibility and more resources. In that sense, this book aims to propose a dismantling of the barriers between theoretical, applied, and what I am calling real-world linguistics with the goal of achieving greater participation in the socio-political, economic, attitudinal, environmental, and other realms of public life. Maybe in the future, language historians will frame this as a fourth phase. The work is unapologetic about my belief that there is no realm of human linguistic experience where applied linguistics should not go.

In terms of theoretical orientations and research methods, my work is equally unapologetic about its interdisciplinarity. Silos-thinking is often responsible for repeated attempts at "discovering the wheel" again and again. For this reason, in this book, applied linguistics partners with disciplines such as sociology, disability studies, speech sciences, and forensics, and makes references to corpus studies, ethnographies, surveys, literary analyses, experiments, and discourse analysis as viable methodological directions and approaches to the investigation of linguistic phenomena as varied as the reductionist language of disability, and the new digital tools for forensic linguistics investigations by the police.

It will come as no surprise to those who have operated within the intersection of the humanities and the social sciences that challenges to the legitimacy of our disciplines are common. While abstract knowledge and its close connection to the development of critical thinking and a better understanding of philosophical and ontological issues are justification enough for the support of theoretical fields, applied linguistics offers the added benefit of solving actual problems, faced by people in the world every day.

To return to the initial point of this introduction, we need experts. It is not difficult to read about situations where the knowledge of linguists could inform policy, economic decisions, political discourse, and everyday life. Many times, linguists are not consulted on issues that are directly connected to language knowledge, but to wait for an invitation to come is not profitable. It is time linguists included themselves further in areas where their knowledge is paramount. It is further necessary that we find accessible language with which to extend our knowledge to a greater audience. However, if you do need an invitation to apply knowledge of language where it has not been applied before, consider this book as a step in that direction.

It is time to move beyond.

Questions and ideas for further research

1. What are some of the ways in which the history of applied linguistics can be systematized?
2. Given different frameworks that present subareas of linguistics in relation to one another, what are intuitive ways to organize them and why?
3. What are some unlikely (according to the literature so far) areas of application of linguistic knowledge that could benefit from this discussion?
4. What are some myths within linguistics and language studies that need to be addressed before more work on language in the real word can be performed?
5. What are some of the challenges that might arise from an expansion of applied linguistics into different realms of knowledge and action?

Notes

1 See https://en.oxforddictionaries.com/word-of-the-year/word-of-the-year-2016.
2 See www.today.com/video/americans-check-their-smartphones-80-times-a-day-study-1093857859881. Retrieved on January 30, 2018.

Works cited and further reading

Bohn, R., and Short, J. (2012). Measuring consumer information. *International Journal of Communication, 6*, 980–1000.

Brumfit, C. J.1995. Teacher professionalism and research. In Cook, G. and Seidlhofer, B. (Eds.), *Principle and practice in applied linguistics* (pp. 27–41). Oxford: Oxford University Press.

Bygate, M. (2005). Calm seas or troubled waters? Transitions, definitions and disagreements in applied linguistics, *International Journal of Applied Linguistics, 15*(3), 282–302.

Cook, G. (2005). *Applied linguistics*. Oxford: Oxford University Press.

Davies, A. (1999). *An introduction to applied linguistics: From practice to theory*. Edinburgh: Edinburgh University Press.

Davies, A., and C. Elder (2004a). General introduction: Applied linguistics: Subject to discipline? In Davies, A., and Elder, C. (Eds.), *The handbook of applied linguistics* (pp. 1–15). Malden, MA: Blackwell.

Davies, A., and Elder, C. (Eds.). (2004b). *The handbook of applied linguistics*. Malden, MA: Blackwell.

Dinneen, F. P. (1995). *General linguistics*. DC: Georgetown University Press.

Emerson, R. W. (1883). *Letters and social aims*. London: MacMillan and Co.

Friedman, T. L. (2016). *Thank you for being late*. NY: Farrar, Straus and Giroux.

Gass, S. M., and Makoni, S. (Eds.). (2004). *World applied linguistics: AILA review. 17*. Philadelphia and Amsterdam: John Benjamins.

Grabe, W. (2010). Applied linguistics: A twenty-first-century discipline. Kaplan, R. (Ed.). *The Oxford handbook of applied linguistics* (2nd ed.). Oxford: Oxford.

Hemforth, B. (2013). *Experimental linguistics*. Oxford Bibliographies. www.oxfordbibliographies.com/view/document/obo-9780199772810/obo-9780199772810-0112.xml. Retrieved on November 22, 2018.

Kaplan R. B. (1992). Applied linguistics and language policy and planning. In Grabe, W., and Kaplan R. B. (Eds.), *Introduction to applied linguistics* (pp. 143–165). Reading, MA: Addison-Wesley.

Kaplan, R. B. (2002). Preface. In R. B. Kaplan (Ed.), *The Oxford handbook of applied linguistics* (pp. v–x). New York: Oxford University Press.

Kaplan, R. B. (2009). Review essay: An introduction to applied linguistics: from practice to theory, by Alan Davies. *Journal of Multilingual and Multicultural Development 30*(2), 167–173.

Kess, J. F. (1976). *Psycholinguistics: Introductory perspectives*. NY: Academic Press Inc.

Meier, H. H. (1969). Lexicography as applied linguistics. *English Studies 50* (1–6).

Ottenheimer, H. J. (2006). *The anthropology of language: An introduction to linguistic anthropology*. Canada: Thomas Wadsworth.

Prideaux, G, Derwing, B. L., and Baker, W. J. (1980). *Experimental linguistics: Integration of theories and applications*. Philadelphia: John Benjamins Publishing.

Simpson, J. (2011a, Ed.). *Routledge handbooks in applied linguistics: The Routledge handbook of applied linguistics*. London, UK: Routledge.

Simpson, J. (2011b). Introduction. In J. Simpson (Ed.), *Routledge handbooks in applied linguistics: The Routledge handbook of applied linguistics* (1–8). London, UK: Routledge.

van Lier, L. (1997). Apply within, apply without? *International Journal of Applied Linguistics* 7, 95–105.

Widdowson, H. (2000). On the limitations of linguistics applied. *Applied Linguistics, 21*(1), 3–25.

2

REVISITING EDUCATION, LANGUAGE ACQUISITION, AND SECOND LANGUAGE TEACHING

Back to basics

> **THIS CHAPTER WILL DO THE FOLLOWING**
>
> 1. Discuss the fluid nature and current state of language use.
> 2. Relate the idea of a diverse, ever-changing environment of languages that are in contact to the role of applied linguistics.
> 3. Argue for a return to rigor in scientific inquiry.
> 4. Argue for a return to basic principles of language understanding.
> 5. Describe and explain the different elements of an applied linguistics engaged with education, TESOL, and SLA.
> 6. Problematize different orientations in the study of English internationally.
> 7. Discuss issues of language and identity.
> 8. Provide ideas for students and scholars who would like to conduct applied linguistics research as it pertains to education and related fields.

Introduction

There is a reason why I am starting this journey through applied linguistics and its interdisciplinary alliances with education, (second) language acquisition, and language teaching. In his comprehensive survey of *History of Applied Linguistics*, de Bot (2015) does a variety of things, which include listing the 14 most influential (picked according to citations by leaders/informants in the field) articles and 25 equally important books. Out of the articles, virtually all of them are about second language acquisition and out of the books, all but seven make overt connections (most of them already in the title) to the pedagogical implications of applied linguistics. While the themes and topics of this book challenge that direct connection by arguing for an applied linguistics that goes everywhere, from forensic investigations to translation studies, and from applied speech sciences to disability advocacy, it seems intuitive to start from what is more established and what has brought in numerous researchers and students to the field. Even if the connection between applied linguistics and real-world problems now spans many interdisciplinary fields, as made obvious by the titles of the chapters in this book, second language acquisition (SLA), Teaching English to Speakers of Other Languages (TESOL), and other branches of education have been linked to it from its very inception.

Indeed, my own introduction to applied linguistics was made possible by my status (at the time) as English as a foreign language learner (even if I stopped using the term many years ago), and subsequently as a TESOL educator. I learned and then taught using audio-lingual and, after that, communicative approaches, and I rejected pedagogies based on grammar translation and fixed models of prescriptive grammar once my education progressed (more on grammar translation later). In time, my interest in issues of language applied to real-world challenges led me to both applied linguistics and world Englishes, often times by way of sociolinguistics, being that the two latter are where I consider to have gained the most insight into the nature of language and where I have conducted most of my research before choosing to expand further. The works of B. Kachru (1983 and after), Hymes (1972 and 1974), Larsen-Freeman (1986), Kramsch (1995), and Canale and Swain (1980) were essential in those formative years, and they continue to be—I had previously been educated in the tradition of the work of Saussure (1997, from the original 1916) and the Prague School, especially Jacobson (2017, of the 1956 original). Communicative competence (Hymes, 1972; Canale and Swain, 1980) arguably became the most important term in my technical repertoire, and the goal of helping students develop their own competence was a high priority on my list. To a certain extent, these formative concepts continue to inspire and cause reflection.

Early in this decade, I was the author of a chapter (Friedrich, 2012) that made a case for renewed attention to the strategic level of communicative competence (Canale and Swain, 1980). My rationale was that situations of communication, varieties of English, and participants in interactions had become so diverse that we would be faced with much complexity—and difficulty—if we tried to decide *a priori* what the linguistic demands of an interaction would be. In that case, the strategic aspect of competence, if well developed, could help make up for practical knowledge, unfamiliarity, or partial familiarity with varieties, and new socio-cultural orientations. This is the case with English, and I would speculate that it is also the case with other languages, especially those used for wider communication. That is, if other aspects of communication break down (e.g., linguistic forms are not all shared, cultural assumptions differ), it is the strategic aspect that will hold communication together. However, what elements of strategic competence are to take front stage will depend on the particulars of a given situation and will be negotiated right then. This is especially true given the diversity and number of users of languages of wider communication, such as English, around the world.

Those sentiments are echoed by Canagarajah (2014, p. 767) who writes that "We are now open to norms being co-constructed intersubjectively in each situated interaction by interlocutors in global contact zones." The key words to me in that quote are our being "open to" *ad hoc* constructions because, as language dynamics go, the dynamics themselves have always been the same: norms have always been co-constructed that way, even if we, educators, tried to prescribe otherwise. Where there is prescriptivism there is often, not far behind, the creative impulse of language users to fulfill their linguistic, identity, cultural, and communicative needs through innovation, negotiation, and co-constructed subjectivity. What has happened is that, given the exponential growth in situations of communication that call for that flexibility and years of research on the nature of languages, we as linguists, and as individuals, are getting a better picture of what this endeavor entails and, at the same time, are—I hope—learning the limitations of our own prescriptions when those are presented to the world. That is, in a classroom, given the authority of the instructor and the relative power of grades, based on defined criteria, which often include such items as "follow the rules of (English) grammar," there exists the possibility for a level of control that disappears once we turn our attention to non-mediated interactions. And while some of those prescriptions may become embedded in the individuals themselves, in actual situations of communication, they will have to exist alongside or in contrast with the needs of the other interlocutors and the demands of space, time, and goal.

Another way to understand this fluidity is through Bauman's concept of Liquid Modernity (2007, p. 1), which the author defines as

> A condition in which social forms (structures that limit individual choices, institutions that guard repetitions of routines, patterns of acceptable behavior) can no longer (and are not expected) to keep their shape for long, because they decompose and melt faster than the time it takes to cast them, and once they are cast for them to set. Forms, whether already present or only adumbrated, are unlikely to be given enough time to solidify, and cannot serve as frames of reference for human actions and long-term life strategies because of their short life expectation.

That liquidity is in many ways also a feature of applied linguistics, perhaps one that makes it challenging for researchers in other areas to understand what we do. If we study phenomena that is fluid and ever-changing, we too need to engage with them in creative, fluid ways rather than with prescriptions. In a manner of speaking, complexity of object requires simplicity of action; finding ways to deal with complex linguistic objects is often a goal in applied linguistics. However, for some, simplicity and dynamism get confounded with superficiality and lack of scientific rigor (as well as a lack of understanding of historical antecedents), and that is not the best way to move a field forward.

Especially when it comes to multilingual settings, and we increasingly study those since in many ways they are the norm rather than the exception, an observation of the strategies and resources that users of language make to achieve successful communication is paramount. Yet, we do not have to think of multilingualism as only applicable to environments where more than one formally recognized language is in action. When it comes to language *ad-hoc* negotiations, in the very least we, as users of language, are negotiating varieties even if we are "monolingual," which means all of us need more than linguistic competence to be successful. This view is presented by Kramsch and Whiteside (2008, p. 664) in their description of symbolic competence. They explain that

> Social actors in multilingual settings seem to activate more than a communicative competence that would enable them to communicate accurately, effectively and appropriately with one another. They seem to display a particularly acute ability to play with various linguistic codes and with the various spatial and temporal resonances of these codes.

The question then becomes how to practice an applied linguistics that is engaged with this fluidity, recognizing this ever-shifting reality of languages while at the same time retaining rigor and a foundationally strong ground on which to build language education, SLA research, related (TESOL, for example) praxis, and the sound theorizing necessary to anchor them. As applied linguists, we must do all of that without complicating approaches to a level at which they become obstructions in our path and pursuit of answers. That is, our methods should facilitate the observation of linguistic phenomena in the world, not hamper it.

I wanted to work in applied linguistics because I always understood it to be driven by questions that originate in the real world. Like the youngster who sits outside and upon seeing a trail of ants asks themselves, "I wonder how they know where to go" or "How can they carry such large leaves?," upon observing language, I wanted to look at it in that kind of wonderment, spellbound by all the things it could and did accomplish, and then follow up, for the most part, with "how" and "why" questions.

For that reason, I find the words of Kramsch (2015, pp. 455–456) regarding theory and practice of applied linguistics so refreshing, for example when she refers to it as "the practice of language study itself, and the theory that could be drawn from that practice." Or yet, "It is an eminently empirical field, from which emerges a theory of the practice." This attention to practice, this recognition that knowledge of the real world is the driving force of discovery makes evident the difficulty in quite a bit of twentieth-century linguistic research, the part that tried to start with theory and then make reality fit it.

Another way to look at complexity leading to practical decision-making can be found in the work of Larsen-Freeman (1997, p. 148) and her groundbreaking application of chaos theory to SLA. Larsen-Freeman suggests that

> language grows and organizes itself from the bottom up in an organic way, as do other complex nonlinear systems. While rules can be used to describe such systems, the systems themselves are not the product of rules.

This is great insight because oftentimes, prescriptively, we, as members of human institutions, try to make language conform to *a priori* rules, and as applied linguists, we know how much that does not work. On the other hand, upon observation of language in the world, we can often offer principles that systematize what is happening, since our human brains do better with patterns than they do without.

In that regard, applied linguistics in the world starts with a sense of curiosity toward a phenomenon, and a wonderment, which is then addressed, taking into consideration what the applied linguist has come to know about the nature and dynamics of languages in context. The possibility that what that same researcher thinks they know about the nature of languages will have to be updated, revised, supplemented, or altogether changed given what they have learned in this investigation needs to always be under consideration as well.

If it is not yet very clear that this "theory of the practice" phenomenon that Kramsch refers to is the orientation of this book, I hope it becomes more so as it progresses and in such examples as the ones provided in subsequent discussion such as the ones on forensic linguistics or disability studies. After all, what could be more a "theory of the practice" than a need to systematize what began intuitively as a real-world need to find answers to "puzzles" that could solve a legal case or establish the authorship of a document/text? Or yet, how important it is to offer people alternatives to the potentially restrictive language often employed to refer to disability.

But fluidity, fast change, and global discussions, while democratic and dynamic in many ways, have also had side-effects. Seemingly paradoxically, our engagement with subject matter has become more superficial (who has time for depth?) and the gap between scientific knowledge and real-world practice has widened. In conversations that are so broad, so global, and so quick, it is harder to tell apart those who have spent extensive time studying and understanding a discipline and those who have had enough access to participate but not necessarily enough background knowledge to consider many aspects of the situation.

This chapter is a call back to basics, to the scientific rigor that must accompany our discussions, analyses, syntheses, evaluations, and applications, but one that does not get confounded with prescriptivism. This encompasses the definition of terms, an understanding of the historical development of disciplines, points of intersection with other disciplinary and interdisciplinary pursuits and of the tensions and disagreements that are still outstanding. It is also a call for applied linguistics research to continue to forge alliances with existing synergetic areas and increasingly with new ones. In the next sections, I will focus on some existing tensions in applied linguistics, especially when it comes to its education alliances and issues that further research could potentially address.

Acquisition, learning, and development in relation to language

The connection between applied linguistics and second language acquisition studies (SLA) has been a close but sometimes disputed one. In 1993, William Rutherford was writing (critically) that it was "quite common to find SLA identified as a kind of 'applied linguistics' itself" (p. 3). Part of the criticism comes from his belief that the knowledge flux in this case is represented as "unidirectional" (p. 3), meaning from applied linguistics to SLA, which then caused him to propose that we instead begin to see the relationship as more of a "two-way street" (p. 4). In his note about applied linguistics in quotes, he mentions with reservation the view of SLA as "an applied science," which he attributes to such scholars as Newmeyer and Weinberger (1988, p. 41).

Besides indirectly pointing to tensions between the concepts of acquisition and learning, for subscribing to one or the other view might make one more inclined to align themselves with more pedagogically-driven fields or to more language-and-the-brain approaches, this discussion reveals once more the reservation some academics have historically had (and may continue to have) about applied knowledge, as I discussed in detail in the introduction. That is, if applied linguistics and SLA were seen as integral aspects of our application of knowledge about language and developed given our observation of what problems in the world this knowledge helps address, it would be less important to discuss which field is fueling which because our focus would be on need ahead of disciplinary loyalty. There are other controversies, however.

In his classic work, Krashen (1981, pp. 1–2) takes a binary stance on the matter of acquisition and learning, two terms that have been much debated over the years. Acquisition, he posits, is the process akin to what children go through when becoming competent in their first and subsequent languages. It is subconscious (Krashen, 1982, p. 10), even in adults. For acquisition to take place, he argues, a few requirements must be met. They include participation in target-language interactions that are meaningful, a focus on the message being communicated (rather than the form), and little attention to corrections. Learning on the other hand, necessitates addressing errors, presenting rules in a clear manner, and typically moving from simple structures to more complex ones (1981, pp. 1–2). Learning, in this view, can be inferred to involve the rational, conscious mind.

Since those observations were written, our understanding of languages, as well as of world dynamics in general, has moved toward a less binary partition of phenomena. When it comes to our personal growth, linguistic and otherwise, it is difficult to isolate variables to the extent necessary for a theory of learning and a theory of acquisition to exist as two separate entities. Perhaps an analogy from a different field of knowledge is that of nurture versus nature in the manifestation of states of health and states of disease. While for a long time the emphasis was on the "versus" part of the phrase, more and more studies in genetics have demonstrated that genes give us an innate tendency toward certain states, but lifestyle, food, toxic exposure, and even stress significantly help turn genes on or off. That is, nature and nurture work much more synergistically than oppositionally. Is it possible to think of learning and acquisition in those terms as well?

It is very hard to imagine that they do not interact or are not juxtaposed, for example, across the many media we use every day and by the many people from different speech communities we get a chance to interact with all the time. Even geographical distance, which was once a limitation, has been reformulated, with the advent of virtual communications, as an asset, since it gives us insight into other cultures and ways of living that were once not accessible to many of us. Therefore, in these complex spaces, virtual classrooms, and worlds so full of linguistic stimulation that is it hard not to merge with the environment, it seems more complicated to vacate one of the slots and argue that, at any given point in time, only acquisition is taking place or only learning is at play.

When defining applied linguistics, de Bot (2015, p. 4) makes reference to language development, which he explains encompasses "acquisition and attrition, instructed and non- instructed learning." Therefore, language development can be seen as a more encompassing concept than acquisition and learning, at least according to this view, one that acknowledges the impossibility of isolating the individual from situations where exposure to languages is happening both organically and systematically at the same time. Often, "learning" is used when overt reference to structured studying is made, and "acquisition" when more unstructured dynamics are at play. One additional advantage of the term "development" is that even when, for example, structured learning is taking place, the learning is not completely isolated from more unstructured forces (and from attrition) which are constantly affecting one's experience anyway. Moreover, while second language development is happening, a person's first language is still expanding too—new lexical items are being incorporated to one's active vocabulary, new structures are being used, creativity is happening, and code-mixing and switching are taking place (I will discuss code-switching and translanguaging later, and more prominently in Chapter 12).

In any case, while terminological discussions often take a lot of space in the research literature, part of our confusion comes, at times, not from the availability of these various concepts but rather by the lack of clear explanations of how they are being used in specific contexts. At other times, we engage in long debates over which terms are best, and, while some of those discussions truly advance the field, others detract us from the main goal of observing, systematizing, and using the knowledge of language in the real world to make someone's life better. In the very least, however, it is important to define how terms are being used in context (this may be a case where the need to strategize in the situation of academic communication mirrors the need to do the same in the real world) and to provide some rationale for those choices.

Meanwhile, as scholars are debating these and other issues, it is not uncommon for practitioners not to be participating in the discussions, which means that when students are being taught, or language development is taking place in the real world, they might be unaffected by the discoveries and advancements of academia in those areas. In turn, if scholars disregard the important role and empirical knowledge of practitioners, their observations might not resonate with real-life experiences and, as a result, might be relegated to an academic exercise.

This gap between academics and practitioners, textbook reality and real-world reality, is pointed out by Kramsch (2015, pp. 458–459) who observes that, "As Applied Linguistics is becoming more and more professionalized in its practice, and intellectualized in its scientific inquiry, the gap widens between researchers and practitioners."

This is a result of the formation of two parallel but almost-never interacting networks but also of time constraints and excess of information. Every time I conduct research to write, I become overwhelmed with the amount of information available at my fingertips until I compromise and accept that my window into the world is merely a small glance at what is there, one that is made more meaningful if it serves as a point of contact with the world.

Another kind of gap exists between textbook writers and researchers. Whereas research has pointed to the multilayered, multiliterate, multimodal, diverse, multi-variety nature of international communications, oftentimes pedagogical materials, with some notable and very worthy exceptions, still reflect a more static view of language in which participants share not only a linguistic variety but also similar understandings of culture and the world around them, and where questions and answers are more predictable (i.e., greater emphasis is placed on linguistic than strategic competence).

Given all of the above, some basic tenets are necessary if we are to practice the kind of applied linguistics that not only displays the rigor we have come to expect of academic undertakings, but also that has an impact on the real world. In the spirit of these items themselves, I offer suggestions and my personal interpretation of the nature of language and teaching rather than prescriptions, which would be completely antagonist to what I am advocating in this book in the first place. They include the following:

1. Individuals have an infinite capacity to add to their linguistic repertoire: therefore, it is counterproductive to dwell on some form of anxiety over the coexistence of different varieties, languages, and linguistic expressions. Language users are capable of making choices appropriate to the different situations of communication they might engage in, and easing them into that process is more productive than trying to limit linguistic expression.

2. Rather than offering prescriptions, teaching is better realized by offering options, rationales, additions, arguments, examples, and reformulations: prescriptions are often the result of external rules (e.g., don't split infinitives, don't end a sentence with a preposition) which do not necessarily reflect the nature of language development or the needs of language users. It is more helpful to focus on the goals of linguistic interactions and the likely outcomes of different choices.
3. Applied linguistics serves its stakeholders better when it dwells on the "add to the repertoire" paradigm rather than the "deficit" paradigm: the linguistic expressions of a person, be they varieties, lexical choices, or "accent," are closely connected to their identity and to their uses of language in the real world, given their communities, roles, and aspirations. To judge a particular feature as "lacking," "insufficient," or "deficient" is to negatively affect the person in their very identity. Furthermore, such a judgment is not only unnecessary for added language development but it might also hamper it. Given our infinite ability for linguistic expression, adding to an existing repertoire not only enlarges the pool of communicative possibilities of a person but also boosts their belief in themselves by reassuring them of the legitimacy of their identity.
4. Purpose and audience are a better guide to (socio)linguistic decisions than some abstract idea of a standard: it is easy to think of situations where the abstraction we call "standard language" might be a deterrent to successful communication. If friends, for example, are chatting in an informal gathering, using slang, sentence fragments, and the like, and someone else arrives using a formal, standard variety, conversations might actually come to a halt. Understanding purpose and audience in this case is as important as using them as guides when crafting an academic article, for example. Since the very idea of a standard is closely connected to linguistic power, the introduction of a variety associated with it often changes the dynamics of an interaction.
5. While once we "know" about languages, we might get an impetus to control it, the very act of knowing should signify we also understand that much in language is beyond our control: applied linguistics has much to contribute to a variety of practices in the real world. That fact notwithstanding, we must reflect on the scope of our ability to have an impact on language phenomena. The degree of our ability to influence the world is proportional to the level of institutionalization of a practice. That is to say, when it comes to educational practices, language policy, translation and other areas where our ability to set parameters is direct, it can be inferred that our level of influence can be greater. On the other hand, when it comes to less structured practices, for example, communication in social media, our role becomes more connected to that of observers and systematizers of a reality that exists beyond us. Unless we are in a position of being trendsetters (including linguistic trendsetters, influencers, etc.,) like some famous people are

(i.e., items of their vocabulary sometimes catch on as much as their fashions), it is difficult to have a direct linguistic influence upon in the fast landscape of digital communications. This is a case where the very idea of (limited) linguistic power applies to linguists ourselves.

Foreign language, second language, international language, lingua franca

In Matsuda and Friedrich (2012), we argue that "foreign" and "second language" do not really refer to how one uses language, but rather, especially in the past, when we were not all so virtually connected, these terms referred to the context in which one originally developed (i.e., learned/acquired) language. That is to say, in a time and place with less fluidity, a person could claim, if they developed English in an educational setting in Argentina or Italy, that they had learned/developed the language as a foreign language because chances are the student was developing their competence to communicate with an international audience, often outside their home country or alternatively with international visitors. Likewise, if they were learners of English in India, having Tamil as their first language for example, they could say they were learning/developing the language as a second language given that English (also) has intranational uses in India. It would, however, even at that time, seem very limiting to think that people were *using* (or speaking) English as a foreign and second language because that Argentine learner could easily travel or go to live in the US. Would they, in that case, still be using English as a foreign language? What if the person from India moved to Australia? Would they be still using English as a second language even if it were their primary language of expression in daily life? And what if one of those individuals were in South Africa, communicating with a group that included an American, a Brazilian, a Singaporean, and an Icelander? Who would claim which foreign, second, additional language label and for what purpose? What if instead of Johannesburg, this conversation was now taking place online?

These examples show that the more fluid, or liquid, our environments become, the harder it is to maintain such labels as foreign and second language, which in turn would provide a good argument for the adoption of such terms as English as an international language (EIL) and English as a lingua franca (ELF). However, as it often happens with our translations from reality into academic models, some challenges arise.

For years now, I have raised questions regarding the phenomenon (or a set of different phenomena) that became known as ELF. For an excellent review, which raises several questions similar to my own, refer to Prodromou (2007). While I am very supportive of the need to study the use of language for purposes of wider communication and have throughout my career advocated for the ownership of language, if we can even call it that, by all who use it (and not just so-called native speakers), I am often confused by the multiple ways in which ELF is described and also by how often it is not defined before it is talked and written about. In my writing, I have privileged the terms "Englishes" and "EIL" because in my view, they encompass respectively, the many varieties of English in use in the world and the function English fulfills when it is used globally/across cultures. That is, through those two terms, I can describe both form and function. In Jenkins (2015, p. 15), the author claims that at the beginning of the ELF model, there was nothing like it to compare it with, acknowledging only that world Englishes (WE) provided a parallel because of its work on postcolonial contexts, but disregarding all the work that WE had already done in expanding-circle countries. Likewise, citing Kachru's 1990s work, Jenkins posits that WE does not account for the fluidity that ELF is able to account for in, for example, online environments. She makes that observation based on the fact that Kachru would often refer to geography as a boundary. This is a surprising claim given that in the early 1990s, when Kachru was describing geographical demarcations, the modes of electronic communication where so much international exchange takes place now did not exist, and therefore could not be accounted for by WE theorizing at the time. Since then, WE has made many references to and research in online environments (see Friedrich and Diniz de Figueiredo, 2016 for examples).

Nevertheless, if I were to use the acronym ELF, I would define it very similarly to EIL as the function of English in which users of language from different backgrounds, parts of the world, and original first languages utilize Englishes for purposes of wider communication. That is, Englishes would be the varieties, and EIL the function these varieties perform in international contexts. Defined this way, the term ELF would have a slight advantage over EIL because it would not so strongly emphasize the international aspect of English(es) communication, given that the language has many intranational uses as well. To me, it is important to highlight the word "function" because I don't believe that ELF refers to a linguistic variety such as American English, Indian English, Chinese English, or even digital Englishes (the Englishes in this paragraph). Rather, I believe users of many different Englishes bring their own varieties (which, in turn, are not static) to situations of communication and negotiate *in loco* the specifics of that interaction. Yet, when I read ELF scholarship, I usually have a hard time finding a working definition against which to test my own understanding of these linguistic phenomena, and when I do, it is often not one that emphasizes that function-of-language aspect of communication. While ELF seems to be quite a liquid concept, to refer back to what is a theme in this chapter, I believe we can take steps to at least concretize a definition.

Seidlhofer (2005 p. 339) has written of ELF as "a way of referring to communication in English between speakers with different first languages," and that does not help narrow down the abstract idea to a working definition. Jenkins (2006, p. 164) claims that "Speakers of European Englishes are typically also speakers of ELF," which would seem to indicate EFL is a linguistic variety. There have also been discussions regarding whether people whose first language is English are "allowed" in ELF communications (see Jenkins, 2007, for the case of reluctant inclusion of native speakers and no data collection from that group, as pointed out by Chapman, 2015). Besides many other problems, this exclusion would pose a significant challenge in real-life scenarios where people are often joining and leaving conversations often (e.g., consider a chat room or a boardroom).

It is clear that the concept has gained momentum, especially within the private language education industry in countries where English is primarily used for international communication. However, in individual papers, conference presentations and interviews, the entity seems to morph and transform without a clear account of its conceptualization. It was interesting, therefore to come across Davies's review (2008) of Jenkins (2007) entitled, "We Are Not Quite Sure What EFL Is." In this call for a return to basics, I would suggest that researchers within the ELF paradigm go back to drafting and communicating a clear definition of the phenomenon they study. Is it a language? Is it a variety? Is it a function of English in multilingual contexts, or is it something else? This would facilitate conversations and discussions regarding points of intersection with other areas and other fields such as applied linguistics and WE. While I will not explore this topic in great detail in this book, I will briefly outline some of my positions regarding ELF when I discuss corpus studies in Chapter 7 and again in Chapter 12.

More globally, I believe an important undertaking for applied linguists at this point is to review the literature of world Englishes, EIL, English as a Global Language, and ELF and have meaningful discussions about what is what, which orientations overlap, what these labels represent (or not), and what they are doing for our understanding of language dynamics. Furthermore, new alliances with SLA need to be forged so that we better account for the difference and potential overlap between stages of language development and the development of new varieties. In this twenty-first century world of hurried, superficial accounts and minute-long understandings, it is time we, in a practical way, engaged again with process and relearned to take our time to define, explain, study, rewrite, and repeat. I have spoken earlier in the book against unnecessary problematizing, yet I believe this particular discussion is absolutely crucial.

Similarity and difference

If philosophically it is our goal to unite us by our similarities rather than separate us by our differences, a premise I am in agreement with, when it comes to the systematic observation of language in use, it is important to consider differences as well as similarities before making assessments, designing frameworks, and crafting taxonomies.

Users of language will, as a matter of course, travel through similar stages of language development. Whether one calls that "making mistakes," "infusing English with features of their existing varieties," "a stage in systematic language change" (i.e., many linguistic innovations started as "mistakes"), or something else depends to a great deal on their theoretical orientation. Objectively they might all be looking at the same manifestation and giving it different meanings. However, acknowledging and documenting such stages, although important and useful in itself, should not preclude us, applied linguists, from investigating meaningful difference, especially if we are observing with a goal of building theory.

When ELF research, for example, focuses on the features of those stages of language development as evidence of the existence of ELF itself (for that, they must think of it as a variety), said research is setting aside much knowledge in SLA enquiry, knowledge that could also serve to highlight differences that are relevant to those discussions. That is, if ELF researchers try to describe a linguistic phenomenon (e.g., dropping of third person –s or the insertion of additional prepositions) as a feature of a linguistic variety and then use this as evidence that EFL exists because there are users of language whose current production reflects these features, they are engaging in circular thinking. To look for order only by finding similarity is to miss all of the difference that can be potentially significant. For example, children in the process of developing their first language often drop third person –s. Does that mean they are users of ELF? Within some "native" varieties of English, users of language tend to drop third person –s as well. Do they use ELF (even though most descriptions by the same researchers exclude native varieties from their corpus)?

Larsen-Freeman (1997, p. 152) puts it well, writing in the context of chaos theory:

> While interlanguages of speakers of various first languages learning English as a foreign language have much in common, they also are distinctive, each constrained by the strange attractors of their L1s, which may be greater than the force of the strange attractor of English.

Though in these 20 years we have revised some of our principles, and, with them, nomenclature (i.e., I mentioned above how the term "foreign language" might now be unnecessary and we do not often use "interlanguages" anymore), the basic methodological idea has remained: investigate and consider difference that is worthy of consideration and is both systematic and outside expected patterns.

As I will discuss later, the association between applied linguistics and forensics has demonstrated that, when it comes to author identification, difference is at least as, if not more, important than similarity. That is, the fact that several common words appear across several texts is much less relevant than a subject's unique use of a vocabulary item or a particular turn of phrase, for example.

It is thus our role as researchers, students, scholars of applied linguistics to identify our own biases, which includes attempts at clustering together elements which present surface-level similarities, by considering language use and change in all its richness and difference.

Critical Applied Linguistics

Critical Applied Linguistics (CAL) is often associated with the work of Alistair Pennycook (2001, for example). In his book by the same name, Pennycook (2001, p. 1) defines CAL as "a critical approach to Applied Linguistics." He goes on to indicate the endeavor to be "self-reflexive" and to delineate an applied linguistics that explores sociopolitical issues in depth.

While the self-reflexive nature of the discipline is one of its welcome aspects, my concerns with some of the tenets are as follows: is to claim there is Critical Applied Linguistics the same as to say that applied linguistics as a whole is not critical? And should not all endeavors in the social sciences and the humanities be self-reflexive?

In Friedrich et al. (2013), my colleagues and I raised these issues and others, including the tendency of CAL—since it places so much upfront emphasis on the critical—to be fault-finding. CAL also leans toward deconstruction and the postmodern notion that much of what we know is "invented." While such confabulations are interesting as academic exercises, they may fall short when it comes to inspiring action in the real world, especially because in an effort to deconstruct, proponents hardly ever offer practical solutions, as those could be easily deconstructed by others as well. The goal is to continue to question without cynicism, to analyze without needing to find that something is lacking.

Growing role of identity in language studies

From the time that language studies were focused on more structural linguistic elements, as Norton (2010) reminds us, to a present infused with notions about society, social forces, social memberships, and social repercussions of language, we have come a long way. Our views of language have been influenced, and have influenced society in its growing complexity. Awareness of diverse ways of living in the world, different cultures, language users and uses, as well as the experience of language contact and change, have led to investigations that, as I mentioned before, tackle dynamics, prejudices, attitudes, perceptions, and certainly identity.

Norton (2010, p. 351) succinctly addresses this relationship between language and identity by stating that "language is thus theorized not only as a linguistic system, but as a social practice in which experiences are organized and identities are negotiated." It was a greater understanding of identity that led us, for example, to reject approaches and methodologies that focus on linguistic deficit. After all, every functional, living language is a complete system in itself, and thus telling a student that their linguistic knowledge was lacking, because of their use of those varieties, only had the effect of hampering learning (besides being untrue); to a great degree, their identity as language learners would have been very attached to the linguistic varieties they already used, and devaluing them is not only morally and ethically questionable, it is also counterproductive when it comes to motivating them to learn more.

Increasingly too, groups and individuals realize that they can choose to highlight certain aspects of their identities: without necessarily knowing the technical terms, they self-assign as members of certain speech communities and communities of practice—they are gamers, poets, millennials, aspiring writers, programmers—and these identities help shape language.

We have a history and many stories

Whether a researcher, student, or scholar has already found lenses through which to look at linguistic phenomena or is still searching, it is important to remember that these conversations, questions, and discussions have a history, and that throughout this history, writers and academics have been telling the stories of language users and their communities. This history—and these stories—cannot be taken for granted. They need to be fully acknowledged and deeply understood before terms and ideas regarding them are written about. A simple superficial glance will not do: in a world full of immediate Google searches, applied linguists must commit to a deeper understanding of and an immersion in language issues.

However, as students' and young scholars' lenses into the world become increasingly fragmented by our multiplying digital windows, we do face the challenge of having to account for breadth and depth in close to impossible ways. It is at this intersection that history and stories often get lost, and it will require effort for mentors and mentees to keep those connections and to ground new work on what came before it. That, of course, does not mean necessarily agreeing with research antecedents, but rather acknowledging their existence and the fact that it is because they exist that new inquiry can occur.

Conclusion

Another quote by Kramsch (2015, p. 457) expresses an achievable and worthwhile program for applied linguistics in years to come. She writes,

> My vision for the future focuses on the recent advances made by Applied Linguistics and their impact on real-world practice, the technical and symbolic dimensions of the field, the spread of English around the world, and the increasingly diverse research cultures in Applied Linguistics.

I hope that in this first disciplinary chapter I was able to offer some thoughts, partial as they may be, on some lines of inquiry, controversies, and alliances with related disciplines which can take us on a course toward these goals. The challenges of our digital postmodernity are many, and they will require much rigor and intent from our profession if we are to move forward, though the possibilities are many and intellectually gratifying. It is my hope that applied linguistics research and its practice equivalent come to contribute significantly to education, the valuing of student varieties, to a focus on enriching students' repertoires, and language policies that are inclusive, just, and inspiring.

Questions and ideas for further research

1. Is current knowledge of applied linguistics making its way into the classroom?
2. How is applied linguistics making diversity a productive starting point in the classroom?
3. How are language pedagogies enhancing one's repertoire by introducing new varieties?
4. What are some of the terminological discussions that have shaped the first two decades of the twenty-first century?
5. What is some productive difference that needs to be investigated if we are to systematize aspects of applied linguistics?
6. What are some methodological decisions that can help ensure that relevant work, and its history, is acknowledged and built upon in applied linguistics research?
7. What are some goals for a critical applied linguistic that questions without cynicism?

Works cited and further reading

Bauman, Z. (2000). *Liquid modernity*. Cambridge: Polity Press.

Bauman, Z. (2006). *Liquid fear*. Cambridge: Polity Press.

Bauman, Z. (2007). *Liquid times: Living in an age of uncertainty*. Cambridge: Polity Press.

Bauman, Z. (2011). *Culture in a liquid world*. Malden, MA: Polity Press.

Blommaert, J. (2010). *The sociolinguistics of globalization*. Cambridge: Cambridge University Press.

Canagarajah, A. S. (2013, Ed.). *Literacy as translingual practice: Between communities and classrooms*. London: Routledge.

Canagarajah, A. S. (2014). In search of a new paradigm for teaching English as an international language. *TESOL Journal, 5*(4), 767–785.

Canale, M., and Swain, M. (1980). Theoretical bases of communicative approaches to second language teaching and testing. *Applied Linguistics, 1*(1), 1–47.

Chapman, R. (2015). The deceiving ELF? Can English really fulfill the role of a *lingua franca*? *Lingue e Linguaggi, 15*, 113–127.

Davies, A. (2008). We are not quite sure what ELF is. *Language Assessment Quarterly, 5*(4), 360–364.

De Bot, K. (2015) *A history of applied linguistics: From 1980 to the present*. NY: Routledge.

Friedrich, P., and Matsuda, A. (2010). When five words are not enough: A conceptual and terminological discussion of English as a lingua franca. *International Multilingual Research Journal, 4*(1), 20–30.

Friedrich, P. (2012). ELF, intercultural communication and the strategic aspect of communicative competence. In A. Matsuda (Ed.), *Principles and practices of teaching English as an international language*. Bristol: Multilingual Matters.

Friedrich, P., et al. (2013). Reading Pennycook critically 10 years later: A group's reflections on and questions about critical applied linguistics. *International Multilingual Research Journal*, 7, 119–137.
Friedrich, P., and Diniz de Figueiredo, E. H. (2016). *The sociolinguistics of digital Englishes*. NY: Routledge.
Hall, C., Smith, P., and Wicaksono, R. (2011). *Mapping applied linguistics: A guide for students and practitioners*. London: Routledge.
Halliday, M. (1978). *Language as a social semiotic*. London: Edward Arnold.
Hymes, D. (1972). On communicative competence. In Pride, J. B., and Holmes, J. (Eds.), *Sociolinguistics: Selected readings* (pp. 269–293). Harmondsworth: Penguin Books.
Hymes, D. (1974). *Foundations in sociolinguistics: An ethnographic approach*. Philadelphia: University of Pennsylvania Press.
Jakobson, R. (2017). *The fundamentals of language*. London: Forgotten Books.
Jenkins, J. (2006). Points of view and blind spots: ELF and SLA. I*nternational Journal of Applied Linguistics*, *16*(2), 137–162.
Jenkins, J. (2007). *English as a lingua franca: Attitude and identity*, Oxford: Oxford University Press.
Jenkins, J. (2015). Repositioning English and multilingualism in English as a lingua franca. *Englishes in Practice* 2015; *2*(3), 49–85
Jenkins, J., Cogo, A., and Dewey, M. (2011). Review of developments in research into English as a lingua franca. *Language Teaching*, *44*(3), 281–315.
Kachru, B. (1983). *The indianization of English: The English language in India*. Oxford: Delhi Oxford Univ. Press.
Kramsch, C. (1995). The applied linguist and the language teacher. *Australian Review of Applied Linguistics*, *18*(1), 1–16.
Kramsch, C. (2015). Applied linguistics: A theory of the practice. *Applied Linguistics*, *36*(4), 454–465.
Kramsch, C. and Whiteside, A. (2008). Language ecology in multilingual settings: Toward a theory of symbolic competence. *Applied Linguistics*, *29*(4), 645–671.
Krashen, S. (1981). *Second language acquisition and second language learning*. Oxford: Pergamon Press.
Krashen, S. (1982). *Principles and practice in second language acquisition*. Oxford: Pergamon Press.
Larsen-Freeman, D. (1986). *Techniques and principles of language teaching*. Oxford: Oxford University Press.
Larsen-Freeman, D. (1997). Chaos/complexity science and second language acquisition. *Applied Linguistics*, *18*(2), 141–165.
Larsen-Freeman, D., and Long, M. H. (1991). *An introduction to second language acquisition*. London: Longman.
Matsuda, A. (2012). *Principles and practices of teaching English as an international language*. Bristol: Multilingual Matters.
May, S. (Ed.). (2014). *The multilingual turn: Implications for SLA, TESOL and bilingual education*. London: Routledge.
Newmeyer F. J., and Weinberger, S. H. (1988). The ontogenesis of the field of second language learning research. In Flynn, S., and O'Neil, W. (Eds.), *Linguistic theory in second language acquisition* (pp. 34–45). Dordrecht, the Netherlands: Springer.
Norton, B. (2010). Language and identity. In Hornberger, H., and S. McKay (Eds.), *Language and identity in sociolinguistics* (pp. 349–369). Bristol: Multilingual Matters.
Pennycook, A. (2001). *Critical applied linguistics: A critical introduction*. London: LEA.

Prodromou, L. (2007). A reader responds to J. Jenkins's "current perspectives on teaching world Englishes and English as a lingua franca." *TESOL Quarterly, 41*(2), 409–413.
Rutherford, W. E. (1993). Linguistics and SLA: The two-way street phenomenon. In F. Eckman (Ed.), *Confluence: Linguistics, L2 acquisition and speech pathology* (pp. 3–14), Amsterdam: John Benjamins Publishing.
Saussure, F. (1997). *Course in general linguistics* (Reprint ed.). A. Bally and A. Sechehaye Peru (Eds.). IL: Open Court.
Seidlhofer, B. (2005). English as a lingua franca. *ELT Journal, 59*(4), 339–341.

3

APPLYING LINGUISTICS TO DISABILITY STUDIES

Ideas for an alliance

> **THIS CHAPTER WILL DO THE FOLLOWING**
>
> 1. Introduce the discipline of disability studies.
> 2. Describe the nature of the work done by humanists and social scientists in disability studies.
> 3. Describe and explain the contribution of scholars in English and related disciplines to disability studies.
> 4. Argue for an alliance between applied linguistics and disability studies.
> 5. Provide examples of work on invisible disabilities through applied linguistics lenses.

Introduction

To my knowledge, this is the first overview book on the use of applied linguistics knowledge in other fields and communities of practice that contains a chapter on disability studies. Given the more closely linguistic associations between the topics of other chapters and linguistic knowledge, I can understand if the reader is surprised at its inclusion. However, I believe there are good reasons to incorporate information on the potential alliance between applied linguistics and disability studies here, and those reasons relate to both the tradition of English scholars to engage in disability studies research (myself included, but see also, for example, Davis, 2009; Bolt, Donaldson, and Rodas, 2012) and the many linguistic aspects of the experience of disability itself.

Simi Linton (2005, p. 518) explains that disability studies is a discipline that,

> introduces a disability reading to a range of subject matter. We prod people to examine how disability as a category was created to serve certain ends and how the category has been institutionalized on social practices and intellectual conventions.

Some of the goals of disability studies according to Linton (p. 518) are "to interrogate the traditional curriculum," "weave disabled people back into the fabric of society," and change the focus from disabled people as having to be "acted on" so that they can fit existing social orders and structures to instead enquire what social changes can be effected so that the environment is conducive to the inclusion, on their own terms, of people living with disabilities. In sum, disability studies transforms the goal of studying disability from one of trying to affect disability on the person to one of addressing environmental problems that make living with a disability harder than it could be. At the same time, the discipline calls attention to language, conceptualization, ideology, and practice that can negatively impact a person with a disability.

There are at least two levels, and I am sure the reader can think of other ones, on which applied linguistics and disability studies intersect. First of all, the way both disabled and able-bodied members of a particular community try to shape the experience of disability is to a great degree done through language. For example, how does referring to an individual's experience of mental diversity as "living with an invisible disability" reshape their own (and others') perception of their own condition, if that had been always referred to as "mental illness" before? How does describing a person as being a "wheelchair user" free them from the restrictive notion of being "wheelchair bound?" (see also Price, 2011, p. 30). How different is the experience of a woman going through some reproductive challenges if the situation is described (and addressed) as one of "reduced hormone levels" as opposed to "*inadequate* levels of progesterone" or a "*defective* luteal phase?" (For this latter example, see Bowker, 2001, p. 603 in reference to a study of the differences in the language of fertility when applied to men and women, also discussed in Chapter 7.)

The experience of disability provides a very large set of examples of language in context and its consequences and ramifications, one that can not only interest applied linguistics to a great degree but also and more importantly, one in which applied linguists can act upon to contribute to meaningful change and, as a result, be a force for good and inclusion.

The second level is that of linguistic disability itself. In that respect, experiences such as hearing impairment, aphasia, dyslexia, challenges in language acquisition/learning/development, dyslalia, the outcomes of cerebral vascular accidents, all have implications for both applied linguistics and disability studies. Note that these experiences are usually framed as some form of impairment, which in general only considers the medical/physical/physiological part of the experience, which is why in the preceding sentence I used the medical terms by which most readers would know these phenomena. Traditionally studied by clinical linguistics—a term that evidences its tight connection to medical views of linguistic elements—these phenomena can also be studied more broadly, and compassionately, through the lenses of disability studies.

Disability, as opposed to impairment, considers the whole person and their sociocultural milieu and frames difference as diversity of experience rather than a departure from a pre-established "norm." As a consequence, disability studies seeks to elucidate and understand what it is like to experience disability not only from a medical perspective but also from the perspective of work, study, relationships, rights, language use, etc. Given that disability studies tends to focus on the environment as the place where social change needs to occur (thus refraining from postulating that the person experiencing disability change to fit social models and expectations), the question may be how applied linguists interested in disability studies can help reframe these experiences to focus on the environment as a locus of transformation and social inclusion of persons with disabilities.

Aided by corpus linguistics strategies, discourse and content analysis, surveys and interviews, as well as observation of naturally occurring language, linguists can seek to explore the many metaphors, discursive practices, linguistic patterns, and attitudes held toward disability, with goals of advocacy, education, awareness raising, and even policy making. Disability in this chapter, as elsewhere in the literature, refers to visible and invisible disability, temporary or long-lasting disability and disability that affects both physical and mental diversity.

Researchers have established three patterns of language used to refer to people who experience disability (Back et al., 2016). One of them, perhaps the oldest form, contains a phrasal structure that starts with the disability and follows with the person experiencing it. Oftentimes, the disability includes an adjectival form, trailed by a noun. Examples include "disabled man," "autistic student," "obsessive-compulsive woman." This kind of label was called into question by disability studies scholars and a number of disability advocates because it seems to privilege the disability over the individual to the point of defining the latter. That is, a person experiencing disability is also and primarily an individual but additionally a mother, an artist, a friend, an athlete, and yet, according to this naming practice, the disability is represented as an all-inclusive identity marker. Back et al. (2016) contend that the disability-first structure conforms more closely to a medical model of disability where the disability (or more accurately, the impairment, which is what medicine studies) is the focus of medical intervention and practice.

The person-first movement (see for example Back et al., 2011 or Blaska, 1993) was born out of discontentment with that emphasis on the disability rather than the person. In that case, proponents suggest that "woman (living) with depression," as opposed to "a depressed woman," which would be considered a disability-first form, is preferable in its valuing of the person before the disability.

Blaska (1993, p. 25) suggests that using a person-first approach promotes "a positive image." A person-first approach can also be seen to promote a sense of empowerment for the individual and a different image for others to consider. However, endorsement of a person-first approach is not universal. The very reasons that are used to justify its adoption (see some in Blaska, 1993) are also at times employed to discourage its use altogether within specific groups. For example, Sinclair (2013, p. 1) argues that "Saying 'person with autism' suggests that the autism can be separated from the person. But this is not the case."

Likewise, in a critique of journal *Adapted Physical Activity Quarterly* guidelines that establish a person-first approach to references to disability in the publication (borrowed from the American Psychological Association), Peers, Spencer-Cavaliere, and Eales (2014, p. 266)

> maintain that universally mandating disability terminologies borrowed from American psychology may serve to either exclude research that does not share the basic cultural and theoretical assumptions of American psychology (as described in more detail below) or force researchers to adopt language that contradicts the epistemologies, theories, methodologies, ethical precepts, or cultural specificities adopted in their research.

They are particularly concerned with different uses of language that are predominant in international contexts given different linguistic and cultural traditions and how limiting participation of these different actors on the bases of terminological disagreements could be detrimental to the discussions at hand.

Thus, it is possible that these views are mediated by issues of identity that can interact with language to different degrees depending on the specific person, their particular disability, their theoretical orientation, and the context in which language is used. For example, one could hypothesize that the relationship between person and disability (and sense of identity) is different for an individual who has, for instance, lived with autism all their life (or being autistic, as many advocates prefer) as opposed to a person who developed a physical disability at an advanced age as a result of aging itself. That is, would a person with a sense of identity that did not include a disability until they were 65 have a different relationship with disability than a person who has experienced it throughout their life? How about individuals who lived with a disability all their lives but did not have a term to name it until they were adults? Would their use of language (and sense of identity) vary as a consequence?

On the other hand, one could also hypothesize that the relationship between individual, identity, and disability is so personal that two people living with the same disability may have very different reactions to the language used to refer to it. These reactions could also be mediated by their past experiences (e.g., inclusion or exclusion, a positive and supportive view of disability within their immediate community, etc.). Finally, could people living with different disabilities belong to different speech communities with different understandings of the terminology used to refer to their particular experience? For example, within the community of individuals with Obsessive-Compulsive Disorder (OCD) community, it is usual for people to refer to the experience of heightened anxiety as a "spike" rather than "panic" or "anxiety attack," whereas those living with Panic Disorder usually speak of "panic attacks." Does language in these cases signal speech-community membership? These are of course only a few of the questions and hypotheses applied linguists could formulate (and test) regarding these linguistic preferences.

Although much of the discussion remains within the people-first and disability-first dichotomy, a third linguistic form of reference to persons living with disabilities exists, and it is that of disability-implicit language (Back et al, 2016). In this case, disability is not directly referred to but is instead alluded to. Saying, for instance, "inclusion students" or "special education" or even "the different needs of students" falls within this category, which can also include, as the authors point out, the omission of reference altogether, which is nonetheless implied in the context, as in "the students," when the context indicates that in that case the expression means "students with disabilities." Those researchers call attention to "context-dependence" and its role in any attempts to explain the use of these different forms and individual preferences, as I also highlighted above.

Back et al. (2016) acknowledge that "language may reflect societal attitudes that are critical in shaping the experiences of people with disabilities, particularly during formative periods." Their study focuses on content analysis of 22 qualitative interviews with a number of stakeholders (high school students, administrators, teachers, parents) about the language that is used to refer to students with disabilities. They explain that,

> As the number of students with disabilities placed in least restrictive environments such as inclusive classrooms increases, language may be especially relevant to understanding the experiences of students with disabilities who are both attempting to engage with their peers and receive an appropriate education.

In their study, interviewees used disability-implicit language the most, followed by people-first language, and finally disability-first references.

Applied linguists have often worked at the intersection of race, ethnicity, class, and gender, formulating, given their observations, theories to explain the use of the language as mediated by these social elements, either by themselves or in combination in what is increasingly greater intersectionality. For example, Deborah Tannen (2017) is known for her work on gender and language, and Kubota (2014) has written extensively about postcolonialism and applied linguistics, touching upon issues of race, ethnicity, and power. It is time that disability be considered too if we want our linguistic investigations to be fully intersectional.

Reclaiming language

As it happens with other minority groups, individuals living with disabilities and their allies also reclaim derogatory terms in the context of disability. For example, crip theory, utilizes a term clipped from "cripple" as a form of both resistance and empowerment; once you reclaim a term as an insider to a particular speech community, you remove some of the linguistic power from people outside those communities who used it in hurtful and "othering" ways. In his own book by that name, McRuer (2006, p. 2) claims that "*Crip Theory: Signs of Queerness and Disability* emerges from cultural studies traditions that question the order of things, considering how and why it is constructed and naturalized." In that respect, crip theory challenges, much as it also does with the experience of heterosexuality as the default, the experience of able-bodies as "the norm," and it uses language as symbolic of this standpoint. Likewise, the movement known as Mad Pride, reclaimed the adjective "mad" to forward the idea that not only do users of psychiatric services have rights, but they also claim for themselves the ability to redefine their disability (with or without medical intervention) in their own terms. Price (2011, p. 10) explains that "Many persons in the mad movement identify as psychiatry system survivors." Mad studies, as derived from that movement (see, for example, LeFrançois, Menzies, and Reaume, 2013), seeks to change perceptions of mental diversity, and reclaiming the term "mad" is part of this process. The aforementioned authors write:

> Grassroots advocates, community groups, and international alliances have been spreading their message of anti-discrimination and inclusion to governments, stakeholder groups, media, and the public alike, in the very discourse of 'mental health' from the reigning biomedical model to a paradigm of social provision, human justice and valorization of diversity.
>
> (p. 9)

In all these cases, what was once a vulnerability, a term that disempowers and diminishes, can become symbolic of resistance, transformation, healing, and self-advocacy. This is another area in which words matter. "Healing" for example, is different from "curing," and "patient," which, besides putting the person involved in a passive position, might not always be true, as not all people experiencing disability are under medical care. "Curing" relates to medical intervention while "healing" involves the transcendence of disability through self-acceptance, social inclusion, human rights recognition, and application of existing and alternative abilities to the empowerment of an individual and the betterment of society as a whole (Friedrich, 2015).

As linguists we have always been aware of the power of words. In the case of disability studies, areas of intersection with applied linguistics go much beyond understanding the motivations and the consequences of naming and referencing practices, as seen above, although those practices are not to be ignored. One other area that has interested me over the years is the figurative, analogous, and metaphorical language used to explain disability within its circles but also in society at large. Such language in the latter case, especially in the context of the media, often reveals biases, misapprehensions, and stereotypes that can be retrieved through linguistic analysis. For example, as I studied the linguistic representation of obsessive-compulsive disorder (Friedrich, 2015), I realized many of the metaphors and analogies used to explain OCD contain references to mechanical and/or electrical components, systems, and models. Common are the references to broken records, looping tapes, stuck systems, malfunctioning transmissions. Whereas these references can contain useful comparisons, analogies, and metaphors, especially to convey meaning and offer shortcuts to those without first-hand knowledge, one also must wonder what the consequences are of understanding human experience as similar to machine malfunction. Does it cause us to see disability, at least in this instance, as a matter of "fixing" a faulty component? Does it take us closer to a pathologized vision of disability, one where body and its individual organs and systems are separate from the mind, as opposed to a humanistic and humanized one?

During the same research project, I also realized that oftentimes terms used to refer to OCD and people living with OCD carried embedded judgment and at the same time minimized the impact of the experience: there were frequent references to OCD thoughts being "bizarre" (even if intrusive thoughts are experienced by about 90% of the population, the one distinction being that in OCD they get "stuck," to use a common term), of OCD being a "quirk," or somewhat "funny" (a perception certainly informed by the construction of characters on TV), and the misleading characterization of its being about "handwashing" and "neatness." Popular use also gives rise to strange grammatical structures such as "He is so OCD" (i.e., *He is so obsessive-compulsive disorder) that do not stand up to scrutiny.

Therefore, one possible task for investigations at the intersection of disability studies and applied linguistics is to conduct both discourse and content analysis of texts used to characterize different forms of disability to find out how linguistic representation impacts understanding, social inclusion and exclusion, self-image, and even willingness to speak publicly of the experience of disability. These analyses can be performed on works of fiction, non-fiction, journalistic accounts, memoirs, movies and shows, as well as everyday oral texts, and also medical texts and scientific papers.

In the latter case, Bowker (2001), for example, shows how language reveals different attitudes toward infertility in men and women, attitudes which are clear in the linguistic choices made, and then reinforced by the same language choices once they become the norm. For instance, Bowker explains that when it comes to comparable challenges to fertility in men and women, "[T]he female focus is described using much stronger and more negative terms than the male focus: men are presented as being below average whereas women are considered inadequate." As evidence, Bowker presents typical adjectives from her corpus study, which in the case of problems relating to male fertility include adjectives such as "poor," "reduced" or "(too) few" [my parentheses] and, in the case of female fertility, include such adjectives as "faulty," "defective," and "deficient."

As it is clear, these linguistic choices sit at the intersection of disability and gender and are mediated by the linguistic and sociolinguistic constructs that are sometimes subconsciously held until revealed in text. That is, it is not too difficult to imagine that collectively, these authors of medical texts that show negative bias toward women (experiencing infertility, for example) are not aware of what their linguistic choices reveal, and that these choices are mediated by cultural institutional practices years in the making. It is up to linguists and disability studies scholars to call attention to these idiosyncrasies and work toward positive change.

In *The Literary and Linguistic Construction of Obsessive-Compulsive Disorder*, I argued for the use of Critical Discourse Analysis (CDA) as an important tool for the elucidation of disability studies linguistic phenomena. I was pleased therefore, to see that another scholar had arrived at a similar conclusion when I read *Mad at School* for the first time, in preparation for this chapter. In it, Price (2011, p. 29) also endorses CDA as compatible with disability studies given "the ways that language is used to construct formations of power and difference." While I focused on the work of van Djik (1993) and Price prefers Ellen Barton's theories (for example, 2002), the commitment is the same: to recognize in the construction of texts our social biases about disability, held collectively and individually.

When we write at the intersection of disability studies and applied linguistics using discourse analysis lenses, we need to take into consideration all of the Discourses (with a capital D) that contribute to our understandings, biases, and political views on our object of analysis when it comes to "impairment" and "disability." Some of those, which I included in Friedrich (2015) are the discourse of medicalization, the discourse of pharmaceuticalization, the discourse of the mind, the discourse of the *Diagnostic and Statistical Manual of Mental Disorders* (DSM), among others. Calling something a "disorder," advocating for a "cure," referring to "chemical imbalances," separating "body," "brain," and "mind" are all discursive strategies embedded in beliefs and values (and political stances) that, can be revealed through and further examined by discourse analysis. Applied linguistics would do well to follow a path of discovery that can positively impact the lives of people with disabilities.

Conclusion

A formal alliance between applied linguistics and disability studies is still in its infancy, which means this is an appropriate time to think of important questions to be asked and crucial research to be conducted. This chapter is only a small sample of themes and areas for further consideration. However, many are the possibilities that arise once we consider inter- and transdisciplinary avenues of investigation. Below I offer suggestions for research questions and research projects. It is my hope that applied linguists accept this invitation to find out more.

Questions and ideas for further research

1. Research the use of people-first and disability-first language among members of different speech communities. Is a pattern possible to identify?
2. What does a discourse analysis of communication within a particular speech community show?
3. What does an analysis of media (movies, TV shows, newspaper articles) regarding a particular form of disability reveal about social perceptions and attitudes and how are those attitudes linguistically formulated?
4. What are further points of intersection between disability studies and applied linguistics?
5. How can applied linguistics, disability studies, and corpus linguistics be combined to reveal linguistic practices within a certain community with regards to a particular disability (e.g., medical professionals)?
6. How does disability (or a particular form of disability), taken intersectionality, reveal different linguistic uses across genders or age groups?

Works cited and further reading

Back, L. T., Keys, C. B., McMahon, S. D., and O'Neill, K. (2016). How we label students with disabilities: A framework of language use in an urban school district in the United States. *Disability Studies Quarterly, 36*(4). Retrieved on August 1, 2018 from http://dsq-sds.org/article/view/4387/4481

Barton, E. (2002). Resources for discourse analysis in composition studies. *Style, 36*(4), Resources in Stylistics and Literary Analysis, 575–594.

Blaska, J. (1993). The power of language: Speak and write using "person" first. In M. Nagler (Ed.), *Perspectives on Disability* (2nd ed., pp. 25–32). Palo Alto, CA: Health Markets Research.

Bolt, D. Donaldson, E. J., and Rodas, J. M. (2012). *The madwoman and the blindman. Jane Eyre, discourse, disability.* Columbus: Ohio State University Press.

Bowker, L. (2001). Terminology and gender sensitivity: A corpus-based study of the LSP of infertility. *Language in Society. 30*(4), 589–610.

Davis, L. (2009). *Obsession: A history.* Chicago: University of Chicago Press.

Dunn, D. S., and Andrews, E. E. (2015). Person-first and identity-first language: Developing psychologists' cultural competence using disability language. *American Psychologist 70*(3), 255–264.

Friedrich, P. (2015). *The literary and linguistic construction of obsessive-compulsive disorder: No ordinary doubt.* London: Palgrave.

Gottlieb, N. (2001). Language and disability in Japan. *Disability & Society, 16*(7), 981–995. https://doi.org/10.1080/09687590120097863

Kubota, R. (2014). The multi/plural turn, postcolonial theory, and neoliberal multiculturalism: Complicities and implications for applied linguistics. *Applied Linguistics, 37*(4), 474–494.

LeFrançois, B., Menzies, R., and Reaume, G. (Eds.). (2013) *Mad matters: A critical reader in Canadian mad studies.* Toronto: Canadian Scholars' Press Inc.

Linton, S. (1998). Reassigning meaning. In S. Linton, *Claiming disability: Knowledge and identity.* (pp. 8–33). New York, NY: New York University Press.

Linton, S. (2005). What is disability studies? *PMLA 120*(2), 518–522.

McRuer, Robert. (2006). *Crip theory: Cultural signs of queerness and disability.* NY: New York University Press.

Peers, D., Spencer-Cavaliere, N., and Eales, L. (2014). Say what you mean: Rethinking disability language. *Adapted Physical Activity Quarterly, 31*, 265–282.

Price, M. (2011). *Mad at school: Rhetorics of mental disability and academic life.* Ann Arbor, MI: University of Michigan Press.

Shakespeare, T. (2010). The social model of disability. In L. Davis (Ed.), *The Disability Studies Reader* (3rd ed., pp. 266–273). New York, NY: Routledge.

Shakespeare, T. (2013). *Disability rights and wrongs revisited.* Oxon, UK: Routledge.

Sinclair, J. (2013). Why I dislike "person first" language. *Autonomy, the Critical Journal of Interdisciplinary Autism Studies. 1*(2). Retrieved on November 22, 2018 from www.larryarnold.net/Autonomy/index.php/autonomy/article/view/OP1.

Tannen, D. (2017). *You're the only one I can tell: Inside the language of women's friendship.* NY: Ballantine.

van Djik, T. (1993). Principles of critical discourse analysis. *Discourse & Society 4*(2), 249–283.

Whitaker, R. (2002). *Mad in America: Bad science, bad medicine, and the enduring mistreatment of the mentally ill.* New York, NY: Perseus Books.

4

PROFILING WORLD ENGLISHES AND LANGUAGES OF WIDER COMMUNICATION

THIS CHAPTER WILL DO THE FOLLOWING

1. Explain the concept of a sociolinguistic profile and position it in relation to applied linguistics practices and goals.
2. Relate the concept of sociolinguistic profile to world Englishes and the practice of describing the users and uses of English around the world.
3. Describe and explain the different elements of linguistic profiles and their application.
4. Exemplify the elements of a profile through published scholarship.
5. Provide ideas for students and scholars who would like to profile English and other languages and their uses around the world.

Introduction

With the expansion of English to many corners of the world, it has become vital to profile countries and regions where that language is used (in its multiple forms) in an attempt to understand social dynamics, political concerns, educational needs, and other aspects of the universe of Englishes. Especially since the 1980s, researchers have been engaged in mapping the world of Englishes through sociolinguistic profiles of the language(s). This chapter will focus on common characteristics of sociolinguistic profiles, the uses of such narratives, examples of existing profiles, and suggestions for future work. While the emphasis in this instance will be on English and its varieties, the guidelines and suggestions provided here are applicable across the linguistic spectrum and can therefore be used to profile any language, particularly languages of wider communication. In multilingual societies, these suggestions are also pertinent when it comes to profiling languages in relation to one another rather than individually, although decisions about scope should as always be motivated by the objectives of the research project itself and the characteristics of the area in question.

Applying linguistic knowledge to these environments—and then using the insight gained through these studies in the real world—is the ultimate goal of country/region/area profiling. In this chapter, I place country/region profiles at the intersection of applied linguistics and world Englishes scholarship. Going back to the idea that applied linguistics is often anchored in practice, one can start the process by contemplating a number of questions. For example, a question could be, "Given that country X's profile indicated that users of English range in the millions who use English for Y functions, and also given that country Z exhibits many sociolinguistic similarities to country X, will the two countries present comparable linguistic features and behaviors?" Further considerations could include theorizing about these aspects of language use given the findings of the profiles or suggesting educational and other practices to facilitate the lives of language users.

World Englishes and sociolinguistic profiles

World Englishes is a field of expertise in which researchers, scholars, and teachers seek to investigate and understand the dynamics of English use, its expressions around the world, the many forms that English(es) takes, the status of different varieties, and the motivations that propel the spread and maintenance of English. Given its stage of development, world Englishes scholarship usually relies on the understanding that languages of wider communication spread because of more than the intrinsic features of those languages and instead are boosted because of socio-economic, political, and attitudinal factors, including users' beliefs about its association with prestige, modernity, economic advancement, and power.

However, world Englishes scholars also understand that once English spreads, it changes. Languages often go through a metamorphosis when they become associated with different cultures, when they mix with other languages, and when they are used for new purposes and in new domains. Additionally, language users will bestow upon the language all their linguistic creativity, causing it to transform further. In that sense, while forces of maintenance exist, causing the language to "stay together" through education, institutional use, and official functions, forces of change pull languages in the opposite direction, causing them to transform and adapt to local needs and local uses (Bakhtin, 1981). Historically (and practically), we know that the forces of change ultimately win; look no further than the history of English itself, with layer upon layer of linguistic innovation being introduced into English, from its Anglo-Saxon origins, through the influence of Old Norse, then Old French, and waves of Latin impact, so that it ultimately took the form we recognize as Modern English.

Thus, our use of "Englishes" in the plural is a way to convey the multiplicity of expressions and the variation of the language at present, which no doubt leads to significant change in the long run.

Other important aspects of world Englishes include the belief that all language manifestations, with their respective communicative purposes, all variations in naturally occurring patterns of pronunciation, changes in vocabulary, code-mixing and loan-word use are valid and legitimate and should therefore be described without prejudice and without a preconception that they are second to standard language. In world Englishes, these varieties are discussed in their richness and communicative potential, with particular attention to the uses that have led to the forms that English or other languages start and continue to take.

Traditionally, and still today, profiles have relied heavily on the framework of concentric circles proposed by Braj Kachru in the 1980s (1983 and after), a model which categorizes countries/regions according to the historical movement of English spread, starting with the Inner Circle (e.g., Great Britain, the US, Canada, Australia, New Zealand); Outer Circle (e.g., India, Malaysia, Nigeria, Kenya, Philippines); progressing to the international communities of the Expanding Circle (e.g., Brazil, France, Mexico, China). The model is useful for profiles because it can help elucidate some of the domains and uses of the language in these places and provide a basis for comparison across other environments. That is, it is intuitive to imagine that profilers will find more commonalities in use and domains between Brazil and Mexico than between England and China, since the first two belong to the same circle and the two latter ones do not. Additionally, profiles can be used collectively to present a more holistic picture of the circles themselves, as well as highlight instances when countries start deviating from the common characteristics of their circle. For example, Berns (1988) has written about how Germany presents characteristics of both the Expanding and Outer Circle, especially given the use of English in the legal domain, even though the country is traditionally understood as belonging to the Expanding Circle. Similarly, it is possible to make an argument regarding the difficulty of placing South Africa neatly in a circle, given the complex linguistic relations there. Note Kamwangamalu (2009, p. 168), for example, who writes,

> Unlike in other former British colonies, in South Africa, English is used both as a native language by more than a million British who, contrary to what they did in other colonies, never left the country when colonization ended, and as second language by a minority of South Africa's population.

Further complicating the matter, is the presence of another European-origin language (Afrikaans, of Dutch origin) and many local languages, several of which are part of the group of 11 with official status in the country. Add to that the fact that many people in South Africa speak more than one language, and profilers have a situation of great linguistic interest, richness, and complexity to describe.

World Englishes profilers are interested in capturing aspects of this kind of variation, kinship, and multiplicity. Focusing on particular environments, profilers set out to record and report on the uses, users, attitudes, innovations, and the possible future of the language in the environments they cover. In turn, they can end up uncovering specific features of the regions/countries they study that have not been systematized yet. The information they provide can be used to draw educational goals and objectives, inform policy, plan international programs among many other real-world applications. Below, I explain what each of the most common elements of a profile entails while giving examples from published profiles and theoretical underpinnings. The chapter then closes with suggestions for students and scholars interested in profiling aspects of English (and other languages) use around the world.

A note of caution is necessary here. While country profiles are an important part of scholarship at the intersection of world Englishes and applied linguistics, world Englishes studies are not limited to profiles. Studies of language variation, attitudes toward language, language policy, the politics of language, Englishes in the media, literatures in Englishes, and many other aspects are well represented in world Englishes scholarship. This chapter will focus on profiles as a springboard to the varied world of Englishes and, by extension, other languages of wider communication.

History of English presence/use

Studying and reporting on the time and means by which English (or another language of wider communication) arrived in a particular area is another task often performed by profilers. Was the language introduced through colonization? Is there history of military presence? Did the language arrive after a significant political event? Was its growing presence related to trade and internationalization? All of these considerations will help a researcher establish the kinds of attitudes held by the users (and non-users) of the language and the domains where the language will be most active. The historical reconstruction, however, does not stop there. Oftentimes, the introduction is not linear but instead episodic, with several defining moments that help explain current linguistic relations.

Domains of use

The idea of domains of use can be traced back to crucial discussions in sociolinguistics such as the ones undertaken by Gumperz (1961 and 1972) and Fishman (1972). The latter author puts forth the matter of domains in terms of role relations (e.g., cleric-parishioner, pupil-teacher, buyer-seller). He goes on to state that,

> It would certainly seem desirable to describe and analyze language use or language choice in a particular multilingual setting in terms of the crucial role relations within the specific domains considered to be the most revealing for the setting.
>
> *(p. 443)*

Sociolinguistic profilers have in general incorporated the idea of these role relations to their profiles, and have thus described in detail the domains of English use relevant in different environments. Within these domains and role relations, as Fishman explains, lies the matter of language choice.[1] Why a function within a domain gets to be performed primarily in a certain language will say a lot about the linguistic relations in the country/region in question. For example, if in a country the functions within the domains of "family" and "religion" by a speech community get performed in language A, but within education and government the primary vehicle is language B, it is logical to conclude that the status (both official/default official and prestige-related) of the two languages will be different, and that language B will enjoy privileges potentially not afforded to language A. On the other hand, if language A leads in all of these domains, our conclusions about the dynamics of language in the place in question will be different.

Combining this knowledge with the world Englishes framework of concentric circles, one is able to observe that the domains of English use and the extent of that use will be different across the three circles but will bear important resemblance among countries within the same circle. In that sense, Brazil and Mexico, countries of the Expanding Circle, will display a strong presence and use of English within international buyer-seller role relations but a much less robust use within parent-child roles and cleric-parishioner interactions. India and Nigeria, on the other hand, will likely display a much more evident use of English within pupil-teacher and government official-citizen communications than either Brazil or Mexico because the former two countries belong to the Outer Circle unlike the latter.

Functions of English

In *The Other Tongue*, Kachru (1992, p. 58) describes four possible functions of English in environments around the world. The instrumental function is performed by English when it is used for learning. Educational uses of the language both as a subject of study, as well as a vehicle of knowledge, fall within this category. The innovative function is performed by creative uses of the language, for example, literary expressions including music, and, I would also incorporate, advertising and the media. Oftentimes, looking at this function will allow profilers to detect great instances of creativity that they can then explore in detail. For example, the use of neologisms, the sedimentation of syntactic forms, instances of borrowing, code-mixing, and switching can often be found and studied within this function, and they make for great subjects of investigation.

The interpersonal function is realized through communication among people. Sridhar (1989) also reminds us that within that function, language works as a symbol of modernity and elitism, and therefore, studying attitudes toward different languages, different varieties, and the motivations people have for using them can be an important aspect of investigating this function of Englishes.

Additionally, how different varieties hold different status and how different people are perceived through the lenses of the differences in their language can also be investigated vis-à-vis the interpersonal function. Finally, the regulative function refers to those uses of English within legal and administrative domains. We know that English tends to have more uses within the legal and government systems in countries of the Inner and Outer Circles. Therefore, changes in the dynamics of English use in such domains in the Expanding Circle, for example, can be worthy of investigation because they likely signal other changes of linguistic and cultural relevance.

Researchers profiling countries or regions where English is used can choose to frame the whole profile based on the model of functions of English, choosing to present a panoramic view of language relations and English through the lenses of these four functions. Alternatively, they can choose to focus on an in-depth analysis of one of the functions or an even more profound evaluation of one element within one of the functions. The possibilities are limitless, and this particular framework offers great opportunities for comparison across different profiles because it has been used often and productively in the field.

Status (official, de facto official)

Part of the reason why countries are clustered in the three circles has to do with the intra- and international functions that English might play in those places. Typically, in Inner and Outer Circle countries English has roles in education, government, and the law, and these roles are made possible because the language has official or de-facto official status. In the US, for example, although no language is named in the constitution, the power of the English language when it comes to performing intra-national functions as an official language would is hard to contest (although that does not mean that proponents of multilingualism accept that reality without challenging it or advocating for space for other languages).

The status of a language as (de facto) official is significant because in instances where a language plays that role, it usually has or develops local models, with local norms. For example, the model of English in the US is an abstraction we call "American English," whereas in India it is "Indian English." While in countries of the Outer Circle, English usually started spreading based on a prescribed outside model, in time local norms started developing, and those norms might have brought innovation and change to grammar, pronunciation, and other linguistic and supra-segmental elements. Part of the job of the profiler is to record, discuss, and bring these linguistic elements to light.

Attitudes toward the language

The study of attitudes toward language(s) is so important that even though it belongs to the discussion about functions of English carried out above, it also deserves its own section and argument. When attitudes toward a language are positive and there are affirmative associations with modernity, progress, and status, more people will likely be willing to embrace that language as their own. Hence, understanding language dynamics through the optics of attitudes is an important step toward figuring out, for example, linguistic ecology and language maintenance; that is, the more positive associations users have regarding a language, the biggest the contribution of attitudes toward the survival of that language (even if other factors—political, economic, and social—will come into play).

I have had an opportunity to profile the users and uses of English in Brazil (Friedrich, 2000), and I noticed that part of the maintenance of the status of the language is justified by users as a matter of better chances of employment, connections to modernity, and overall optimistic beliefs in the power of English to provide its users, including those who learned the language as a foreign language (the issues regarding this term notwithstanding), with opportunities for growth and access to knowledge. This was the case with both people who already had a level of communicative competence in English as well as those wanting to learn. That latter group is the main reason why I am including this information in a section about attitudes. Several of the respondents to my survey *hoped* that English would bring them certain advantages, thus highlighting the value of attitudes and expectations in language use and spread. In this case, they were willing to study and acquire the language given those expectations.

A sociolinguistic profile can rely on a variety of methodologies to gauge attitudes toward a language. They include but are not limited to surveys, interviews, ethnographies, analyses of media materials, reviews of books, and investigations of educational practices. In a separate study (Friedrich, 2002), I looked at uses of English in advertising in Brazil by studying magazine articles and found similar associations with modernity and status motivating the use, although there was clear acknowledgment that the use of English could not mediate the primary message of most ads, given that the overall proficiency of the Brazilian population is often estimated to be around 5% (population over 16, as estimated by the British Council and Data Popular Institute, 2014). For that reason, English texts and expressions often appeared in the secondary text of these messages, in terms such as "high tech" and "light," which strengthen the association of the product with those desirable traits without compromising intelligibility.

This low number of actual users combined with the high frequency of English in advertising secondary texts further illustrates that the power of a language can be felt in its presence even when it is not being actively employed. This can be confirmed when one studies the history of English and the layering of French terms brought into the language by the Norman invaders, who for centuries formed the upper class; even the everyday people, who did not speak French, in time started making associations between that language and status and prestige. To this day, French-derived words in English carry a connotation of sophistication and status when compared to more "casual" Anglo-Saxon terms. Contrast, for example the Old- and Middle-French derived sentence, "Literary endeavors necessitate vigilant consideration" as opposed to the Old English-based, "Writing needs careful thought." It is all in the attitudes.

Attitudes can also be an important element in one's understanding of why a language spreads to certain domains and why one cannot simply look at the intrinsic elements of a language (i.e., syntax, vocabulary, supra-segmentals) to try and determine its long-term prospect and viability.

Number of users (and how to count those)

It is very difficult to precisely measure how many people speak a language of wider communication, to a great degree because it is very hard to decide and then to apply our criteria to who counts as a user of language, especially if the person is not a first language user (i.e., from first-language users there is an expectation of proficiency, however flawed that concept may be). Is it the person who can hold a survival-level conversation; is it a person who is completely fluent; and what does having communicative ability at these two levels, for example, mean? Does "using English" necessitate that a person be competent in all four skills (i.e., speaking, reading, writing, and listening) or does it suffice that a person be able to engage with one skill? Even if one decides for a particular level of communicative competence, how does one go about assessing language users' fulfillment of the requirements for that level of linguistic skill? Asking language users themselves might not be all that elucidating because their attitudes toward their own communicative ability will be mediated by their beliefs and cultural orientation. For example, in cultures where being modest about one's ability is an important social value, language users might underestimate their linguistic fluency.

On the other hand, in more individualistic contexts, where it is not only acceptable but also expected for one to talk openly about their accomplishments, people might even exaggerate their skills a bit. As a consequence, estimates, especially those that take into consideration the sum of native language users, users who acquired the language as a second or additional language, and those who learned in environments where English is mostly used for international communication, are notoriously unreliable.

In the beginning of the century, David Crystal (2000, p. 3) estimated that about one and a half billion people around the world spoke English. Since then, scholars can speculate that the number of users has grown although we don't know by how much. There is more agreement when it comes to the number of first-language users of English: estimates are around the 350-million mark (Ethnologue, online, for example). English is still considered the primary language of the Internet with almost one billion users, but Chinese is now quickly catching on, almost reaching the 800-million point (Internet World Stats). These latter numbers appear to be more reliable since Internet language use can be tracked and computed. What these numbers show almost unequivocally, nonetheless, is that the number of first-language users of English is significantly smaller than the number of users of English as an additional/second/foreign language, which makes non-native users a strong force in language change. This phenomenon is one of the important reasons for profiles of these environments to be drawn.

Estimating the number of users in a particular country or region can be a part of a sociolinguistic profile, but it is important to qualify that estimate in your work because of all the reasons provided above. Those numbers can then be revisited in following years for a notion of how English is further impacting local language relations and/or is being affected by larger socio-economic and political factors. It is important to remember, however, that numbers are but one element in the big picture drawn by sociolinguistic profiles, in part because profiles assume that even people who are not fluent in the language in question can be affected by its presence in the country and region profiled. When I profiled learners of English in Brazil (Friedrich, 2000), I realized that it was actually beginner learners that overvalued the power of English in changing their lives. That is, not yet being members of the speech community labeled "users of English," they were the ones with the highest expectations, and hopes, as to what English would do in their lives. While some of them would likely go on to indeed become members of that community, their power in shaping, for example, the role of English in educational realms cannot be understated, and would make itself felt even before they became active users of the language.

Local ecology of languages

One of the aspects that greatly complicates the crafting of a sociolinguistic profile is the existence of an ecology of languages (and varieties) in the regions or countries a profiler might be studying. This is even more clearly the case in multilingual societies, or within multicultural groups, as explained by Kramsch and Whiteside (2008, p. 646):

> In the many places around the world where multiple languages are used to conduct the business of everyday life, language users have to navigate much less predictable exchanges in which the interlocutors use a variety of different languages and dialects for various identification purposes, and exercise symbolic power in various ways to get heard and respected (Rampton, 1998–1999). They have to mediate complex encounters among interlocutors with different language capacities and cultural imaginations.

It would therefore be presumptuous for a profiler to ignore that whatever window they have into the environment they are portraying is only that—a window—and it is worth reminding the reader that it is best to acknowledge the limitations of this kind of study, being specific about what it can and cannot provide, instead of attempting to create a sweeping image of English and other languages, one that cannot withstand scrutiny. Furthermore, if a researcher is entering the environment through the lenses of English, they are already establishing a linguistic bias that will affect the picture they paint. While they may be an insider to the culture(s) of English, and even a user of one or more local languages, their own position vis-à-vis these languages is a strong force in determining the shape the profile will take. In itself, these facts are neither negative nor positive, provided the profiler is willing to acknowledge them and use their existence as an informative and reflective springboard.

The very nature of an ecology of languages means that linguistic relations, symbolic meaning, and power struggles are in a constant fluid state, often hard to capture and systematize. Embedded in the metaphor[2] is also the idea that languages, as living organisms, are affected by and affect one another; hence, local socio-political decisions can tip the linguistic balance at any given point in time.

Given these many variables and the great diversity that users of language process every day, especially now, in a world that is in flux, characterized by great migrations, humanitarian crises, resettlement of refugees, etc., it seems it is an appropriate time to reconsider the boundaries of a profile. In certain environments, it might be more productive to profile cities, rather than countries, or speech communities, rather than regions. Even cities might be too broad a scope, depending on their characteristics and the goals of the profile.

Take the example of Kramsch and Whiteside (2008, p. 647), who describe a bit of the sociolinguistic reality of the projected 25,000 Yucatecans who live in the San Francisco Bay area. These language users reside in an area of great linguistic diversity, and being that many work service jobs, in the restaurant industry for example, they come in contact with a linguistic reality that includes many languages in daily contact. The authors posit that in some restaurants as many as eight languages are commonly spoken alongside English. A complex sociolinguistic reality follows, one according to which certain languages are deemed appropriate for public use while others are reserved for the home; certain languages further acquire symbolic meaning as languages of solidarity among minority groups.

How much of this reality is transferable to other speech communities in the San Francisco area is certainly very debatable, which means that far-reaching generalizations about the status of English and other languages in the US, California, or the Bay area would apply to a larger degree (or not at all) depending on the scope of the profile and the ways it was framed, and it is therefore the job of the profiler to establish these boundaries and discuss the limitations of their investigations in some detail.

Linguistic innovations

Investigating linguistic innovation in a particular context is not only a great way to find out and highlight what matters to a people, but it can also be a very rewarding and interesting activity. While some universals apply to the way cultures deal with the introduction of new languages to their repertoire, where users of language focus their attention and what form and function these innovations serve can help draw a much better picture of a community than relying on "standard language" ever could. For example, it is expected that in the interaction between two languages, if a term is borrowed, it will in time conform to the grammatical norms of the receiving language. In that way, the English verb "to click," became "clicar" in Portuguese because a vowel + r combination indicates infinitive in that language, whereas the dropping of the K allows the written form to conform to the Portuguese alphabet, which does not contain the letter K (Friedrich and Diniz de Figueiredo, 2016). However, the fact that so many terms from English, in the domain of computers and technology, come into Brazilian Portuguese through English points to a cultural association between modernity, development, and the English language. Through triangulation, I arrived at the same result when I asked language learners why they were learning English, and they themselves spoke of its association with progress and modernity. Notice, in this case, that whether the association is "true" in the stricter sense of the word is less important than the attitude and perception that it is because the attitude is the driving force for linguistic change. This process can be considered analogous to economic dynamics, where a belief that an economic crisis is coming would bring about an economic crisis (whereas a belief in economic stability would cause consumers to behave in the very manner capable of bringing stability). Thus, profilers can call attention to such elements and discuss them both in the context of individual countries/regions and in their combination to indicate trends and tendencies.

The future of English

Will English continue to develop into new varieties? Will it break apart into many languages? Will these languages become unintelligible to one another's speakers? These are all pertinent questions for world Englishes (WE) researchers, scholars, and students to ask. While we have many historical examples of lingua franca antecedents to use as predictors of the future of English, those languages, however widespread, did not have a crucial element that contributes to a great degree to the uniqueness of English: global and digital communications. As languages such as Latin spread, they became more and more different given geographical distance, cultural differences, linguistic needs, and other region-specific variables. In time, the varieties become so distinct that they are perceived as different languages especially if they become associated with different nation states. While English may share the characteristic of spreading over vast territories, it is, on the other hand, pulled back together more readily given the power of Internet communications, worldwide media, and instant access to varieties other than one's own.

Some lessons from existing profiles

While certain characteristics of countries in each of the circles can be taken for granted, profiles have an opportunity to highlight peculiarities of different countries given their unique geographical, cultural, and even climate-related specifics. For example, Aguilar-Sánchez (2005, p. 166) explains how "the number of foreign English-speaking retirees and immigrants who settled in Costa Rica," help, among other factors, explain the need for media, including radio, in English. It is the case that given ecotourism in Costa Rica and the relative proximity to the English-speaking countries of North America, people looking for a more relaxed, beach-style life move to the country and change their linguistic landscape. Were it not for its geographical location, beautiful coast, and amenable weather, the linguistic reality could be quite different, mirroring more standard dynamics of the Expanding Circle. The author also explains that with international investments, certainly boosted by this move of retirees and second-home owners from the Inner Circle, came academic and economic expansion, which goes to show the interconnectedness of social and linguistic phenomena that the profile can highlight.

Likewise, Dimova (2005) states that, with regards to English in Macedonia, there are elements particular to the socio-political makeup of the country that contribute to the spread of English there. These are quite different from the reported reasons for the spread of English in Costa Rica, even if both countries can be claimed as part of the Expanding Circle. She writes,

> The number of users of English is expanding also due to political developments in the country, which have resulted in a vast presence of commissioners, military officers, diplomats, business people, and other foreign representatives.
>
> *(p. 197)*

Profilers, therefore, fulfill the important task of balancing what characterizes a country in terms of their English use both when they further insert those countries in a global community of users with similar motivations, and when they point to distinguishing characteristics of specific environments. Further studies can elucidate the ways in which the uses of language in individual countries reinforce our theorizing of language dynamics and the refinement of theories necessary to explain dynamics that are specific to given contexts. Because tension often exists in languages to both expand/change and at the same time maintain a sense of cohesion for the sake of communication, profiles help us identify in what respects languages such as English are affecting and being affected by these dynamics and what the future likely holds for them.

Profilers-to-be will need to decide what kind of relationships between languages they will attempt to unveil. Haji-Othman and McLellan (2014, p. 486), for example decide to emphasize the linguistic ecosystem aspect of English in Brunei. They explain their take relies on a "vertical perspective," that is, on further exploring the relationship between English and other languages locally, as opposed to, for example, a "horizontal perspective" which would likely result in a comparison between English in Brunei and in neighboring countries.

Not every profile will, in the end, focus on the functional and practical uses of English in a city, country, or region. Writing about English in Congo, which is considered an Expanding Circle country, Kasanga (2012, p. 64) highlights that in that African country, where French serves many of the purposes that English does in Outer Circle counterparts in the continent, the role of English is much more symbolic than informational. This, of course is not a deterrent to the building of a strong profile, as symbolic roles are as relevant in world Englishes as are informational ones.

Finally, keeping a sense of continuity with the literature allows profilers to immerse their work in a network of information by their peers. Utilizing some of the frameworks described in this chapters, and others, employed across several profiles makes comparisons across profiles and overtime easier. In her profile of English in Kenya, Michieka (2005) has used the above-described functions of English (e.g., interpersonal, regulative) making it easy to establish similarities and differences between that country and others in the WE literature.

Methodologies

To achieve the goals of a profile, researchers often engage mixed methods of research, both qualitative and quantitative, and ideally triangulate data by accessing information from a variety of perspectives, referring to a number of different language users. It is also important to be upfront about the scope and limitations of the study, especially in environments displaying great diversity of population and access to language and/or large geographical areas. Although the possibilities are endless when it comes to choosing methods and procedures, oftentimes methods borrowed from sociology, anthropology, and other social sciences fulfill the goals of the profile well. Some of the most used (but this is definitely not an exhaustive list) include the following.

Surveys

Questionnaires and other survey instruments can be used for a variety of purposes within a profile. Often, they are used to gauge language users' attitudes toward English and other languages, the domains of use of different languages, learning experiences of those profiled, among many other possible sociolinguistic elements.

Interviews

Speaking directly with language users within a speech community allows for clarification, subsequent questions, triangulation (i.e., imagine, for example, speaking to students, teachers, and administrators within a certain educational context), authentic language utterances, answers about preferred linguistic forms, pronunciation, etc. Again, the possibilities are endless.

Ethnographies

Among the most thorough ways of investigating cultures, ethnographies can insert the research within the community they aim to investigate. Ethnographies have been very productive tools in linguistics, allowing a field linguist great access to authentic samples of language, attitudes towards languages and varieties, and the larger social milieu that contributes to language dynamics within the group and between the group and society at large.

Review of local documents including legislation, school curricula, and syllabi

Some profiles or profile elements do not rely on information that is accessed through conversations with users and learners of English. Local documents can add to profiles by offering broad-scope information of practices, policies, educational mandates, etc.

Evaluation of media including print and Internet advertisement, availability (or not) of newspapers and magazines in the target language

In the Inner and Outer circles, media in English tend to be available to a large or medium portion of the population. In Expanding countries, chances are local media in English will be a lot more restricted, which can in itself provide interesting information to the profile. Establishing the target audience and the goals of media and advertisement and then analyzing the content of the material can elucidate among other things whether English is being used for communication or more likely for its symbolic meaning.

Investigation of the history of education

A look into the history of language presence in education and other formal institutions of the country of region in question can help determine other aspects of English use and attitudes toward the language. Was English imposed given the larger political milieu? Were students barred from learning in their local languages? Were there moments when the power of languages shifted? These and other questions can help elucidate elements of the current presence and use of individual languages.

What could be done in future profiles

Country profiles are about many things. Above all, they are about our humanity as users of language—our motivations, prejudices, expectations, and innovations. Our capacity for creativity in light of linguistic imposition and our propensity for linguistic survival against all odds. It is, however, the case that although we are poised to continue changing language and modifying it so that it stands the best chances of endurance, very many languages qualify as endangered at present, in numbers never before recorded. While the efforts of some linguists and populations will go toward the worthy goal of giving these languages a fair chance at resisting, including creating a written script if they lack it, teaching it to children, or designing online depositories and instructional materials, the profiler can help by documenting the uses and users of those languages and the dynamics of interaction especially with global and regional dominant languages. These data can then be used in conjunction with language policy and educational initiatives to provide the best chances of a positive outcome.

Yet, it is not only in the case of endangered languages that future profiles can help. Every situation of language use, every user of language, and every language used is worthy of further investigation and discovery.

Topics and ideas for future profiles

Here are some ideas for work on profiles:

1. Research what areas of the world have few or no sociolinguistic profiles available. Look for explanations for such a gap. In the case of English, is the language not very relevant there? Is it a matter of access of local scholars to media where they could report their findings internationally? Is there a lack of awareness of the possibilities afforded by linguistic profiles themselves? Are linguists from other parts of the world not interested or not knowledgeable of the specific situations of that context to be able to profile it?
2. Choose an area that has not been profiled yet, and draw a profile of English (or another language of wider communication) there. What are some of the uses and users of English in the place? What are the functions performed by English? What domains present the most significant engagement with English and why? What are some of the varieties present and what is the perceived status of each? What is the history of contact between English and other languages?
3. What are some of the attitudes held by users of English vis-à-vis that language and other languages? How about the attitudes of non-users?
4. Consider a city or a speech community that has not been profiled and whose dynamic sociolinguistic reality would yield an informative profile. What would a descriptive account of its features look like?
5. What theorizing can be done from your thorough profiling of a particular country or region?
6. Compare and contrast the use of English(es) among members of two distinct speech communities or communities of practice in a given place. What does the thorough study of these uses tell us about language in context?

Notes

1 Notice that the word "choice" here is used with much greater latitude than the concept of individual choice would mandate. A professor teaching in a US institution cannot individually "choose" to teach Physics, for example, in a language other than English. There would need to be a special reason (a group of visiting international students from the same linguistic background for example) for that choice to be exercised.

2 I am aware of the criticism the metaphor has received in some circles.

References and further reading

Aguilar-Sánchez, J. (2005). English in Costa Rica. *World Englishes, 24*(2), 161–172.

Bakhtin, M. M. (1981). *The Dialogic Imagination*. Austin, TX: University of Austin Press.

Berns, M. (1988). The cultural and linguistic context of English in West Germany. *World Englishes*, 7(1), 37–39.

Crystal, D. (2000). Emerging Englishes. *English Teaching Professional, 14*, 3–6.

Data Popular Institute (2014, for The British Council). Learning English in Brazil: Understanding the aims and expectations of the Brazilian emerging middle classes. São Paulo: British Council.

Dimova, S. (2005). English in Macedonia. *World Englishes. 24*(2), 187–201.

Fishman, Joshua, A. (1972). Domains and the relationship between micro- and macrosociolinguistics. In: Gumperz, J., and Hymes, D. (Eds.), *Directions in sociolinguistics. The ethnography of speaking* (pp. 407–434). New York: Holt, Rinehart and Winston [originally 1971, several reprints].

Friedrich, P. (2000). English in Brazil: functions and attitudes. *World Englishes*, 19(2), 215–223.

Friedrich, P., and Diniz de Figueiredo, E. H. (2016). *The sociolinguistics of digital Englishes*. NY: Routledge.

Garcia, O., and Schiffman, H. (2006). Fishmanian Sociolinguistics. In O. Garcia, Peltz, R., and Schiffman, H. *Language loyalty, continuity and change* (pp. 3–68). Bristol: Multilingual Matters.

Haji-Othman, N. A. and McLellan, J. (2014). English in Brunei. *World Englishes, 33*(4), 486–497.

Internet World Stats. Internet world users by language. Retrieved on October 15, 2016, from www.internetworldstats.com/stats7.htm

Kachru, B. (1983). *The Indianization of English: The language in India*. New Delhi: Oxford University Press.

Kachru, B. (1990). World Englishes and applied linguistics. *World Englishes, 9*(1), 3–20.

Kachru, B. (1992). *The other tongue: English across cultures*. Urbana, IL: University of Illinois Press.

Kamwangamalu, N. (2009). South African Englishes. In B. Kachru, Kachru, Y., and Nelson, N. *The handbook of world Englishes*. Oxford: Blackwell-Wiley.

Kasanga, L. A. (2012). English in the Democratic Republic of Congo. *World Englishes, 31*(1), 48–69.

Kramsch, C., and Whiteside, A. (2008). Language ecology in multilingual settings: Toward a theory of symbolic competence. *Applied Linguistics, 29*(4), 645–671.

Michieka, M. (2005). English in Kenya. *World Englishes, 24*(2), 173–186.

Nielson, P. M. (2003). English in Argentina. *World Englishes, 22*(2), 199–209.

Schaub, M. (2000). English in the Arab Republic of Egypt. *World Englishes, 19*(2), 225–238.

Uistinova, I. P. (2005). English in Russia. *World Englishes, 24*(2), 239–252.

Velez-Rendon, G. (2003). English in Colombia. *World Englishes, 22*(2), 185–198.

5
PLANNING LANGUAGE

THIS CHAPTER WILL DO THE FOLLOWING

1. Explain the rationale of language planning and policy.
2. Relate the concept of language planning and policy to educational and other activities at the macro or micro level.
3. Describe and explain the different elements of language planning as well as the recent history of research in the field.
4. Discuss how applied linguistics can contribute.
5. Provide ideas for students and scholars who would like to conduct research in language planning and policy.

Introduction

It can be argued that the field of language planning and policy (LPP) *is* applied linguistics. Often defined as "deliberate efforts to influence the behavior of others with respect to the acquisition, structure, or functional allocation of their language codes" (Cooper, 1989, p. 45), language planning requires all of the expertise that applied linguists have developed throughout the history of the discipline. I make this claim based on my estimation of the knowledge of linguistic theory, language acquisition, language education, the sociology of language, and the politics of language necessary for one to propose, with a minimum level of authority, educational and other far-reaching policies involving language. And yet, this is, in itself, one of the biggest challenges of LPP: that it be authoritative in its effort to establish policy without being authoritarian; that in manipulating language access and availability, policy makers and language experts (who should always be consulted but not always are) do not disrupt the very delicate balance of languages—one already so precarious given the incredible differences in power, reach, and accessibility of different languages; that they rely on expertise of language dynamics and yet be involved in a localized, grassroots-inspired activity; that they do not become biased by interests other than the wellbeing of the populations language planning serves. Furthermore, as Wiley (2015, p. 16) points out, even under the assumption that language policy and planning exist to solve language problems (which is, in itself, a big assumption), it is unclear who gets to decide what is a problem and for whom it is a problem. Through the many challenges and competing interests in language planning, applied linguists are in a crucial position to contribute if they 1. Remain true to the goals of fostering linguistic understanding and access; 2. Engage local populations who constitute the most important stakeholders; 3. Are humble in their understanding that language dynamics are very powerful and thus sometimes beyond their capacity of influence and change.

Yet, despite the challenges, we, as human beings, members of communities, and linguists are always planning language. From the individual student who decides to learn French, to the family that enrolls their kids in private English lessons, to educators choosing language and approaches, to lawmakers writing articles and amendments in constitutions and other legal documents that indicate which languages are to perform which function (the absence of those deliberations is also a form of language planning), we make language planning decisions all the time. The choices we make at the individual and collective level about the place of languages in our communities have far-reaching ramifications for all involved and because of item three above, these decisions are not always completely under our control.

Such a situation begs the question: is it possible for a critical and well-informed applied linguistics to promote attainable, sustainable, and fair goals for LPP, both recognizing the demands of a world that, given its state of interconnectedness, needs languages of wider communication (and will use them with or without linguists' "permission") and at the same time respecting the rights of linguistic communities and minority groups?

It is certainly a tall order, especially given that language planning is one of the most ideology-driven things one can do with language. The decisions involved in it tend to be informed by beliefs about language, inclusion, access. Still, the beyond-the-functional aspects of the activity have only taken a more center-stage position in the literature in recent times. Johnson and Ricento (2013, p. 9) recognize that the enquiry originally had its focus elsewhere, when they claim that "the ideological nature and sociopolitical ramifications of language planning were only hesitantly and theoretically considered, even up until the early 1980s." They also explain that early work in the field (e.g., Haugen, 1959) involved corpus planning consisting of the manipulation of language forms, as if such manipulation (conducted in the real world) would not have long-lasting social implications (and, I would add, unintended consequences). They further explain that the work of Kloss (1969) moved the field into the area of status planning, and thus allocated different functions to different languages on that basis, while Cooper (1989) concerned itself with acquisition planning. Nevertheless, preoccupation with and consideration of an ecology of languages, linguistics rights of language minorities, and the effects of regional languages on minority languages are much more recent foci of awareness and action.

History

Ricento (2000, p. 196) abstracts three historical moments and theoretical perspectives in LPP research: 1. A phase and theoretical orientation (1960s) toward decolonization, structuralism, and pragmatism; 2. A phase and theoretical orientation (1970s–1980s) toward (recognition of) the "failure of modernization," critical sociolinguistics, and access; 3. A phase and a theoretical orientation (1980s–present) toward the "new world order, postmodernism, and linguistic human rights."

These phases and ways of seeing the linguistic landscape are of course in tandem with what was/is happening elsewhere in society and resonate with the historical developments and social challenges of a particular era. While they were not always recognized at the time, in part because it is so much easier to see them in retrospect than in the moment, the ideological underpinnings of LPP were there from the beginning. Pragmatism (and structuralism), in the first phase led theoreticians to consider languages viable for planning and formal functions if they presented a high degree of codification, if they were written languages, and if they were perceived as highly adaptable to technological development (Ricento, 2000, p. 197). This of course introduces significant political biases to the process, as these tended to be European languages or economically powerful regional languages (and corresponding varieties more closely associated with economic and political power). Furthermore, this kind of approach takes away the power from local and indigenous populations. As Hornberger (1998, p. 452) explains, "it is not the number of speakers of a language, but their positioning in society, that determines their patterns of language use." In this first phase, it becomes clear that the positioning of large regional languages and powerful technologically adaptable languages such as English was seen, in practical terms, as a benefit while the possible social, attitudinal, and identity-related consequences of those choices were less examined.

Some acknowledgment of the more overtly social aspect of policy and planning started to happen in the second phase, though not to the degree that would occur later, in the third phase. Ricento (2000, p. 202) also explains that "Rather than studying languages as entities with defined societal distributions and functions, sociolinguists focused on the status and relations of *speech communities* in defined contexts." [Emphasis in the original]. The negative effects of planning started being more noticed in this phase, as did the complexity of language use in context (Ricento 2000 p. 202). Issues of critical sociolinguistics and a concern for access made for a change in landscape.

As with most spheres of life, fragmentation became the operational concept of postmodernism, more evident in the third phase. The relativization of life and experience—and or truth itself—as well as greater awareness of rights of all communities informed and informs language planning in the third phase. Historically, this third phase saw issues of linguistic imperialism (Philipson, 1992) and Critical Applied Linguistics (CAL, Pennycook, 2001) reshape understandings of language in context, with far-reaching implications for language planning.

If anything, in this third and current phase, we are more aware of the tension and of the possibly unavoidable conflict (of interest, point of view, perception and attitude) that LPP can bring about, given the different stakeholders and what is at stake for different people. We are also aware of how much issues of language speak directly to one's sense of identity and how unevenly distributed linguistic power is. That can partially explain the greater focus on micro-level planning since the 1990s (Liddicoat and Taylor-Leech, 2014). The same authors explain that micro-level planning refers to the local implementation of macro-level policies, resistance at the micro-level to the implementation of macro-level policies, planning at the micro-level to address local needs, and policies at the micro-level to open new linguistic possibilities.

That does not always mean that macro-level policies are problematic and micro-level action is problem-solving. As the authors further elaborate, "the influence of local decision-making is not always supportive for language learning and actions taken at the micro-level may constrain the implementation of macro-level policies that favour multilingual education" (p. 7, online version).[1] For example, schools may, through their individual practices, limit a student's access to multilingualism even if the macro-level policy has made provisions for it (p. 7). Furthermore, informal ideas about what language to use, and where to use them, can, when taken as a cluster of decisions, impact both individuals and their whole communities.

The example of Brazil comes to mind. The current *Lei de Diretrizes e Bases* (1996, Art.26.5),[2] which is the law that establishes guidelines for national education states that,

> *Na parte diversificada do currículo será incluído, obrigatoriamente, a partir da quinta série, o ensino de pelo menos uma língua estrangeira moderna, cuja escolha ficará a cargo da comunidade escolar, dentro das possibilidades da instituição.* (Within the diversified part of the curriculum, as of fifth grade, at least one modern foreign language will be compulsorily included, and its selection will be the responsibility of the school community, given the possibilities of the institution in question). [my translation]

While the law makes room for the individual selection of languages, in practice, the default choice is English because, on the one hand, it is more difficult to find teachers of other modern languages, and, on the other, English is often connected with the kind of prestige (Friedrich, 2000) students and parents will want to associate themselves with. A small cluster of private schools exists that chooses other languages (e.g., French and German) because of the origin of the schools and highly specific population they serve (e.g., children of diplomats, executives, and foreign service personnel), but often those languages are taught in addition to English and to populations that would, given their wealth, have access to language resources outside of school anyways. However, the decision to teach English, taken by innumerous schools at the individual level, has consequences at the macro level. The teaching of English is still very restricted to grammar-translation lessons, communicative methods being perceived as difficult to implement especially in public-school settings where 30 or more students are assigned to each class. It is not too far-fetched to imagine that teaching Spanish, a language that shares a significant portion of its vocabulary and structure with Portuguese, would bring more tangible benefits (similarity could mean that students would advance further and be potentially more communicatively competent at the end of high school), but the individual decisions of thousands and thousands of schools, result in a national policy that, although amenable to multilingualism in its official form, in practice has different results.

The extent to which attitudes toward languages—as well as the different status these languages hold—affects language choice is significant. Wiley (1996, p. 121) calls our attention to the matter of status ascription in the US in the following:

> Depending on to whom one talks, bilingualism in the United States tends to be seen as either an asset or a curse. This ambivalence is reflected in educational policies that attempt to provide a transition for language minority students from their native languages to English as soon as possible and attempt to teach monolingual English speaking students foreign languages. [emphasis in the original]

The author posits that in the first case, acquiring a second language is associated with remedial work, whereas in the second with elite education. It is interesting, therefore to notice that while in one context a language might have relative higher status than others, those other languages can be the high-status ones in other contexts.

Take the example of Paraguay. Ito (2012) explains that in the country, where a very large portion of the population (80% or more) speak Guaraní, and where that language has acquired official status, a situation of diglossia exists, in which Spanish holds high status, and in which education ultimately fails to be all it could be to students whose first language is Guaraní. Ito argues that,

> while Paraguayans may have "more" positive attitudes toward Guaraní now due to the officialization of Guaraní and the introduction of

> Guaraní-Spanish bilingual education in the early 1990s, they may still have "even more" positive attitudes toward Spanish because Spanish remains dominant in official domains and is considered socioeconomically more beneficial than Guaraní.
>
> *(pp. 5–6)*

The author also points to the "dilemmas of sociolinguists," (p. 9) namely weighing "integrative and instrumental values of" the languages in question to propose a course of action that could potentially enhance the presence and increase the number of users of certain languages in specific domains. All of that is mediated by attitudes and perceived "worth" (including socioeconomic importance) of the languages, which brings me back to the original point: while in the US first-language users of English are often told, or start to believe, that Spanish holds less status than English, the former, in many Latin-American contexts, holds a high-status position in relation to other local languages. Perceived status, which is relative and determined contextually and on-site, has a very important role in the use (or not) of languages chosen for planning. In the case of indigenous languages, as Hornberger (1998, p. 439) puts it, there is the pull of "seemingly irresistible social, political, and economic pressures." Those pressures, I argue, are as important or in some cases more important than the "practical" considerations the first phase described by Ricento attempted to be about.

Language planning, thus, we now know, has several angles to it (Baldauf, 2006, p. 147 and pp. 150–151): status planning (e.g., making a language official), corpus planning (e.g., reforming spelling), education (language) planning (e.g., changing curricula), and prestige planning (e.g., using a language for diplomatic purposes). These aspects work at time independently, at other times in tandem with one another, and at other still because of one another—or even despite one another (p. 152).

Therefore, in the case of Brazil, outlined above, despite national policies that would point toward the possible presence of an ecology of "foreign" languages (international, additional, wider-communication languages), individual actions at the micro-level create a hegemony of English in education. Another interesting case—involving the Portuguese language in Brazil, Portugal, and other former colonial Portuguese contexts—illustrates the difficulties in language planning, this time more specifically in corpus planning. In 1990, all countries where Portuguese is an official language signed a "spelling agreement" in Lisbon. The goal was to unify spelling conventions to facilitate the spread and circulation of texts in Portuguese, which many times had to be edited or republished before circulating in different countries, given differences in spelling conventions (and especially accent marks). This move spoke both to corpus planning and prestige planning, since it was believed that the greater circulation of texts in Portuguese would benefit the language and its users in terms of presence and influence. However, not all countries (eight, in total) ratified the resolution, and until 2004 no further decisions were made. Finally, at that latter date, it was decided that if three of the eight countries ratified the resolution, the agreement would take effect. While at this writing Brazil has made the changes official, the lack of implementation in other countries means that differences, of the kind that triggered the decision in the first place, are likely still causing the problems the reform was originally designed to address.[3]

Finally, a third case of significant language change in Brazil, and somewhat of a diglossia marker, this time involving the so-called Brazilian "urban educated norm" (something akin to Standard American English) and a more colloquial, working-class variant, became widely known as the "gerundism" phenomenon and exemplifies forces to be acknowledged and considered in language policy and planning.

Starting in the 1990s and more evident in the 2000s, the alleged overuse of the future continuous tense led to both strong critical reactions and to stigmatization of this verbal form. Uncommon in standard Portuguese, the use of the future continuous in situations where the simple future is sufficient has been informally traced to mistranslations from English telemarking manuals adopted in Brazil. Thus, a telemarketer would, in what sounds like an overcorrected, unnecessarily cumbersome form, say for example, *Eu vou estar checando a informação e vou estar retornando sua ligação ainda hoje* ("I will be checking the information and will be returning your call still today") instead of the much simpler and more common *Eu vou checar a informação e vou retornar sua ligação ainda hoje* ("I will check the information and will return your call still today.") Since this form in English is not that uncommon, it is difficult, in translation, to convey just how unnecessary it sounds in Portuguese. Yet, for a while now, its use has become very widespread among speakers of specific urban dialects and has at the same time often been ridiculed by users of the educated urban norm. The hypothesis of attempted politeness and saving face through the use of this tense, along with other linguistic strategies such as changes in intonation, has also been raised (Appa, 2005, p. 69–73). Telemarketing is considered to be somewhat of an invasive practice, and the use of a softening device, such as the continuous tense, could be seen as an attempt to ameliorate that situation.

In time, gerundism became a marker of diminished status, and possibly a setback in efforts of formal education to create linguistic leverage for all people; users of the form, more than likely believe they are engaging in the use of a highly institutionalized (and therefore status-holding) form. However, the result tends to be exactly the opposite, as evidenced by the innumerous news columns and humoristic texts written about the matter. I provide this as an example of additional forces that play a significant role in language change and maintenance that at times have not really been sanctioned either at the macro-policy level or at the micro-planning level, but which still have to be considered as powerful *ad hoc* elements in language use, influencing policy and planning and the outcomes of language education.

Either in cases of deliberate language policy or institutionalized forms possibly introduced by the private sector as shown above, some level of education is at play. Education is also at play in attempts to revitalize languages or to stimulate the use of multiple languages. Knowing the power of face-to face interactions, Edwards and Newcombe (2005) emphasize the importance of including members of communities beyond education to participate in projects that aim to increase bi- and multilingualism. For example, they describe how the Twf Project in Wales relies on professionals in health, including midwives and health visitors (who provide post-birth advice and counsel), in who participate in conversations on language choice with the community members they work with (p. 140). While a cause-and-effect conclusion about the efficacy of the program is difficult to reach, given many other elements contributing to language choice, the authors acknowledge that plenty of anecdotal information exists and that "Parents, health professionals and other partners were all able to cite individual cases of change in language behaviour following exposure to the project" (p. 145).

Translanguaging

A chapter about language planning is as good as any an opportunity to discuss newer developments in our formulations of what it means to use and teach language. One of the most controversial terms in this regard might arguably be translanguaging, a concept that Otheguy, García, and Reid (2015, p. 283) define as "the deployment of a speaker's full linguistic repertoire without regard for watchful adherence to the socially and politically defined boundaries of named (and usually national and state) languages."

There are several elements to unpack in this quote. The way it is written, much is taken for granted as agreed upon that actually needs to be discussed. First of all, in situations of communication, interlocutors are faced with, on the one hand, the possibility of their full linguistic repertoire and, on the other, the reality that, given the way our cognition operates, choice is actually much more limited than we once thought (see Schwartz, 2003, for analysis of how cognitive science has demonstrated we often and in reality choose among a small set of items to preserve energy). Therefore, the idea of the whole repertoire being available for us to make a selection is an abstraction: in real life, we are considering a few likely, suitable alternatives based on such elements as the background of the participants (and the less we know the more restricted our choices will be), previous experience with similar interactions, the situation of communication, the context, what was said before, etc.

Translanguaging scholars typically reject the ideas of multiple codes and languages as traditionally construed, and therefore multilingualism tends to also be out of the picture too, since rather than different languages that are then part of a multilingual repertoire, these academics tend to privilege one unique code which encompasses all linguistic expression of a person and which in turn forms their idiolect (notice that to escape "code," one ends up with "code" yet again).

This poses an interesting conundrum. To create this version of the idiolect, researchers have to deny languages as stand-alone units, and then, by doing so, end up recognizing the existence of languages themselves. One cannot deny something before first acknowledging its conceptualization, in the very least in abstract terms. They also deny code-switching and code-mixing; if languages do not exist independently, then they cannot be combined or alternated. This creates another interesting dilemma: linguistics is the study of linguistic codes, however porous and precarious the boundaries between codes can be. In fact, it is the very fact that these codes are dynamic and interact with social, political, psychological phenomena that makes applied linguistics possible. To deny switching and mixing codes becomes a necessity for translanguaging advocates, since they do not recognize the existence of distinct codes in the first place. That is, you cannot switch or mix a variety of codes if only one "supercode" (i.e., your entire repertoire) exists, which in practical terms brings us back to the idea of code one more time.

Yet, we all know what we mean when we say "language," "code," "variety," "dialect;" in the very least, we know we use these various terms because linguistic expression is fluid. Pennycook (2006, p. 66) writes that "The idea that languages somehow exist as ontological entities within their attendant structures, boundaries, grammars, and forms, has become an almost unquestioned given." However, such confabulation is absolutely not true for anyone who has operated in applied linguistics, sociolinguistics and related disciplines in the real world. Formulations such as rhetorical grammars, descriptions of code-mixing and code-switching, the frameworks of world Englishes, conversations about purpose and audience, and discussions of the politics of language and digital languages are but a few examples of awareness that, in languages, very little is static and bound. In linguistics, these terms do not refer to fixed, immutable, and non-exchanging entities. They are certainly abstractions and mental representations we use to facilitate representation of the learning/classifying/storing away of information, but they are representations based on the observation of language as it occurs in the world, with all the diversity, complication, and interest that languages generate.

It is also not true that at all times all selections from our linguistic repertoire are available to us (even beyond the cognitive point I made above). To write this book, I am making only selections among the items marked "English" in my mental file, even though a rich repertoire consisting of vocabulary, grammar, pragmatics and sociolinguistics knowledge, syntax in other languages is available to me. In certain cases, an item is present in more than one mental file; in others, an item is exclusively labeled "Portuguese" or "English." At other times still, if I am in conversation with users of English and Spanish, items marked both "English" and "Spanish," as well as their creative combination, will be at the forefront of my selection menu. These mental files will grow to include new items, some of which are borrowed from other languages overtime, but to assume that they are all stored together, that somehow our nonawareness of their closer relationship to certain groups, histories, and situations of communication would make for better language politics is somewhat naive. Would such a system mean that with a frequency that is pretty much unheard of, users of language would be including items in their language production that are completely undecipherable to their audience (i.e., one would randomly be throwing in terms associated with Spanish or French even when speaking to a monolingual user of English) just because theoretically they all belong to the same super-repertoire?

Next, we must consider the part of the quote that refers to the politics of language. If someone was carefully adhering to social and political borders of language, as the passage suggests, they would likely not be code-mixing and code-switching in the first place, since these are symbolically speaking a way of "breaking the rules" prescribed by traditional grammars. When we code-switch and code-mix, we indicate that language is available to us at different times, with different audiences, in different terms, that are mediated by our cognition but also by the affective domain, and thus susceptible to autonomous systems of the mind. That is, not always does one consciously consider the full range and effect of their linguistic contribution in any given situation of communication, but they often consider such items as the linguistic repertoire of those they are interacting with to make an educated estimation of the effectiveness of their own input. So "watchful adherence" would, if it existed, mean we had absolute control over language production and likely then would choose to use the most highly codified or "proper" variety for a situation. If people were being funny, we would automatically be amusing too, adhering to all the spoken and not-spoken rules of humor; we would never say anything we later regretted; and we would be so convincing, no one would ever disagree with us. In reality, our language use is much more *ad hoc* and spontaneous, and we code-switch and code-mix constantly for a variety of reasons (see Friedrich and Diniz de Figueiredo, 2016), both across what is traditionally understood and defined as languages (however shaky and permeable their boundaries might be), but also across varieties, and, if one accepts the concept of idiolect as dynamic, across different manifestation of our individual varieties as well. A broad conceptualization of code-mixing/switching already encompasses all those possibilities, and, if by any chance the fact that is does is not clear, we can always polish our definition, expand it to different domains, apply it to actual situations of communication, as applied linguists do.

Then, there is the use of "named languages." We can use code-switching narrowly and broadly. We can elect to tell students that we code-mix on and off all the time, that such dynamics are normal, effective, creative, welcome. One defines what "code" means. It could be large "national" languages, but it could also be the group of forms one uses in the home, the group of forms one uses with friends, the group of forms the use with family members who are users of multiple languages. The selections we make are to a certain extent based on the awareness we have that we share that code with others (and mediated by the aforementioned cognitive models). As I mentioned earlier, there is a reason why I have chosen (for the most part) forms only from the group of terms broadly associated with English (and explained, translated, and contextualized the ones from other languages) to write this book even though I have a lot more available in my repertoire. I relied on the very idea of code to make those choices, and the choices went beyond choosing English: they included my best estimation of what constitutes an academic register and style as well as the preferences and repertoire of a community of practice I mentally labeled "linguists."

Finally, one can raise issues regarding the naming of languages and the association between language names and nation states independently from an acknowledgement that languages exist as somewhat defined entities—not bound, as Pennycook (2006) charges, but delineated, with fluid, permeable, and changing borders. Not only would their dissolving of languages cause us to have to deny ideas of code, mixing, and switching, the next steps would involve rejecting as non-entities dictionaries, grammar books, and corpus studies as well. This is not to say that dictionaries and grammar books contain exhaustive "truths" about language, but rather that they serve as proxies, however incomplete, of recognizable entities we call languages. Additionally, as MacSwan (2017, p. 177) points out when speaking of the work of Makoni and Pennycoook (2007), gone too would be, according to the latter authors, the concepts of language rights and multilingualism. As MacSwan then concludes, "the existence of these phenomena depends not on whether named languages are political constructs but on whether we may reasonably speak of discrete speech communities by *any* name or for *any* purpose." (emphasis in the original). He continues later in the same passage, "Whether we can reasonably speak of discrete languages or speech communities depends on the analytic utility of these constructs, not their political associations."

For all these reasons outlined above and because I firmly believe in the "analytic utility" of the construct "languages," I prefer the historically employed and long-researched terms *code-mixing* and *code-switching* over *translanguaging*, whether we are describing naturally occurring language or pedagogically engaged practices. In the real world, the former has currency. What are the implications for language planning and education of the acceptance or not of this translanguaging paradigm? MacSwan (2017) has expressed it best:

> we cannot both rely on codeswitching scholarship to support a positive view of bilingualism and simultaneously deny multilingualism and codeswitching exist, and by choosing to do the latter over the former, we lose the empirical case against a deficit perspective on bilingualism and are left only with an ideological one.

This is indeed the greatest hurdle a translanguaging perspective faces in the real world. In starting from an ideological, political stance rather than an empirical observation, its proponents create an impossibility: a theory that needs to rely on reference to many aspects of linguistic knowledge only to then deny the very existence of those aspects and elements in the first place.

Pedagogically, what is useful is the idea that students rely on the many codes (and their combinations) they might have access to when developing their linguistic and sociolinguistic repertoire without having to worry about negative attitudes toward their varieties and languages because of linguistic prejudices and deficit perspectives. That is where we, as linguists and educators, can have the greatest impact.

Conclusion

This chapter presents but a brief account of some of the areas of contribution of applied linguistics toward the practice of language policy and language planning. There is of course a much broader field for applied linguistic research to engage with the matter of planning. Below are a few suggestions in that regard. This is yet another aspect of application where observation of what happens to languages in the world is paramount.

Questions and ideas for further research

1. Given a particular linguistic community, what are some of the implications of the language policies that have been implemented, for example, in education?
2. What are the historical antecedents of research on translanguaging and what are some of the consequences of these antecedents for language research?
3. What are the implications of the way one constructs the concept of the idiolect for language policy and planning?
4. What are some case studies of individual linguistic phenomena (consider the case of telemarketing and Portuguese) that influenced the linguistic landscape of a particular group or speech community?
5. What current educational policies in a particular area or country can be further investigated in light of the considerations in this chapter?

Notes

1 Liddicoat, A. J., and Taylor-Leech, K. (2014). Micro language planning for multilingual education: Agency in local contexts. *Current Issues in Language Planning, 15*(3). Retrieved on November 22, 2018 from www.tandfonline.com/doi/full/10.1080/14664208.2014.915454?scroll=top&needAccess=true.

2 *Lei de Diretrizes e Bases* (1996). Retrieved on June 12, 2017 from www.planalto.gov.br/ccivil_03/leis/L9394.htm.

3 To read more, in Portuguese, refer to Faraco, C. A. Novo Acordo Ortográfico. Retrieved on December 14, 2017 from https://s3.amazonaws.com/academia.edu.documents/35095872/novoacordo2.pdf?AWSAccessKeyId=AKIAIWOWYYGZ2Y53UL3A&Expires=1513292662&Signature=BSuXUJyJkCTgnB7xEvg9jAreB5k%3D&response-content-disposition=inline%3B%20filename%3DNovoacordo2.pdf.

Works cited and further reading

Appa, R.C. (2005). *Polidez Linguística nas Conversações de Telemarketing*. Dissertation. Universidade de São Paulo.

Baldauf, Jr., R. (2006). Rearticulating the case for micro language planning in a language ecology context. *Current Issues in Language Planning*, 7(2), 147–170.

Canagarajah, S. (2011). Translanguaging in the classroom: Emerging issues for research and pedagogy. *Applied Linguistics Review*, 2, 1–28.

Cooper, R. L. (1989). *Language planning and social change*. New York: Cambridge University Press.

Creese, A., and Blackledge, A. (2010). Translanguaging in the bilingual classroom: A pedagogy for learning and teaching? *The Modern Language Journal*, *94*(1), 103–115.

Edwards, V., and Newcombe, L. P. (2005). Language transmission in the family in Wales. *Language Problems and Language Planning* 29(2), 135–150.

Friedrich, P. (2000). English in Brazil: Functions and attitudes. *World Englishes*, *19*(2), 215–223.

Friedrich, P., and Diniz de Figueiredo, E. H. (2016). *The sociolinguistics of digital Englishes*. New York: Routledge.

Garner, M. (2005). Language ecology as linguistic theory. *Kajian Linguistik dan Sastra*, *17*(33), 91–101.

Haugen, E. (1959). Panning for standard language in Norway. *Anthropological Linguistics*, *1*(3), 8–21.

Haugen, E. (1966). Linguistics and language planning. In Bright, W. (Ed.), *Sociolinguistics* (pp. 50–71). Berlin: Mouton.

Hornberger, N. H. (1998). Language policy, language education, language right: Indigenous, immigrant, and international perspectives. *Language in Society*, *27*, 439–458.

Hornberger, N. H. (2000). Bilingual education policy and practice in the Andes: Ideological paradox and intercultural possibility. *Anthropology and Education Quarterly*, *31*(2), 173–201.

Hornberger, N. H. (2009). Multilingual education policy and practice: Ten certainties (grounded in indigenous experience). *Language Teaching* *42*(2), 197–211.

Hornberger, N. H., and Johnson, D.C. (2011). *The ethnography of language policy*. London: Routledge.

Ito, H. (2012). With Spanish, Guaraní Lives: A sociolinguistic analysis of bilingual education in Paraguay. *Multilingual Education* 2(6), 1–11. Retrieved on June 12, 2017 from https://link.springer.com/content/pdf/10.1186%2F2191-5059-2-6.pdf.

Johnson, D. C., and Ricento, T. (2013). *Conceptual and theoretical perspectives in language planning and policy: Situating the ethnography of language policy*, (219), 7–21.

Kircher, R. (2016). Language attitudes among adolescents in Montreal: Potential lessons for language planning in Québec. *Nottingham French Studies*, *55*(2), 239–259.

Kubota, R., and McKay, S. (2009). Globalization and language learning in rural Japan: The role of English in the local linguistic ecology. *TESOL Quarterly*, *43*(4), 593–619.

Loss, H. (1969). *Research possibilities on group bilingualism: A report*. Quebec: International Center for Research on Bilingualism.

Liddicoat, A. J., and Taylor-Leech, K. (2014). Micro language planning for multilingual education: Agency in local contexts. *Current Issues in Language Planning*, *15*(3), 237–244.

Makoni, S., and Pennycook, A. D. (2007). Disinventing and reconstructing languages. In Makoni, S., and Pennycook, A. D. (Eds.), *Disinventing and Reconstituting Languages*. (pp. 1–40). Clevedon: Multilingual Matters.

MacSwan, J. (2017). A multilingual perspective on translanguaging. *American Education Research Journal, 54*(1), 167–201.

May, S. (2003). Rearticulating the case for minority language rights. *Current Issues in Language Planning, 4*(2), 95–125.

Otheguy, R., García, O., and Reid, W. (2015). Clarifying translanguaging and deconstructing named languages: A perspective from linguistics. *Applied Linguistics Review, 6*(3), 281–307.

Pennycook, A. D. (2001). *Critical applied linguistics*. New York: Routledge.

Pennycook, A. D. (2006). Postmodernism in language policy. In T. Ricento (Ed.), *An introduction to language policy: Theory and method* (pp. 60–67). London: Blackwell.

Phillipson. R. (1992). *Linguistic imperialism*. Oxford: Oxford University Press.

Ricento, T. (2000). Historical and theoretical perspectives in language policy and planning. *Journal of Sociolinguistics, 4*(2), 196–213.

Schwartz, B. (2003). *The paradox of choice: Why more is less*. New York: HarperCollins Publishers.

Wiley, T. G. (1996). *Literacy and language diversity in the United States*. Washington, DC and McHenry, IL: Center for Applied Linguistics and Delta Systems.

Wiley, T. G. (2005). *Literacy and language diversity in the United States* (2nd ed.). Second Edition. Washington, DC and McHenry, IL: Center for Applied Linguistics and Delta Systems.

Wiley, T. G. (2015). Language policy and language planning in education. In W. E. Wright, Boun, S., and Garcia, O. (Eds.), *Handbook of bilingual and multilingual education* (pp. 164–184). Hoboken: John Wiley & Sons.

6

BUILDING BRIDGES AND CONSTRUCTING MEANING IN TRANSLATION STUDIES

THIS CHAPTER WILL DO THE FOLLOWING

1. Briefly comment on the discipline of translation studies.
2. Highlight important historical stations of its development.
3. Describe the work of translators and different subsets in areas of expertise (e.g., subtitling, dubbing, interpretation).
4. Discuss the importance of Contrastive Rhetoric to translation studies.
5. Comment on the intersection of translation studies, technology, and applied linguistics.
6. Provide ideas for students and scholars who would like to develop projects combining applied linguistics and translation studies.

Introduction

The field of translation/interpretation in all its manifestations has advanced significantly in recent years, becoming more professionalized and hailed as a recognized area of special expertise, boosted by a need for intercultural communication to take place in an increasingly globalized world. At the same time, the contributions of applied linguistics, contrastive rhetoric and cross-cultural communication, among other disciplines, to the practice of translation have become more evident as we strive to negotiate the use of artificial intelligence in translating against the nuanced practices that can be effected by human beings. This chapter will explore that intersection to argue that an appreciation of applied linguistics is a fundamental aspect of translation studies and practice. It will also discuss the role of computer technology in translation and the interplay of human and machine translation as a possible area of further investigation and inquiry. While we need to make a distinction between the practice of translation itself and the area of study that focuses on a more abstract and theoretical appreciation of those practices (i.e., translation studies), I will often switch between one and the other in this chapter since both theory and practice are connected to applied linguistics issues and considerations. Williams and Chesterman (2008, p. 13) make this fluidity between theory and practice even more obvious by suggesting that any person who has not had practice doing translation should first engage with it before attempting to do work in translation studies, risking otherwise becoming someone akin to a "stereotypical back-seat driver." That is, translation studies is a pursuit that starts with translation itself, the intuition we get for the interpretative role translators play, and then continues toward an investigation of what those discoveries mean for translation best practices themselves but also for applied linguistics and a great understanding of how humans communicate. I would further argue that those individuals involved in the development of machine translation and artificial intelligence should also try translation in practice to understand its nuances and details. Whether in interdisciplinary teams with computer programmers and applied linguists or attempting to do this from a computational linguistic perspective, professionals should look to applied linguistics for insight and directions.

As it is the case with many applied disciplines, I believe translation is more than the transposing of linguistic elements from one language to another (Díaz Cintas, 2012). Translation, when done well, is an art, a reading of the world, an assessment of the necessary interpretations and adaptations to be made so that communication, not only of objective meanings but also of that reading of the world can be achieved across languages and cultures. Great translation and interpretation make it possible for us to appreciate literary prose, poetry, technical texts, film, and oral production (among others) that would otherwise be not accessible to us, for having been written originally in a language we do not share; it helps us bridge the distance between sound and sign; it aids peace processes and diplomatic talks; it gives us a window into cultures that would perhaps otherwise remain distant.

More than playing an auxiliary role, translators—we should acknowledge—stand in a position of power, from where they make decisions, some of them quite immediate, about what and how to communicate across cultures, understandings of the world, and language ideologies. To translate in ways that are linguistically sound, ethically responsible, and culturally sensitive is not a small feat, and applied linguistics should be looking into ways to help make the practice the best that it can be.

Therefore a first step in this process is to decide what one hopes to derive from an investigation of translation and its practices: is it a greater understanding of translation itself so that new insight can contribute to new practices? Is it better insight into the essence of cross-cultural communication and the features that need to be adapted so that communication is better achieved across geographical and linguistic boundaries (even if they are porous?) Or is it a clearer comprehension of the nature of language itself, its dynamics, and challenges? Whatever the goal, the study of translation and its related areas has much to offer applied linguists, and I hope this chapter will cause a few readers to consider what aspects of the practice could do with further scrutiny and awareness.

Translation studies in the context of translation

The word "translation" is usually primarily associated with the general transformation of text in one language into text in another. Nevertheless, it is possible to make many more nuanced distinctions about what the practice entails and to also highlight that often when one uses the general term "translation" they might be thinking of activities that include translation, interpretation, dubbing, and subtitling individually or in a number of different combinations. Munday (2012, p. 8) reminds us that translation refers to a subject area, the product of the work of the translator, and the process by which text in one language is transformed into text in another. Additionally, the practice can include intralingual translation (as in turning a text in a given language into another version of it, for example less technical, within the same language), interlingual translation (which is what we generally associate with translation), and even intersemiotic (which would involve a translation into a nonverbal form of communication) (p. 9), ranging from expression in a sign language to artistic representation in visual creations or music.

Each of these dimensions of translation has its own complexities and sets of necessary skills. What makes translation great, as well as what considerations one should have in mind beyond the linguistic while translating, is an issue for translation studies, as are the more political, ideological, ethical, and philosophical considerations. As Munday (2012, p. 10) points out, what we often refer to as translation studies is the scholarly endeavor that deals with the issues germane to the area in a broad sense. The discipline developed especially after the mid twentieth century, and now brings together the contributions of scholars and researchers in many related and different disciplines.

Munday (2012, p. 11) notes, regarding the UK that,

> The study of modern languages at school and university has been in decline but the story of postgraduate programs in interpreting and translating, the first of which were set up in the 1960s, is very different.

This phenomenon in a way mirrors what is happening to other disciplines in English departments (and foreign language departments) everywhere: whereas the study of literature proper is declining in terms of numbers of students[1] (and modern language departments were traditionally anchored in literary studies), the more applied disciplines of ESL, ESL writing, editing, and second-language teaching as well as many areas of applied linguistics and of writing, continue to show potential for further development both in themselves and in partnership with other areas (as this book illustrates) to a great degree because they are applied in the first place. In fact, given the perceived or real "crises in the humanities," these associations are a natural and very welcome way to show just how vital disciplines that stand at the intersection of the humanities and social sciences, such as applied linguistics, really are. That is not to say that there is not a cyclical quality to heightened interest in certain areas of study: there is nothing to indicate that in the pendulum-like movement of disciplinary attention and notice, we could not be right back to much interest into areas that are now having to reconsider their stance in the academic cosmos.

Nevertheless, the insight gained throughout the years in these areas can and should continue to be utilized in combination with more nascent areas of enquiry. For example, literary scholars can contribute very significantly to conversations on the nature, characteristics, and status of literature in translation. Those working on poetry can highlight the intricacies of rhyme and rhythm when works are represented in a language other than the original. And those scholars with an interest in historical development can investigate the changing practices in the translation of literary texts throughout the centuries.

Munday (2012, p. 24) acknowledges that "potential for a primary relationship" exists between translation studies and other areas of language interest, especially in such subject areas such as applied/contrastive linguistics, language studies, cultural studies, among others. Newmark (2009, p. 20) goes even further by stating that translation,

> [a]s an interdiscipline […] must take into account its essential components and their applications, namely a theory of writing well and of stylistic and ethical language criticism, as well as the subjects of cultural studies, applied linguistics, sociolinguistics, psycholinguistics, logic and ethical philosophy.

Echoing both scholars, I myself believe that the contributions of contrastive rhetoric, discourse analysis, cross-cultural communication are, alongside all the subjects cited, essential in translation studies, which, given its scope and importance, can only be practiced interdisciplinarily. The key words here are "practice" and "interdisciplinarity." While, conventionally, practice was considered second to theory, and traditional disciplinary silos were created to garner greater status to certain areas, the complex world we live in today, full of complicated problems, requires an appreciation for both innovative and inventive collaboration and problem solving and an understanding of diverse areas (which is the very premise of this book). Perhaps we are coming full circle: the polymath of the renaissance gave way to the disciplinary expert of the nineteenth and twentieth centuries, who is now giving way to the multidisciplinary practitioner again.

History of translation studies

Because the aims of this book include inquiring on the possible further partnerships between applied linguistics and other language-related disciplines, this chapter will not contain a thorough recounting and investigation of translation studies and its goals and aims. Rather, it will offer very brief commentary on the history to then focus on points of common interest between the subjects and areas of study. For the reader that would like a thorough historical and disciplinary understanding of the field, *The Routledge Handbook of Translation Studies* might be a good place to start and *The Map: A Beginner's Guide to Doing Research in Translation Studies* a good place to continue, the latter being especially suitable for those who, upon reading this brief reflection, decide that investigations that delve into translation studies might be for them.

Newmark (2009, p. 2021) explains that the development of translation theory can be seen as divided into four cumulative stages, depending on what the concerns of the time were. In the first, linguistic stage which is pre-1950s, some of the central discussions involved the question of literal versus less literal translations, their merits and challenges. The second, communicative stage, lasting from the 1950s to the 1970s, was marked by the application of linguistics to translation studies and concern with different registers. The third, functionalist stage, which encompasses the 1970s through to the year 2000 had its focus on the intention of the text and the commercial relationship between translation and client. Finally, the stage since 2000 adds a preoccupation with the ethical dimension of translation and representation in texts.

These stages run parallel to the foci of attention in other areas of language study and general socio-philosophical preoccupations of the times. For example, in English Language Teaching (ELT) (see Griffiths, 2004), the period before the 1950s was marked by the widespread use of the grammar-translation approach, which was very focused on the equivalence of linguistic forms between two languages. While students might end up with large vocabularies and a grasp of the syntactic features of the two languages, the fact that the first language was a strong intermediary in communication made the process difficult and fluency very elusive. Grammar translation seemed more like an exercise in scholarly translation than a mechanism to make a person able to use a language other than their first. Its format, also for practical reasons, was suitable to large classrooms, for example middle and high school contexts, in which 30 or more students can be "trained" in grammar translation but to whom it would be hard to introduce more communicative methods that rely on individualized instruction and longer student-talking-time (STT) as opposed to teaching-talking-time (TTT). This latter reason might explain why grammar translation still persists to this day in school classrooms (and their counterpart in the teaching of Spanish, for example, is still quite present in American classrooms) not always helping students achieve goals of communication in the target language.

While a variety of methods and approaches developed after grammar-translation and as a direct reaction to it (Griffiths, 2004), one of the most salient, especially in the 1960s was the audio-lingual approach. It did have a strong aspect of application, just like translation at that time was exploring. It was based on drilling and repetition and a strong connection to wartime translators (Griffiths, 2004, p. 7), the same kind of applied practice translation studies was also striving for at the time. It should also be highlighted that under audio-lingual approaches, it was common for language labs to be created, where students could repeat the drills, replay their own oral production, improve their fluency, and receive feedback from a monitoring teacher when they ran into issues. This period was marked by a much greater use of technology in teaching (including not only the aforementioned labs but also computer-mediated exercises) in a move that would also be paralleled by greater use of technology in translation.

Starting as early as the 1970s and extending until our own time are more communicative approaches that take into consideration not only the linguistic aspects of communication, but also those extra linguistic ones—sociolinguistic, pragmatic, strategic—strongly influenced by Canale and Swain's concept of communicative competence (1980) and recognizing that language is embedded in culture, context, and situation of communication (see Griffiths, 2004 for more). Given that translation and translation studies are interdisciplinary endeavors, it is not hard to imagine an overlap not only in methods and approaches but also of professionals working in both language teaching and translation (and theorists describing them) and therefore practices circulating from one field to the other, with applied linguistics mediating this conversation. At the same time, we became increasingly aware of the responsibility embedded in language use, not only at the individual level, but also—and in a more impactful way—at the societal one. As ethical-linguistic considerations rise in our consciousness, it is to be expected that they would also permeate the world of translation. Note that these phases do not start and end in clear-cut ways. While ideas about new ways of thinking of language may spread in academic circles and localized practice, they continue for quite a while to exist alongside existing practices elsewhere. That means that until this day it would be possible to find practices such as grammar translation (as originally construed) and communicative practices cohabiting the same institutions at the same time.

However, as maligned as grammar-translation was, especially after the advent of communicative approaches, its importance is beginning to be discussed again, as it often happens once participants of a given community are given the advantage of time and a little distance. Cook (2010, p. 15), for example, has come to a sensible acknowledgment of grammar translation in both its limitations and possibilities in the following:

> Grammar Translation undoubtedly has weaknesses, and cannot provide a holistic course of study for students who want to attain a rounded proficiency. However to use criticism of Grammar Translation as an argument

> against *any* and *all* use of translation is a logical sleight of hand. Grammar translation is by no means the only way to use translation. [Emphasis in the original]

Cook is referring more specifically to pedagogical uses of translation, but I do not think the issue is completely separate from that of translation as a professional activity, especially because many translators will have started on their path to professionalization by being students of language and subsequently teachers of language. In fact, what reflections such as these show is that those among us who are language teachers often assume we know what the ultimate goal of learning is for those students we serve. If a student's objective includes learning to translate, shouldn't our classroom practice reflect that possibility? And shouldn't the study of translation focus not only on the more philosophical and abstract elements of the field (we read words such as immateriality, materiality, and technicity, for example, in Littau, 2016) but also in the very practical and pedagogical aspects of teaching one how to translate? While these considerations are not self-exclusive, it seems at this later stage of translation studies, more philosophical abstraction is taking center stage, and applied linguistics can help and offer a more concrete language-based balance that takes us back to real-world insight into best practices and sensible professional training.

Goals and aims of translation studies

Is translation just an intuitive process based upon one's deep knowledge of two languages or does it require reflection, theorizing, and systematization? In case it does, what does translation studies as a discipline do? In reading academic texts about translation, I am often surprised that, as a trend, the theorizing aspect of it takes precedence over the applied theory. There are many discussions on text, context, and elements such as coherence and cohesion, but there is less direct application, the kind that dwells on what to do now that we know what we know. This leaves ample space for applied linguistics to exercise its basic function, which I described at the beginning of the book as observing what goes on in the world (in this case, the very act of translating), formulating ideas about what is observed, and returning with further recommendations and suggestions for an improved practice.

Applied linguistics is also in a good place to explicate the close connection between culture, rhetorical patterns, and language, especially through contrastive rhetoric, which I consider to be an applied linguistics discipline. It always amazes me to observe, for example, how collectivism (Hofstede, 1980), high-context orientation (Hall, 1976), and deductive patterns of presentation (i.e., starting with maxims and then moving on to practical observations rather that starting from empirical evidence) correlate with certain language families (e.g., romance languages) and wonder how translators in practice deal with translating to a language that manifests in different ways—through individualism, high-content orientation, inductive patterns (e.g., American English). In that regard, despite individual differences, a Brazilian, for instance, would likely have started a meeting by engaging in small talk for many minutes, used first-person plural even when he/she meant to say "I" (a move that indicates humbleness), explained the basic reasoning behind a line of thought, only then to tell the group what the problem is. An American, on the other hand, would have more likely started right on time with the subject matter of the meeting, used the pronoun "I" without difficulty, and presented the issue right away. What is a translator/interpreter to do? That is a question for translation studies but also for applied linguistics.

At the same time, translators have the privilege of peeking into the specificities of a language, those that make it poetic, beautiful nuanced. In Portuguese, for example, the sun "is born" every day (*O sol nasce*), and a woman does not simply give birth, but instead "gives light" to a child (*Dar a luz*). Living in the intersection of different worlds allows the translator to partake of and appreciate both. Do these preferred forms of expression offer us insight into the worldview of the people who use them and if so, what do we learn? That is another question for applied linguists to help explore alongside translation theorists.

I now move to a short exploration of areas related to translation but deserving individual attention.

Subtitling

Subtitling, while intrinsically connected to translation, offers the researcher many possibilities of further enquiry given not only its oral language/written text duality but also the specifics of the medium where it appears.

Díaz Cintas (2012) provides a useful definition of subtitling which involves,

> a translation practice that consists of rendering in writing, usually at the bottom of the screen, the translation into a target language of the original dialogue exchanges uttered by different speakers, as well as all other verbal information that appears written on screen (letters, banners, inserts) or is transmitted aurally in the soundtrack (song lyrics, voices off).

As the author later points out, subtitling is interesting because the original text (commonly oral although if a scene includes an image of a written text, that can get subtitled too) remains available for viewers/readers alongside the subtitled translation, thus "adding an extra layer of information." That means, he continues, that many levels and interacting elements need to be taken into account including timing/speed, space (not to disrupt the viewing of the material), and how loyal to the original translations need to be in light of the former and in light of the viewer's access to both texts (for the purpose of comparison).

The idea that both the original and the subtitled texts would not be available to the viewer/reader at all times because the use of subtitling itself is connected to an impossibility to access the original text can be easily contested. First of all, subtitles can be used as a tool for learning. The viewer with intermediary listening-comprehension ability, for example, might find the combination of both texts very useful when it comes to getting a holistic understanding of the original text. Secondly, a user of sign language and subtitling might be at the same time accessing visual cues and lip reading while reading the subtitles. Finally, other environmental factors such as the quality of the audio, noise, etc. may cause viewers to rely on both subtitles and sounds/voice in a complementary manner, whether they are a written "translation" of oral language or provide information in an additional language they also use.

These factors are probably part of the reason why Díaz Cintas (2012) writes of the uniqueness of this translation form:

> Subtitling is not only an unusual form of translation because of its cohabitation with the original text, but it also stands out as a unique translational type because of its asymmetric endeavour of rendering original speech into written target text.

These intricacies, as well as the applicability of translation and its tools to language learning, is good reason for applied linguistics to pursue further research in dubbing and to derive meaning and conclusions from what works and what does not.

Dubbing

As a child in Brazil, I often watched dubbed American cartoons. It was a welcome practice: three- and four-year-olds are cognitively able to enjoy these stories but too young to have acquired the literacy skills necessary to read and follow subtitles. As children, my friends and I were not even aware of what the original voices would have sounded like: we were so familiar with the tone, accent, and mannerisms of the actors that dubbed our favorite cartoons that they might as well have been the original ones. Years later, when I first traveled to Portugal, I was surprised to find out that our fellow Portuguese speakers there watched subtitled cartoons instead, and that trip raised questions for me about how children were able to understand what went on in the stories if they did not know the original language. I wondered if they developed different skills such as inferring from context, or simply focusing all of their attention on the visual cues, but I was never able to conduct research on those cartoons to find out more (although I believe this remains an interesting question for an applied linguist to ask). It was therefore noteworthy to read in Chaume (2012) and Tveit (2009) about countries that were, historically, reluctant to use dubbing, Portugal among them.

Chaume (2012, p. 288) explains that the practice of dubbing is now much more widespread, in Portugal as well, and part of a menu of options available to those who enjoy audiovisual media. As with several areas within translation studies, there seems to be tension between research on the linguistic components of the craft and the more ideological aspects, such as how to adequately translate culture, what some of the challenges to freedom of expression might be, and how powerful groups can use (or misuse) translation and its related practices, such as dubbing, to keep information from the public (see Chaume, 2012, p. 293), since, in the case of dubbing, the original text could be quite different from what is presented and viewers/listeners would never know.

Yet, a whole other area of study might open up to applied linguists. The fact that dubbing has to take into consideration so many aspects of linguistic and extra-linguistic production, from the length of the utterances, to how close those utterances are, to the need to lip-sync the actors, to the background noises, to the overlap of voices in dialogue, makes it both a complex and a compelling subject for linguistic investigation. In that respect, dubbing is not a direct activity, as Martínez (2004, p. 3) explains:

> The audiovisual dubbing process comprises several closely linked phases, which must follow an established order and rhythm, something akin to a production line. If one of these phases is delayed or runs into problems the entire line may be affected. Also, so many different people are involved that problems do tend to occur.

Chaume (2012) also mentions that there are few studies done on attitudes of viewers toward the dubbed product, and thus having applied linguists ask questions directly from viewers might help determine what are the *sine qua non* features of successful dubbing, especially those that can be extrapolated and applied to other contexts.

Interpreting

Pöchhacker (2008, p. 128) explains that interpreting occupies a paradoxical space in translation studies as both a subdiscipline and an independent field of study, given not only the oral characteristic of this form of translation (not enough in itself to encompass or explain its complexity) but also and more importantly its "'real-time' human translation in an essentially shared communicative context." This crucial variable, the quality of being a synchronic form of translation, confers interpretation many important characteristics. There is no consultation of other texts, of dictionaries and thesauruses for the best and most historically accurate version of a term or utterance. There are no revisions, peer-review, or self-editing after a few days. There is an urgency that influences affective responses and linguistic production. And there is quick decision-making and immediate choice selection. We can add to it that a lot of interpretation takes place in high-stakes situations: diplomatic talks, governmental meetings, conferences, medical situations.

Davidson (2000) makes a statement that once read might seem evident enough, but whose importance might otherwise go unacknowledged:

> Interpreters interpret for a reason, because there is some communicative or social goal that needs to be met; they do not simply wander upon two speakers shouting at each other in different languages and offer their services. From this point of view, the measure of the interpreter's success may not be an abstract count of how 'accurate' they are, but rather the degree to which she allows, through her actions, the speakers first to negotiate and then to achieve their goals for the speech event in question.

Granted that this statement applies more to professional interpreters than occasional ones, the significance of this reflection lies in the recognition that interpreters are called that because what they do requires their judgment and because their choices occur in ways that are much more complex than a simple transposing of terms from a language to another; they involve the creation of meaning on the spot, meaning resulting from knowledge not only of the codes involved but also and more importantly of the sociolinguistic reality of the languages and cultures represented.

Another interesting aspect of interpreting that Pöchhacker (2008, p. 129) highlights is that its studies have very much been driven by professionals working in the area and explaining what they do. Such explanations are not given in an attempt to seek endorsement or justification for the practice but rather to inform, thus providing a roadmap to those wanting to engage with the profession themselves. Translation has so many inherent applied purposes that it manifests as a primarily applied discipline. This observation has reminded me of the dynamics of the genesis of forensic linguistics, which basically developed because forensic professionals and investigators realized that language could be a tool to understanding, answering questions, and solving mysteries, thus being less driven by the postulations of academics. While the insight of academics does help a lot, this is yet another aspect of translation (as well as many of the areas of study and action presented in this book) in which it is best to align theorizing with real-world practice.

Contrastive rhetoric and cross-cultural communication

My introduction to studies in contrastive rhetoric was through the milestone work of Ulla Connor (1996). I was drawn to ideas of not only different rhetorical patterns but also their connectedness to cultures and multiculturalism. Besides, a new attention to writing production in second language matched my own experience as a second-language writer of English, my experience as an ESL teacher, and thus informed my practice and education in new, important ways. Connor explains:

> It is fair to say that contrastive rhetoric was the first serious attempt by applied linguistics in the United States to explain second language writing.

> It is only within the past twenty years, however, that writing skills and the role of transfer in particular have been of interest to applied linguistics researchers. For decades, writing was neglected as an area of study because of the emphasis on teaching spoken language during the dominance of audiolingual methodology.
>
> *(p. 5)*

Having taught both through audio-lingual methodologies and with an emphasis on oral communication—the latter often favored quite openly by students—I found Connor's assertion to be true and important. Around the same time, I also started reading the work of Geert Hofstede (1980)—which by then, in the late 1990s was already almost two-decades old—including his comparison of cultural values and beliefs across countries and regions. The juxtaposition of the insight I acquired from those texts informed the empirical work I was doing at the time (it still does), and I went on to survey and write about the different cultural beliefs across five Latin-American countries, which are often erroneously portrayed as being similar to one another in those regards. The results were published in journal articles (Hatum et al., 2006 and Friedrich et al., 2006) and demonstrated how different beliefs affected interactions, produced clashes, and influenced the outcomes of business negotiations. Some of the highlights were the fact that even though these countries have many points of historical and cultural intersection, the particulars of their communicative styles and social beliefs (which we can infer are influenced by everything from geography to economic crises) still generated confusion and clashes if one was not aware of them. There were variations in time elasticity, gender perceptions, past and future orientation, level of collectivism, and even levels of bureaucracy, items that ultimately influence rhetorical patterns and linguistic choices. What is more, we speculated that given commonalities in histories and original cultural influences in those countries, people might be less likely to consider cultural and linguistic beliefs as a source of tension or at play in any given interaction. That is, when a person from Japan communicates with a person from Argentina, they expect that some linguistic beliefs and cultural values will be different given their different histories, influences, and geographical distance, and they are more likely to watch for them and respond from that perspective of awareness. On the other hand, when a person from Argentina and another from Colombia communicate, they are potentially more likely to expect that a somewhat shared culture will facilitate their communication (i.e., they tend to be more aware of their similarities than their differences), and thus they are more likely to decode any clash as the other person's "fault," unwillingness, or problem rather than consider that they might be speaking/writing from different cultural standpoints.

The lessons I leaned at that time stayed with me and caused me to spend quite a bit of time investigating issues in cross-cultural communication, but it was only years later that I started considering that the impact of what we found could have implications for translation practice and translation studies. Take that same context and reflect, for example, on what our findings would mean for communication between Argentines and Brazilians if that interaction was mediated by translation/interpretation. How would an interpreter deal with the potentially different linguistic and cultural values that might show up in conversation? And consider those same countries, where Spanish and Portuguese respectively are the most prevalent languages, but where other native languages coexist: what, for instance, would an interpreter/translator between Spanish and Guaraní in Paraguay (also official in that country) have to take into consideration regarding rhetorical and cultural patterns while interpreting/translating in that context? How do such variables such as politeness, directness, inductive presentation manifest in these different contexts especially given the expectation of commonality?

These are not questions with simple answers but they are certainly some that a partnership between professionals working in those fields and applied linguists can help address. More specifically, reports from professionals in the area as well as academic work in translation studies, contrastive rhetoric, cross-cultural communication, second language acquisition (because many translators will be using a language that they acquired additionally to their first), second language writing, negotiation, peace linguistics and language for diplomatic purposes (as a subfield of language for specific purposes (LSP) and even more specifically, English for specific purposes (ESP)) can interdisciplinarily arrive at insight that benefits the practice and also informs linguistic theory.

Child interpreters, language brokers, and natural translation

Writing about brokerage in broad terms, Stovel et al. (2011, p. 1) explain that brokers usually serve as,

> intermediary links in systems of social, economic, or political relations who facilitate trade or transmission of valued resources that would otherwise be substantially more difficult.

This concept of brokerage applies to many uses of language and in this case the use of translation too can be considered a form of brokerage, although much more complex than the concept might initially give away. So far this chapter has been dedicated to professional uses of translation and interpretation, but the fact is that another reality also exists—one in which people, many times young people, given real-world situations, are called upon to translate and interpret without having been professionally trained to do so. Many are the possible instances in which this can happen: an emergency situation when immediate information is required, such as a medical emergency in a public place; a traveling customer in a shop, aided by another customer who shares the same language; and, as this section will show, immigrant situations, where many times children with a higher level of communicative competence in the target language mediate communications between community members/institutions and their (the child's) parents.

This is what is called "natural translation" (Harris and Sherwood, 1978), a case in which a person's intuition about language and existing knowledge about the languages and varieties involved dictates choices made during translation/interpretation. While accurate in general terms, Stovel's et al.'s businesslike description of brokerage does not give away the intricacies that accompany facilitating this kind of interaction.

Tse (1995) uses the term "language brokers" to refer to these individuals (a great portion of the work refers to child translators); Stovel et al. (2011, p. 4) add that these young interpreters are a type of "captured brokers" meaning that they are not neutral intermediaries in those interactions but rather "span the boundary between a solidary group and the outside world." "Captured" here means having their loyalty captured by one of the sides, that is, the side the interpreters are solidary to, in the case of children, their families. Finally, Orellara et al. (2003, p. 508) describe these interpreters' activities as follows: "They often mediate between mono-lingual speakers, advocating for or supporting their families in some manner," while being careful to point out that "this term also obscures the power imbalance between participants, for example, between a store owner and a child, or between a school teacher and an immigrant parent."

This latter observation could be a central point of research for applied linguists and sociolinguists when it comes to this form of interpretation, namely, how language and linguistic-related decisions in translation on the one hand reflect and on the other address the paradoxical condition of having the power to make linguistic decisions while not holding an equal position of authority in linguistic interactions with counterparts who are older, likely know more about the register, and linguistic specificities of their areas of knowledge, and who hold greater institutional and hierarchical clout. That is, consciously or subconsciously, and/or as a result of feedback and outcomes, these young translators are making active decisions and many times serving as sociolinguistic supporters for their family. Orellara et al (2003, p. 508) go further when they use the term "para-phrasing" (which alludes to the word para in Spanish, meaning "for" or "in order to") to describe what language brokers are doing:

> We believe this term emphasizes that what children do is purposeful; they are taking action in the world, not simply moving words and ideas or explicating concepts.

Sociologists and psychologists should research, write about, and actively engage with this phenomenon as there are obvious implications for social interactions and social constructions as well as emotional and cognitive ramifications in taking the responsibility of spokesperson and mediator from a young age. Ideally, as a society we should be providing these families and these young translators with the necessary support to make these interactions easier and/or to think of multilingualism as a social condition where more help is available to those who need it. These interactions also take place with obvious repercussions for linguistic and sociolinguistic development as well as for attitudes toward the languages involved. For example, one can wonder if the role of translator in this case accelerates language acquisition (or has other forms of impact on language production) and an understanding (and use) of pragmatics since these interpreters are getting to talk and negotiate subject matters that are not common preoccupations until later in life (benefits, healthcare, commercial exchanges, etc., see Stovel et al., 2011, p. 5). Additionally, if the interactions are perceived as successful and the results benefit the family unit, are attitudes toward the target language influenced by such outcomes? What if results are less than optimal? Where do language loyalties go and how do they change overtime?

Perhaps it is Urciolli (1998, p. 4, cited in Reynolds and Orellana, 2009, p. 212) who expresses best the ramifications of the position so often faced by immigrants, minorities, and those with potentially diminished power, linguistic and otherwise:

> When people migrate, become political minorities, or become colonized, they find their lives structured in ways that force them to work across languages and place on them the burden of understanding and responding correctly.

The notion of language brokerage, when not combined with this kind of awareness and action in the world to facilitate communication and access, hides the hardships involved in cross-language interactions and may lead newcomers to the discussion to believe in a simple-flow-of-information, neutral and equitable exchanges involved in interpretation. However, these young translators live this reality and dwell at this intersection, trying to negotiate not only language and the immediate needs of communication of their families but also their own identity and linguistic destiny. I am using linguistic destiny to mean the makeup their linguistic repertoire and idiolects will have and how much this experience as interpreters will influence such a future and their sense of agency and power.

Reynolds and Orellana (2009, p. 215) show through case studies how anxiety provoking some of these interpretation situations can be. On the one hand, family members being represented in translation by young interpreters do not always understand that knowing a language does not mean knowing and being able to decode all of the possible registers, styles, and vocabulary (including jargon) that different speech communities and communities of practice may demand. On the other, there will be the very demands of the institutions and interlocutors trying to communicate the most diverse pieces of information about medicine, finances, insurance, and all the many professional and societal linguistic norms that accompany them. It is in this space of power/disempowerment that this form of interpretation takes place, and it is in this context that applied linguistics questions should be asked and ways to attenuate the problem found. Ultimately, linguistic awareness means understanding that no one knows a "whole" language and that many decisions about language are made at the time communication takes place, mediated by the expectations and background of interlocutors.

Conclusion

Translation, both its realization and the formal study of the practice itself, presents the applied linguist with a host of opportunities for research and reflection, including the pursuit of questions regarding the nature of language itself. Seeing translation as a creative, multifaceted process allows researchers to ask interesting questions about it and about the social spheres where translating takes place. The advent of more and more digital spaces of relevance to the topic should only encourage linguists to take a closer look.

Questions and ideas for further research

Here are several suggestions for research questions involving applied linguistics and the study of translation. For the sake of inclusiveness, they are formulated in a generic way, but the researcher would of course be better served by adapting them to more specific contexts and a more manageable scope. For example, instead of asking "What does a case study of translators in the field teach us about the practice and its challenges?" the question in a real research project could be "What does a case study of Brazilian translators working at the Argentina border teach us about the necessary rhetorical adaptations to be made between these two closely related romance languages in this part of the world?

Below are ideas for honors theses, master theses and applied projects, and dissertations:

1. What is the rate of acceptance of papers written in other languages and translated for the purpose of submitting to journals? Does the strategy work? For example, follow the road to publication of a group of academics from the conception of the work to the submission of article in a second language (through translation), to feedback from journal.
2. What are the features of dubbing that make the practice particularly successful (according to the interpretation of viewers)? What interferes with communication in that context in viewers' estimations? What are viewers' attitudes toward dubbing?
3. What are some of the linguistic consequences for children serving as translators for their parents? What are some of the sociolinguistic consequences? How does linguistic power figure in this scenario?
4. What insight can applied linguistics offer when it comes to deep rhetorical patterns embedded in text and the best way to translate them?
5. In a survey with interpreters, what are some of the biggest challenges they relate when it comes to practicing their profession? What are some of their best insights?
6. What further insights can we derive from contrastive rhetoric and its application to translation/interpretation?

7. What are some crucial issues in cross-cultural rhetoric and cross-cultural communication affecting the practice of translation?
8. What are some lingering questions in (a specific area of) translation studies?
9. What are some points of disagreement or contention within translation studies?
10. What does a case study of translators in the field teach us about the practice and its challenges?
11. How can the study of specific features of translation inform applied linguistics and linguistic theory?
12. What might the future of translation and translation studies hold?

Note

1 I would argue that there are ways of teaching literature as a more applied discipline that would potentially make it possible for it to attract more students at this difficult historical moment for the humanities.

Works cited and further reading

Baker, M. (2003). Corpus Linguistics and translation studies: Implications and applications. In Baker, M., Francis, G., and Tognini-Bonelli, E. (Eds.), *Text and technology*. Philadelphia: John Benjamins.

Baker, M., and Malmkjaer, K. (2009). *Routledge encyclopedia of translation studies*. London: Routledge.

Canale, M., and Swain, M. (1980). Theoretical bases of communicative approaches to second language teaching and testing. *Applied Linguistics, 1*, 1–47.

Chaume, F. (2012). Research paths in audiovisual translation: The case of dubbing. C. Millán, and F. Bartrina (Eds.), *The Routledge handbook of translation studies*. Routledge. Retrieved on April 7, 2018 from www.routledgehandbooks.com/doi/10.4324/9780203102893.ch20.

Connor, U. (1996). *Contrastive rhetoric: Cross-cultural aspects of second-language writing*. Cambridge: Cambridge University Press.

Cook, G. (2010). *Translation in language teaching*. Oxford: Oxford University Press.

Davidson, B. (2000). The interpreter as institutional gatekeeper: The social-linguistic role of the interpreters in Spanish-English medical discourse. *Journal of Sociolinguistics, 4*(3), 379–405.

Díaz Cintas, J. (2012). Subtitling. In C. Millán, and F. Bartrina (Eds.), *The Routledge handbook of translation studies*. Retrieved on April 7, 2018 from www.routledgehandbooks.com/doi/10.4324/9780203102893.ch20.

Friedrich, P., Mesquita, L. F., and Hatum, A. O. (2006). The meaning of difference: Beyond cultural and managerial homogeneity stereotypes of Latin America. *Management Research 4*(1), 53–71.

Griffiths, C. (2004). Language learning strategies: Theory and research. Auckland: AIS St. Helens, Centre for Research in International Education (pp. 1–26). Retrieved on June 27, 2018 from www.crie.org.nz/research-papers/c_griffiths_op1.pdf.

Hall, E. T. (1976). *Beyond culture*. Garden City, NY: Anchor Press.

Harris, B., and Sherwood, B. (1978). Translation as an innate skill. In Gerver, D. and Sinaiko, H. W. (Eds), *Language, interpretation and communication* (pp. 155–170). New York: Plenum Press.

Hatum, A., Friedrich, P., and Mesquita, L. (2006). Más allá de los estereotipos: decodificando los estilos de gestion en latin America, *Harvard Business Review* (Latin American Edition), *84*(6), 40–50.

Hofstede, G. (1980). *Culture's consequences: International differences in work-related values.* London: Sage Publications.

Littau, K. (2016). Translation and the materialities of communication. *Translation Studies, 9*(1), 82–113.

Martínez, X. (2004). Film dubbing: Its process and translation. In P. Orero (Ed.), *Topics in audiovisual translations* (pp. 3–7). Philadelphia: John Benjamins.

Millán, C., and Bartrina, F. (Eds.). *The Routledge handbook of translation studies.* Retrieved on April 7, 2018 from www.routledgehandbooks.com/doi/10.4324/9780203102893.ch20.

Munday, J. (2012). *Introducing translation studies: Theories and applications.* New York: Routledge.

Munday, J. (2009). *The Routledge companion to translation studies.* New York: Routledge.

Newmark, P. (2009). The linguistic and communicative stages in translation theory. In J. Munday. (Ed.), *The Routledge companion to translation studies* (pp. 20–35). NY: Routledge.

Orellana, M. F., Dorner, L., and Pulido, L. (2003). Accessing sssets: Immigrant youth's work as family translators or "para-phrasers." *Social Problems, 50*(4), 505–524.

Pöchhacker, F. (2008). Issues in interpreting studies. In J. Munday (Ed.), *The Routledge companion to translation studies* (pp.128–140). New York: Routledge.

Reynolds, J. F., and Orellana, M. F. (2009). New immigrant youth interpreting in white public space. *American Anthropologist, 111*(2), 211–223.

Stovel, K., Golub, B., and Milgrom, E. M. M. (2011) Proceedings of the National Academy of Sciences, *108*(4). Retrieved on July 14, 2018 from www.pnas.org/content/pnas/early/2011/12/13/1100920108.full.pdf.

Tse, L. (1995) Language brokering among Latino adolescents: Prevalence, attitudes, and school performance. *Hispanic Journal of Behavioral Sciences, 17,* 180–93.

Tveit, J.-E. (2009). Dubbing versus subtitling: Old battleground revisited. In J. D. Cintas, et al. (Eds.), *Audiovisual Translation.* New York: Palgrave-Macmillan.

Urciolli, B. (1998). *Exposing prejudice: Puerto Rican experiences of language, race, and class.* Boulder, CO: Westview.

Williams, J., and Chesterman, A. (2008) *The map: A beginner's guide to doing research in translation studies.* New York: Routledge.

Wolf, M., and Fukari, A. (2007). *Constructing a sociology of translation.* Philadelphia, PA: John Benjamins.

7

COMBINING CORPUS LINGUISTICS AND COMPUTATIONAL LINGUISTICS

THIS CHAPTER WILL DO THE FOLLOWING

1. Explain the concept of corpus linguistics.
2. Relate the field of computational linguistics to corpus linguistics tools.
3. Call for a great partnership between applied linguistics and computational linguistics.
4. Exemplify the use of corpora studies across different areas of applied linguistics.
5. Provide ideas for students and scholars who would like to develop projects combining applied linguistics, computational linguistics, and corpus analyses.

Introduction

Imagine these real-world situations: a company would like to know what adjectives its clients are using in social media to describe its products. Or teams of computer scientists and linguists work together in the development of artificial intelligence and language tools, or even, a group of researchers wants to find out whether words from a language they have been trying to revitalize are being spread through Twitter. A linguist wants to investigate large-scale linguistic innovation in social media or wants to find out the geographical location of certain linguistic features (lexical items, for example). Finally, a peace researcher wants to find out what words resonate the most with people doing field work on conflict and peace. What all these situations have in common is the employment of corpus linguistics tools of investigation and the potential use of computational linguistics to achieve the goals.

According to Weisser (2016, p. 23), "[a] corpus (pl. corpora) is a collection of spoken or written texts to be used for linguistic analysis and based on a specific set of design criteria influenced by its purpose and scope." In this broad definition, Weisser includes all texts that have been "systematically assembled" even if the collection is modest. Therefore, for example, if I were to write down all slang that a class of 20 students uttered during a one-hour discussion session to discover which one is the most frequent item and which is the rarest and most unique, I would be engaged in the study and analysis of a corpus of language. By the same token, if I were to input in a computer program the text from all Jane-Austen novels to establish patterns in paragraph formation and word use, I would still be engaged with corpus analysis even though this set and my list from the previous example are very different in length of text and number of words.

Corpora can be gathered to represent historical data, contemporary data, or data that shows historical progression over time. For example, one could investigate the diminishing frequency of the pronoun *thou* in canonic works of English literature in a given century, or the context of use of singular *they* in contemporary texts, or even syntactic variation and innovation in Shakespeare's plays. The larger the data set and the more complex the analysis, the more computational linguistics can help.

Lappin (2014) explains that computational linguistics is "the study of natural language in the intersection of linguistics and computer science." This means using computers and big data analyses to deal with the increasingly complex and large corpora that the digital age has made available to researchers. For example, in the past, one might have transcribed interviews by hand and followed up by counting the number of times the filler "like" appeared in the transcript. This was very time consuming and therefore, researchers were usually restricted to examining small sets of data and looking for single variables or spending a decade in a single, larger project. Aided by computer technology, we can now look for that same feature, or its combination with adjacent terms, in sets of data that are significantly larger (e.g., a whole section of Twitter or the life work of a particular writer) and yield results in a fraction of time. In addition, researchers can now ask many follow up questions about the variable(s) in question and receive almost immediate responses. To use the same example of the filler "like," one can design a model that helps established the age, gender, and geographical location of those who use it the most. Of course, the human component that helps us make sense of the data we find continues to be crucial. Therefore, if we want to discuss the significance of the increased frequency of the "like" filler, we still (thankfully, I believe) need to do that part of the work ourselves.

In this context, major functions of computational linguistics include seeking,

> to develop systems that facilitate human-computer interaction, and to automate a range of practical linguistic tasks. These tasks include (among

> others) machine translation, text summarization, speech recognition and generation, information extraction and retrieval, and sentiment analysis of text.
>
> *(Lappin, 2014)*

Lappin also reminds the reader that understanding how human beings process language in the brain is also a goal for computational linguistics. I would like to briefly discuss "sentiment analysis," which is the practice of extracting and compiling the prevailing mood within a corpus. My brief detour has the goal of ensuring that I don't contradict myself in stating that subjectivity still requires a human touch when it comes to finding meaning in data. While "sentiment analysis" does indeed deal with expressions of emotion and impression, the characteristics of the data are not very different from those of other corpus studies. Ultimately, it requires that a researcher at the end of the process interpret the data to attribute significance to it.

Nguyen et al. (2016) argue that until recently, computational linguistics tools had been used more readily within the informational dimension of language and much less so in helping us to understand its social dimension. They argue that attention and interest in social media has started to change in a sustained way (and sentiment analysis has found fertile ground in social media). They point out, as one of the difficulties of a more sociolinguistically informed collection and analysis of large data, the great variation that occurs in online environments, much of which, as this book shows, engages with a lot of linguistic creativity and less standardized linguistic forms. The authors thus argue for a greater partnership between computational linguistics and sociolinguistics in an effort to conduct corpus studies that are more engaged with the social dimensions of language.

Predicting behavior, creating better translators, designing programs that can be used in forensic investigations, building models that can aid research, identifying idiosyncrasies in professional or research practices are all worthwhile goals for corpus studies. As applied linguists, we should be asking how we can positively influence the development of tools and conversely too what kinds of information we would like to generate for our field(s) of study. At the same time, we should be advocating for the ethical use of these tools and exploring the potential pitfalls of their simply becoming instruments of commercial exploitation. Issues of privacy, linguistic and otherwise, should also be pondered.

I will not spend time in this chapter on the methodological and sampling aspects of corpora studies; many great works exist that describe best practices in that regard (please refer to the works cited and further reading at the end of the chapter). I will also not spend much time on natural language processing (as a feature of artificial intelligence, the kind that allows us to speak to our phones) as its study ventures into complex, specialized territory that is not always within the larger scope of applied linguistics and sociolinguistics (i.e., many times its predictive models do not take into consideration the socio-cultural environment of the subject, though they should). I will offer, however, that although not explored here, there are interesting questions to ask about that interface, for example, what meaningful sociolinguistic factors help explain miscommunication with machines. But instead, I would like to explore some ideas regarding why corpus linguistics should matter to applied linguists and in what places a partnership with computer scientists can help.

However, knowledge of a few basic concepts that linguists/computer scientists utilize in their investigations is important if we want to consider how we can use computational tools to conduct applied linguistics. For many studies requiring advanced computational skills and ability to build models, it is best to work with interdisciplinary teams to which each member brings their expertise. This can be thought of in similar terms to the way many linguists have regarded (traditional) statistics thus far: every linguist can benefit from an understanding of statistics that allows them to both create studies that answer the questions they want to ask and read quantitative research conducted by others. However, when a complex statistical model has to be written, it is often wiser to work with a statistician. Likewise, a working understanding by linguists of what is behind computational models and a primer on language dynamics for computer scientists are welcome additions and good working tools. While my expertise is certainly in linguistics and not in the more technical aspects of computational models, I would like to offer a few concepts that might help language researchers start thinking of projects that might be designed in interdisciplinary partnership by these teams.

The first one of such concepts is neural networks, which are a series of functions that help one predict dependent variable y from independent variable x. Neural networks rely on decision nodes that go in multiple directions. For example, the ultimate question "were these texts written by person A?" is a yes/no question possibly based on nodes with such variables as vocabulary, sentence structure, paragraph structure, syntax, etc.

The creation of neural networks is a step in the application of deep learning. Through them, you can decide the significant functions and significant facts that predict known outcomes so that in the future when the outcomes of the same kind are not known, we already have the model to predict them. Take for example the use of the filler "like" from my example above. By inputting more and more data and refining the parameters of a model, a scientist can ultimately decide whether geographical location should be an element of a predictive tool that looks at the distribution of that feature or whether it does not matter (perhaps the process will show that age and social network are more significant).

Deep learning is based on a brain model (thus the name "neural" network for the application it uses). Perhaps the easiest way to describe it is as a subset of machine learning that utilizes neural networks to create predictive models. Machine learning, in turn, is a subset of artificial intelligence practices. The subfield of computer science that deals with machine learning is data science (in itself a form of applied statistics). Simple machine learning is used to predict y from x. In neural networks, the number of correlating elements can be much larger, and part of the process of deep learning is to establish which correlations are more important, as in the example of "like" above. By inputting more data, one tries to improve results and better the model. Ultimately, one is trying to find which variables from a set are predictive and which can be discarded.

Here is another simple example from forensic linguistics. If a researcher tries to build a model to establish if a set of suspect texts were written by an individual for whom they have five known texts, they will have a much harder time building that model from such a small sample than if they had 100 known texts by the same individual. Part of the problem might be the restricted number of correlating elements and the very few occurrences. That is, if they were to only have available five known texts, they might also have an equally restricted set of linguistically meaningful elements (e.g., acronyms for "be right back" as BRB appearing once, and laughing expressed as "lol" twice). However, if the number of known texts were much greater, the same researcher might have a much larger set of linguistic items to try and correlate (e.g., acronyms for "be right back" as BRB appearing dozens of times, laughing expressed as "lol" consistently, sentences often ending in prepositions, kisses and hugs represented as "xxoo" as opposed to "XXOO," a repeated grammatical or spelling mistake, etc.). It is just like identifying fingerprint points: it is much harder to find a match with three points than with a full, clean fingerprint containing all its distinctive bridges, ridges, and bifurcations. Not only that, but with a larger data set, the researcher can better predict which elements actually matter. For example, it might turn out that the acronym BRB is not a meaningful correlating element if in the larger set it appears in free variation as all "BRB," "brb," and "be right back." On the other hand, if across 100 texts "lol" appeared consistently as such, it might help eliminate an author if in the suspect texts it only appears as "lawl" (an attempt at phonetic representation of the sound of "lol" if read as a word, not an acronym).

And here is a more complex example to illustrate these concepts and frameworks (for more information, refer to Virginia Hughs's blog in National Geographic's *Phenomena*, 2013).[1] A few years ago, the alleged story goes, working on a Twitter tip, *Sunday Times*'s editor Richard Brooks figured out that the pseudonymed author of *The Cuckoo's Calling* (Robert Galbraith), was no other than best-selling J.K. Rowling, author of *Harry Potter.* One of the things Brooks did to substantiate the tip he received was confirm that the publisher and agent of the two authors was the same, but more importantly, he consulted two computer scientists, one of whom, Patrick Juola, looked for linguistic similarities between the texts. Hughs (2013) mentions that among the foci of the analyses were considerations of how words are paired and what adjacent words a particular lexical item recurrently has. The scientist also looked for the most frequent words in each book, differences in the frequency of these words, as well as frequency of words of different lengths. Another researcher, Peter Millican conducted analyses that went from sentence and paragraph length, to specifics of punctuation, to lexical usage. The combination of these analyses made the researchers confident that the books were by the same author. I can also speculate that by adding more and more data to the data set (i.e., more books by Rowling) as well as by adding factors to analyze, these researchers were creating or refining a program that would have increasingly good predictability results, not only being capable of establishing that further books were Rowling's (if so be the case) but also being able to input other books by other authors and do the same when they were compared to known works.

This is a potential and real use of neural networks and deep learning for linguistic research: deep learning means that with the subsequent addition of factors for statistical analysis (i.e., determining correlation, establishing factors that are the most important, discarding elements that are not) one can create fine-tuned models to analyze increasingly complex sets of data. After all, it is called deep learning because it has multiple activation layers.

Other predictability applications of models resulting from deep learning can include establishing, for example, the profile of consumers who would like a certain kind of language in a commercial or identifying characteristics of an individual or group depending on their language use. As I mentioned earlier, the ethical use of these tools is of extreme importance and a topic I hope many linguists will pick up in the future.

Corpus studies in linguistics

This section will necessarily and purposefully touch upon areas of application for corpora studies in applied linguistics that include many of the subject-matter areas of other chapters, for example, forensics, translation studies, medical humanities, world Englishes and associated disciplines, and digital Englishes. This not only helps bring this book's parts together but also and more importantly helps showcase applied linguistics as methodologically and philosophically consistent (I hope the reader can extrapolate other methodological possibilities across chapters). In that sense, this chapter is different from the others because its application and methodological considerations are pertinent to different subareas and therefore do not constitute a subarea in itself.

Twitter and language

Twitter is very popular with language-and-society researchers because it is possible to access a large amount of data in short, self-contained segments. The datasets created for analysis can be as large or as small as needed for the goals of the project. One can select criteria ranging from interests to geography, to gender. One can follow retweets, replies, the formation of communities as well as the characteristics of viral posts of the impact of particularly important news events. The flexibility and scope of the medium makes it very attractive for research studies.

The first such study I will discuss was conducted by Pak and Paroubek (2010, p. 1320) with the goal of sentiment analysis. Of the advantages of using Twitter I mention above, they added others, including how much contributions in Twitter involve opinions; the fact that all segments of society are represented, from celebrities to urban professionals, from politicians, to teenagers and intellectuals;

and the representation of many languages. Because Pak and Paroubek's goals mirrored the development of programs capable of learning to do the job rather than focusing on answering specific questions about specific data sets, their method included collecting data that would create a training set. Ultimately, the set would involve the use of emoticons such as :-) for positive emotions and :-(for negative ones as well as posts for news outlets known for a certain neutrality to train for neutral ones, among other elements.

While many of the authors' comments are methodological in nature, since they are interested in developing the best possible model, some commentaries on the linguistic elements themselves are of interest to applied linguistics. In a partition between objective and subjective texts, the former presented more common nouns and proper nouns while the subjective ones presented more personal pronouns. Negative texts contained more past, past participle, and adjectival forms ending in -ed, for example, "lost," "gone," and "bored" (p. 1322). On the other hand, positive texts contained many instances of "whose," which upon further scrutiny was discovered to be a mistaken use taking the place of "who's," as in "who's in?" (p. 1322.) This unexpected result shows that these kinds of analysis can be used to establish trends in language change and items for teaching, besides fulfilling their original goal of establishing the general mood within a data set. However, they also raise questions. The assumption that a frowning emoticon means a negative emotion overlooks how what we say/write, and what we mean should be analyzed taking in consideration concerns about humor, sarcasm, banter, exaggeration, etc. For example, a person could write a tweet that ends in a sad face to joke with the person to whom they are responding:

A: (posts a picture of a chocolate cake and captions it "dessert today.")
B: What?! You baked this delicious cake while I'm not there? :-(hahaha.

In this example, one would be hard pressed to label this as a negative text, yet an analytic tool might do exactly that. Repeated instances of such use might influence the outcome of the analysis as, for example, negative even if overall it is not.

Other considerations include how these programs can (or cannot) be trained to tell connotative from denotative meaning as well as understand hyperbole and other figures of speech. For example, in:

A: I won't be able to go to the movies with you all tonight.
B: That's the worst thing I've ever heard!

it is hard to imagine that indeed the failed movie date is the worst thing speaker B has ever heard. Simply, on the internet, exaggerations are very much a part of discursive practices. Likewise, in:

A: Look at the new computer I bought.
B: Sick!

the word "sick" works as a synonym of "great" or "awesome," and thus has a positive meaning. The question remains whether through deep leaning, machines can be trained to understand that difference and decide when it has been applied.

Having become curious about this last example, I entered the English version in a popular online translator, and in turns, asked for versions in Spanish, Portuguese, and French, languages that I speak and for which I could, therefore, check the results without further consultations. Interestingly enough, the translator got it right one out of three times. For Spanish, the translator rightly assigned, in context, the word "increíble" (i.e., incredible) as a possible translation. On the other hand, the same dialogue translated to Portuguese and French resulted respectively in "doente" and "malade," that is, "sick" in the "ill" sense of the word. The program did not offer, as it sometimes does, secondary meanings.

One wonders if the continued partnership between computer experts and linguists will increasingly bridge this gap between the more objective and the more sociolinguistically and pragmatically mediated use of language. After all, machine translators have already come a long way from their beginnings. Aspects such as the immediate context of use of the word, including surrounding terms, as well as punctuation, frequency, and other extra-linguistic aspects will likely help. As their technology becomes more sophisticated, deep learning follows, and research on social media also moves forward.

In my own classroom, students have used Twitter to investigate how varieties of world Englishes, such as Irish English, South African English, and Australian English are being represented, especially when it comes to the use of slang and more colloquial language (in the world Englishes framework I subscribe to, not only new Englishes but all Englishes are included). In the process, they learned new words, new expressions, and made connections between culture, language, and audience. The fact that utterances are short allows linguists-in-training to survey a large number of language users.

English as a lingua franca inventories: VOICE and ACE

The Vienna-Oxford International Corpus of English (VOICE, see www.univie.ac.at/voice and the work of Seidlhofer, 2010) is a corpus of English language, capturing the linguistic interactions of users of English for whom English is not a first language. The corpus contains over one million words by over one thousand and two hundred speakers and has what is ultimately a descriptive goal. The inventory focuses on European varieties. The availability of such a corpus is of great interest for linguists because of naturally occurring quality of the data, which can then be accessed when one has specific questions that need answering.

Similarly to VOICE, the Asian Corpus of English (ACE, see Kirkpatrick, 2013) has gathered together data by speakers in Eastern and Southeastern Asian countries such as China, Vietnam, and Japan. According to Kirkpatrick (2013, p. 19), the project "aims to provide a truly representative sample of English as used as an Asian lingua franca."

Much has been written about the controversy regarding the term English as a Lingua Franca (ELF) itself (Friedrich and Matsuda, 2010). Great work and advancement have resulted from these fruitful discussions, and the reader will find elements of that important phenomenon elsewhere in this book. For the purpose of the current conversation, I will only mention a few of the points that evidence where I currently stand in this exchange:

1. ELF is a function of language given the needs of users of English everywhere, who use it as a first or additional language to communicate with one another. The presence of native speakers in the interactions does not take away from the function of ELF. It is the need to communicate across cultural, geographical, and linguistic boundaries that defines the function "English as a lingua franca." It is English at the moment, given its perceived power and scope, but the function takes precedence over the language. Lingua-franca functions have been performed by Latin, French, and other languages before (and concomitantly with English), including the original lingua franca," from which we draw the expression, a now elusive pidgin of the Mediterranean spoken from medieval times for about 300 years (Nolan, 2015, p. 99).
2. The particulars of each interaction are negotiated given the cultures, the idiolects, the purpose, and the audience of the exchanges. While there might be similarities among the varieties used, given the very nature of language acquisition and production themselves, diversity of expression continues to be a value and a reality in international communication in lingua franca situations.
3. The very existence of different inventories of language based on geography and to a certain degree first-language family or proximity is evidence that we are speaking of function rather than simply form. In this case, form is a result of similarity in other sociolinguistic characteristics, hence an Eastern Asian inventory such as ACE and a mostly Western European one such as VOICE, as a separate one. Were the linguistic aspects of the inventory completely consistent across cultures, we would only need a world-wide corpus.
4. This is not to say that the varieties represented through ELF inventories are any less significant, important, or functional than native-speaker varieties. This is another reason to emphasize function over form while at the same time investigating what forms are defying native-speaker norms in the users' own quest for communication and self-expression.
5. In the discussion over forms that can be found among users of English as an additional language to fulfill a lingua-franca function, and whether the ones that deviate from native-speaker norms are mistakes or not, ELF proponents tend to defend the perspective that to consider them to be errors would be

to advocate for the superiority of native varieties. On the other hand, it can be argued that many of these forms can be what they are because of developing competence and necessary stages of language acquisition. In this regard, I wonder why these two aspects of language acquisition and use would be thought to be self-exclusive. The distinction between an error and language variation that leads to change is usually drawn on the bases of time and systematization, in a continuum. We know from the history of the English language that the mistake of yesterday is the standard language of tomorrow (e.g., "If I was," "one chicken," "a pea," which were once "If I were," "one chick," and "a pease"). What separates the two sides of the continuum is wide-ranging use. Therefore, an inventory of naturally occurring language will likely contain elements that at a given point in time can be considered mistakes while it will also contain others that, although different from whatever the imagined standard is, will be widely used and do not interfere with communication. Asking questions about this distinction can be a worthwhile pursuit vis-à-vis language inventories such as VOICE and ACE.

6. The terms world Englishes (WE), English as a Lingua Franca (ELF), and English as an International Language (EIL) should not be used interchangeably. Not only do they point to different phenomena, they also have very different histories which should be acknowledged and understood by researchers and practitioners if they want to do justice to the many insightful advances made especially in the last 40 years.

Corpus of language such as VOICE and ACE are full of promise and possibility for applied linguists. Not only do they help us answer the questions we have but they are also catalysts for the design of new ones. To add to the worthwhile goal of mapping varieties of English and their characteristics around the world, it would be important to develop parallel projects in the Americas, in Africa, and elsewhere around the globe. It is in the detailed study of different realizations and the comparisons across regions that further answers to questions about the dynamics of English can be found.

Language studies of medical corpora

After years and years of work and new iterations of scientific research, the biases and choices regarding how a phenomenon is written about can become invisible to those practicing in the field. Studies of linguistic corpora can help shine a light on language that might be having unintended consequences for those described in the literature and that might be unwittingly skewing practices that are meant to be helpful. This is what Bowker (2001) demonstrates in her corpus study of medical language used in the context of infertility. In analyzing ten years of semi-specialized (i.e., for educated laypersons) and specialized (i.e., for medical professionals) literature on infertility (almost five-hundred thousand words), Bowker discovered that the language referring to disorders and conditions resulting in infertility in men tended to be much more neutral than the language used to describe infertility in women. For example, the uterine environment described often as "hostile." Terms such as "abnormal," "incompetent," or "failure" were often used to describe women's organs, cycle, or reproductive processes. In the case of terms referring to conditions leading to male infertility it was much more common to find such terms as "retrograde" instead of "incompetent," "dysfunction," and "impaired" (with impairment standing in for "failure," in this case), terms that are not only more neutral but which also do not carry any connotation of blame, as "failure" does.

What Bowker so aptly manages to demonstrate is that corpus studies have the capacity to, in a much more definitive way, confirm (or not) what intuition and anecdotal evidence can only suggest. In this case, Bowker concludes with the recommendation that theorists and terminologists start investing in the long process of proposing new terms for new phenomena in a way that takes gender sensitivity into consideration while aiming for the transformation of existing insensitive language in the long run.

I had the opportunity of experiencing the advantages of corpus studies myself as part of a team (Files et al. 2017) that investigated the use of titles as forms of address for male and female doctors during grand rounds. Doctors who are women had long suspected that they were addressed as doctors less often than their male counterparts, being instead referred to by first name, even in formal situations of professional introduction and even when other doctors, who were male, were referred to by title in the same interaction. Through the study of a corpus of more than 300 introductions we were able to confirm the following:

> Female introducers were more likely to use professional titles when introducing any speaker during the first form of address compared with male introducers (96.2% [102/106] vs. 65.6% [141/215]; $p < 0.001$). Female dyads utilized formal titles during the first form of address 97.8% (45/46) compared with male dyads who utilized a formal title 72.4% (110/152) of the time ($p = 0.007$). In mixed-gender dyads, where the introducer was female and speaker male, formal titles were used 95.0% (57/60) of the time. Male introducers of female speakers utilized professional titles 49.2% (31/63) of the time ($p < 0.001$).
>
> *(p. 413)*

Because of the corpus study, we are now able to point to quantitative evidence that there was an imbalance (probably subconscious for many people) that might result in women feeling less valued in their professional capacity, which is the first step in changing that reality.

The possibilities for corpus studies of medical data (and sociolinguistic data related to medical practice) are limitless. This is of course just a very short commentary and micro-sampling of what is possible. I hope other researchers and students will feel encouraged to ask questions and look for answers in linguistic corpora. There is much to learn and a whole society to benefit from such knowledge.

Questions and ideas for further research

1. What are the best predictive linguistic elements in a comparison between novels by the same author?
2. What are some ethical questions faced by linguists when they consider the use of computational linguistics to find out specific information about large populations?
3. How can corpus linguistics analysis be used to further peace initiatives?
4. What does the study of literary corpora with works of fiction authors tell us about the nature of our linguistic fingerprint?
5. What does a corpus investigation of language used to describe fictional characters of different genders tell us about the construction and representation of women in particular time and place?
6. What does a corpus analysis of words used to describe disability in a particular set of medical texts tell us about the state of the discipline?
7. What are some of the lingering linguistic challenges when it comes to improving online translators and machine learning?
8. What pedagogical practices can be adopted in different classroom environments to foster a possible collaboration with computational linguistics?

Note

1 Hughs, V. (2013). *How Forensic Linguistics Outed J.K. Rowling (Not to Mention James Madison, Barack Obama, and the Rest of Us)*. Retrieved on June 16, 2018 from http://phenomena.nationalgeographic.com/2013/07/19/how-forensic-linguistics-outed-j-k-rowling-not-to-mention-james-madison-barack-obama-and-the-rest-of-us/.

Works cited and further reading

Baker, M. (1993). Corpus linguistics and translation studies: Applications and implications. In M. Baker, Francis, G., and Tognini-Bonelli, E. (Eds.), *Text and technology: In honour of John Sinclair* (pp. 233–250). Amsterdam and Philadelphia: John Benjamins.

Biber, D., Connor, U., and Upton, T. (2007). *Discourse on the move: Using corpus analysis to describe discourse structure*. Amsterdam: John Benjamins.

Biber, D., Conrad, S., and Reppen, R. (1998). *Corpus linguistics: Investigating language structure and use*. Cambridge: Cambridge University Press.

Biber, D., and Kurjian, J. (2007). Towards a taxonomy of web registers and text types: A multidimensional analysis. In M. Hundt, Nesselhauf, N., and Biewer, C. (Eds.), *Corpus linguistics and the web* (pp. 109–132). Amsterdam: Rodopi.

Bowker, L. 2001. Terminology and gender sensitivity: A corpus-based study of the LSP of infertility. *Language in Society, 30*(4), 589–611.

Carter, R., and Adolphs, S. (2008). Linking the verbal and visual: New directions for corpuslinguistics. In Language and computers [Special issue]. *Language, People, Numbers, 64*, 275–291.

Davies, A., and Elder, C. (2004a). General introduction: Applied linguistics: Subject to discipline? In A. Davies, and Elder, C. (Eds.), *The handbook of applied linguistics* (pp. 1–15). Malden, MA: Blackwell.

Davies, A., and Elder , C. (Eds.). (2004b). *The handbook of applied linguistics*. Malden, MA: Blackwell.
Eagleson, R. (1994). Forensic analysis of personal written texts. In J. Gibbons (Ed.), *Language and the Law* (pp. 362–373). London: Longman.
Files, J. A., Mayer, A. P., Ko, M. G., Friedrich, P., Jenkins, M., Bryan, M. J ... Hayes, S. N. (2017). Speaker introductions at internal medicine grand rounds: Forms of address reveal gender bias. *Journal of Women's Health, 26*(5), 413–419.
Friedrich, P., and Matsuda, A. (2010). When five words are not enough: A conceptual and terminological discussion of English as a Lingua Franca. *International Multilingual Research Journal, 4*(1), 20–30.
Gass, S. M., and Makoni, S. (Eds.). (2004). *World applied linguistics: AILA review*, 17. Philadelphia and Amsterdam: John Benjamins.
Gibbons, J. (2004). *Forensic linguistics*. Malden, MA: Blackwell.
Hughs, V. (2013.) How forensic linguistics outed J.K. Rowling (not to mention James Madison, Barack Obama, and the rest of us). Nationalgeographic.com. Retrieved on June 16, 2018 from http://phenomena.nationalgeographic.com/2013/07/19/how-forensic-linguistics-outed-j-k-rowling-not-to-mention-james-madison-barack-obama-and-the-rest-of-us/.
Hundt, M., Nesselhauf, N., and Biewer. C. (Eds.). (2007). *Corpus linguistics and the Web*. Amsterdam: Rodopi.
Hunston, S. (2002a). *Corpora in applied linguistics*. Cambridge: Cambridge University Press.
Kennedy, G. D. (1998). *An introduction to corpus linguistics*. London: Longman.
Kirkpatrick, A. (2013). The Asian corpus of English: Motivation and aims. *Learner Corpus Studies in Asia and the World, 1*, 17–30.
Lappin, S. (2014). What is computational linguistics? The British Academy. Retrieved on November 22, 2018 from www.thebritishacademy.ac.uk/blog/what-computational-linguistics.
McEnery, T., and Wilson, A. (2001). *Corpus linguistics* (2nd ed.). Edinburgh: Edinburgh University Press.
Nguyen , D., Doğruöz, A. S., Roséand, C.P., and de Jong, F. (2016). Computational sociolinguistics: A survey. *Computational Linguistics, 42*(3), 537–593.
Nolan, J. (2015). Lingua franca: A not so simple pidgin. *SOAS Working Papers in Linguistics, 17*, 99–111.
Olohan, M. (2004). *Introducing corpora in translation studies*. London and New York: Routledge.
Pak, A., and Paroubek, P. (2010). Twitter as a corpus for sentiment analysis and opinion mining. *Proceedings of the International Conference on Language Resources and Evaluation*, LREC 2010, May 17–23, 2010, Valletta, Malta.
Seidlhofer, B. (2010). Giving VOICE to English as a lingua franca. In Facchinetti, R., and D. Crystal. (Eds.), *From international to local English and back again* (pp. 147–164). New York: Peter Lang.
Thomas, J., and Short , M. (Eds.). (1996). *Using corpora for language research*. London: Longman.
Weisser, M. (2016). Practical corpus linguistics: An introduction to corpus-based language analysis. West Sussex: John Wiley & Sons, Incorporated.

8

INVESTIGATING THROUGH FORENSIC LINGUISTICS

THIS CHAPTER WILL DO THE FOLLOWING

1. Explain the concept of forensic linguistics and position it in relation to applied linguistics and sociolinguistics.
2. Relate the concept of idiolect to the practices in forensic linguistics.
3. Describe and explain the different elements of forensic linguistics.
4. Exemplify the elements through the changing characteristics of text messages.
5. Provide ideas for students and scholars who would like to develop tools for the forensic study of language.

Introduction

The success of such television shows as *CSI*,[1] with its many versions, has provided the public with a specific, fictionalized take on forensic sciences as applied to crime solving. In the show, laboratory analysis is often conducted in a futuristic environment, where test tubes share space with computers. There are many consequences to the popularity of these shows, which include greater visibility of forensics and a larger number of students seeking careers in related areas. Another is that, if asked what forensics looks like, most members of the audience are likely to think of the aforementioned laboratory tubes, fingerprint dusting, ballistics, and other "hard sciences" elements exclusively when questioned about methods and directions of investigation.

It was therefore refreshing to realize that another popular series, *Criminal Minds*,[2] introduced the concept of forensic linguistics through one of its main characters in season eight: Alex Blake, portrayed by actress Jeanne Tripplehorn, is a FBI agent and professor of linguistics. The gesture has caused forensic linguistics, perhaps for the first time in its decades-long history, to be considered outside academic and scientific realms by a more general audience.

Nevertheless, even within those learned circles, and much more so in the "real world," forensic linguistics is yet to realize its full potential and to be fully considered a sister science to the ones that involve chemical, physical, and biological analysis. Just like other social sciences such as psychology, whose contribution in profiling is now widely recognized, forensic linguistics has the potential to play a significant role in forensic investigations.

In this chapter, I describe some of the antecedents of forensic linguistics, its uses and methods, and argue that the age of digital communications has offered both new possibilities for this applied science—through the documentation of otherwise oral/undocumented texts and the creation of digital programs of collection and analysis—but also challenges, many of which are likely to become more evident given the increasing influence of automatic text editors and other forms of electronic revision. These new developments have the risk of eliminating author-specific traits of texts (which are key in forensics) and therefore of making what were once creative uses of language more homogeneous. Finding new ways of identifying traits of authorship means much work ahead for applied linguists. On the other hand, the greater partnership of forensic linguistics with computer scientists can allow for the development of programs that look at large quantities of linguistic data with the goal of solving linguistic puzzles in the real world.

What is forensic linguistics?

If forensic linguistics was to be summarized in one sentence, it would be that it is the science of author identification. Relying on the assumption that individuals have idiolects (i.e., individual dialects, however multi-layered), forensic linguistics postulates that if you identify and isolate the features of that idiolect in a text (written or oral), and compare and contrast those features in a text of known authorship with those in a suspect text, one can arrive at the author or discard the possibility that a particular individual is the author. This can be done at a more individualized level (e.g., comparing one suspect text message to 25 known texts by a given person) or, in corpus studies, against a large database of texts (e.g., features of a novel against many works from that period).

While this is an extremely simplified summary of what forensic linguistics can do, it brings what is a rich, complex application of linguistics to a concrete level. Ariani et al. (2014, pp. 223–224), provide a much broader picture by expanding the realm and the possibilities of forensic linguistics (as applied to legal domains) to include, besides author identification, "forensic stylistics, discourse analysis," linguistic dialectology, "forensic phonetics, forensic transcription," and the study of variation (both intra- and inter-author variation). I would contend that these are different foci, linked to different methodological decisions, that in the end point to author identification anyway.

Although it is intuitive to think of forensic linguistics in relation to the solving of crimes (i.e., analyzing ransom notes, text messages of missing persons, etc.), as a science serving the purpose of author identification, forensic linguistics can also be used to authenticate texts of a non-criminal nature, for example, works of fiction, essays, or historical documents, and to detect plagiarism, which now with the aid of computer programs can be done on a large scale. What all these texts have in common is that they carry the rhetorical and linguistic fingerprint of their authors—they store the features of their idiolects, which are then available for researchers to unveil and codify. Reflectively, these investigations in the real world can lead to theorizing about the idiolect itself and the individual features of language that one might be able to identify.

Even people who have not heard of an idiolect, have experienced its power. It can be felt in the fact that, at times, one can pick up the phone and within a few words know who is speaking. It is also crucial in political satire: good comedians are funny when acting out as public figures in part because they have a talent for exaggerating features of idiolects. It is in the way one remembers peculiarities of the speech of a dear relative, or catches themselves repeating the same expressions, fillers, and exclamations over and over.

While many understandings of the idiolect exist, in this chapter the following description by McMenamin (2002) is appropriate:

> The idiolect has been referred to as a personal dialect. No two individuals use and perceive language in exactly the same way, so there will always be at least small differences in the grammar the person has internalized to speak, write and respond to other speakers and writers. The idiolect is the individual's unconscious and unique combination of linguistic knowledge, cognitive associations, and extra linguistic influences.
>
> *(p. 53)*

By adopting this definition, I am not implying that the idiolect is a monolithic entity, which manifests itself as the "same" language all the time. Layered here are the context of situation, the speech community or community of practice in question, the genre, the other participants of the interaction, and so many other elements that play a part in linguistic output and performance. Nevertheless, within variation, there are markers of one's unique experience with language. Of particular interest in this definition is the idea of "unconscious and unique," which means people cannot always make conscious decisions to disguise language, and even when they do, certain features remain, unbeknownst to them. This makes it possible for forensic linguists to analyze texts and determine with various degrees of accuracy, the likelihood of a particular individual being the author of a text. I say various degrees because several variables will influence the result of the investigation, including the following:

1. The amount of data present—the longer the texts, the greater the likelihood that it will contain relevant and unique features of a person's idiolect. This applies both to the known texts as well as to the suspect texts. This is a principle that applies to data, of all kinds, in research in all fields. Whereas it is great to have a large amount of known text, if the suspect text is simply "How are you?," a very unmarked kind of greeting, it will be much harder to find idiolectal variations than if, for example, a lengthy essay is available (although the more marked version "how RU?," although short, would be more auspicious, of course).
2. The genre of the known and suspect text—because users of language will make context-specific dialectal adaptations depending on the situation of communication, if the known text and the suspect text belong roughly to the same genre, it will be a lot easier to look for similarities and meaningful differences than if they belong to very different genres. For example, comparing text messages to an academic essay will likely reveal less than comparing two sets of text messages or two academic essays pertaining to the same discipline.
3. The presence of marked social and regional dialects—If the person in question belongs to a social or regional speech community with marked dialectal features likely to appear in that individual's idiolect, the precision of the linguist will likely be greater. For example, a classic case, now widely known,[3] regards how forensic linguist and investigator Roger Shuy solved a kidnapping case by noticing a kidnapper's note contained the expression "devil strip" in reference to the patch of grass between the sidewalk and the curb (the man had also used unlikely spellings for "kan" (can) and "kop" (cop), trying to look less literate than he really was.[4] The investigator asked if there was, among the suspects, a well-educated person from Akron, Ohio. The officers were stunned because one of the suspects fit this description precisely (the case happened in Illinois). It turns out the expression "devil strip" is very specific to that area, and the misspellings looked too intentional to be the result of actual mistakes, especially because the general register of the message was that of a formally educated person.
4. The presence of an unusual turn of phrase—an especially fortuitous occurrence in the realm of forensic linguistics is that of wrong word, especially when the slip turns out to be peculiar enough to be significant. Forensic linguists can look for consistent fossilized mistakes that can give away authorship, though individual words unique to one's repertoire can be "planted" too, just like other forms of forensic evidence.
5. The existence of a close set of potential authors—as pointed out by MacLeod and Grant (2012), descriptive methods work best in situations where a closed group of potential authors exist, whose idiolectal features can be compared

and contrasted to those of suspected texts. See for example the case of "devil strip" above. It was only the preexistence of a closed pool of suspects, one of whom presented the matching features that made the resolution of the case possible.

6. A methodology that allows that more subconscious decisions by authors of text—involving for example type, frequency, and placement of prepositions, or length of sentences, or even role and shape of function words—be considered and analyzed.

While crucial for forensic linguistics, the idea of an idiolect is not always universally endorsed, within the discipline, which can be quite a conundrum. Olsson and Luchjenbroers (2014, p. 226), for example, who wrote one of the most popular textbooks of forensic linguistics, question its very existence in the following:

> Not only should we avoid the use of inappropriate technical devices—such as the idiolect—but we should not hesitate to take advantage of contemporary linguistic assets, such as language corpora, decades of sociolinguistic research and the work of Bakhtin, Barthes and other theorists of language and culture.

This can be a problem, and the statement is a bit surprising, because without the idea that individual varieties of language exist (the idiolect is also a construct, not a technical device), we could not really practice forensic linguistics. It would be equivalent to trying to use fingerprints to identify suspects while acknowledging that many people could have the same exact groves in their fingers. Furthermore, a closer look at sociolinguistics and the work of language theorists points to both collective dynamics (toward linguistic change, or the formation of speech communities, for example) but also to individual preferences and layered influences (based on the interaction of such elements as age, gender, ethnic background, geography, education, and so many others that form the constitutive parts of the idiolect). Finally, corpora studies, as seen in Chapter 7 directly or indirectly rely on the idea of the idiolect to offer researchers the opportunity of observing which elements tend to be differential across texts and which are common across a particular genre. For example, studies show that elements that are often subconscious such as frequency and type of function words vary greatly across authors while having a much greater level of intra-author consistency (Argamon and Levitan, 2005).

Part of the problem is that when people outside sociolinguistics and applied linguistics think of the idiolect they often think of elements such as content vocabulary and surface items such as punctuation, to the exclusion of elements such as syntactic structure, position and type of prepositions and other function words, patterns of coordination and subordination, and even use of loanwords or code-mixing. Once one thinks of the idiolect as containing not only obvious and superficial variations, although those help too, they will realize that all the features they use in forensic analysis can ultimately be connected to the concept of the idiolect. They tend to also describe it as a static construct while in practice the idiolect can be quite dynamic.

Of course it would not be good science to use the idiolect as a construct simply because it would be convenient, if we did not have evidence that its use is actually theoretically and methodologically sound. That is, we cannot start at the construct and fit the data to it if the construct is an inaccurate element in the first place.

However, good evidence exists that the idiolect can indeed be used for analytical purposes. The very fact that cases have been solved on the basis of "unconscious and unique" elements of the idiolect (consistent with McMenamin's definition) points in the direction of its usefulness. Finally, the fact that we might not have identified all of the intricacies of the idiolect as well as all its practical applications does not mean they are not there. DNA analysis can be seen as an analogous case. Even when forensic sciences didn't know their particulars, DNA markers were already present, waiting to be unveiled and utilized, so much so that science has retroactively analyzed materials (stored for years) for those markers. Nowadays we even take DNA data for granted as an obvious element of analysis. It is as if it had always been employed, and we forget that it was only in the 1980s that DNA made it to court.

Given that, and compared to other branches of forensic science, forensic linguistics is still young. We can hope and take steps to guarantee that the features of individual varieties will one day become as commonplace and will be as thoroughly understood and systematized in forensics as DNA, ballistic, and fingerprinting evidence currently is. Our effort as linguists should be to further theorize and systematize the features of the idiolect (as a multilayered, dynamic, and situation-morphing element) that can be used for author identification, research, and investigation. Both qualitative and quantitative methods of analysis, as well as their combination in mixed methodologies, have a place in the development of forensic linguistics.

The history of forensic linguistics

According to the Forensic Linguistics Society (FLS) the term forensic linguistics was first used in 1968 by linguist Jan Svartvik. Ariani, Sajedi and Sajedi (2014, p. 223) explain that "In the 1980s, Australian linguists discussed the application of linguistics and sociolinguistics to legal issues." The authors further describe how in 1988, the Federal Police in Germany organized a conference on the topic. Subsequently, in Britain, evidence pertaining to authenticity of statements was first given in a criminal trial in 1989 (FLS), so when in the past I have asserted that comparatively speaking forensic linguistics is a newer applied science, I was making reference to its pragmatic uses as a set of knowledge items and methodological approaches. On the other hand, our human interest in looking for clues of authorship and unveiling the author of messages is very old. It also starts early in our own personal history: the reader can probably think of a situation early in their cognitive development when they were curious about a text of unknown authorship—whether they were playing Secret Santa or were the recipients of a note in school—and intuitively looked for elements that could help detect the author of the message. It might have been through the vocabulary used, or trying to figure out who would have had the specific knowledge or information contained in the text. In any case, that will have been an intuitive appeal to forensic linguistics.

Many of the first questions addressed in practice and in courts by forensic linguistics had to do with Miranda rights (to use the American expression) or collusion and authenticity of police reports. For example, when more than one police officer writes a report of the same incident, it is expected that certain types of information will coincide. On the other hand, were they to remember a defendant's utterances *ipsis litteris*, or were they to remember events that, given their position or role, could not possibly have been witnessed, those occurrences would be of interest to forensic linguists (see Olsson and Luchjenbroers, 2014, pp. 4–7). Investigators can then go on to try and determine whether the reports were written independently or not, authentically or not.

In time, the uses of forensic linguistics were expanded to include analyses of ransom notes, phone calls, appeals to the public, and communications claimed to be by missing persons, among many others. One can argue that the UK has incorporated forensic linguistics into its legal system to a greater degree and extent than its US counterparts. The Parliamentary Office of Science and Technology, for example, provides background information, procedures and techniques, and a bibliography on its website.

In general, we can speak of three different areas of application for forensic linguistics when it comes to courts and the legal system (Olsson and Luchjenbroers, 2014): cases where plagiarism is in the center of the investigation (and thus language is both the object and the tool of investigation), cases where language is used as an auxiliary of investigation, including surveillance and intelligence (e.g., trying to decide if a set of text messages could be from a missing person), and analyses of the language of the law itself (i.e., legalese). These uses overlap in terms of theoretical underpinnings with other applied branches of linguists, for example sociolinguistics, in that they try to establish the relationship between social phenomena, what we know of language dynamics, and how language manifests in the "real world."

While each of these areas deserves careful and in-depth consideration and research, in this chapter, I will focus on the second, that is the use of linguistics as auxiliary in the investigation and argumentation in cases. Given our reliance on technology and the ways we now document both synchronic and diachronic communications, which many times in the past would have not been recorded, many possibilities for linguistic research currently exist. That is also true of our ability to gather large amounts of data through corpus studies, which then can be used for comparative terms against suspect texts. For example, if a group of forensic linguists is tasked with analyzing the legitimacy of an appeal to the public (e.g., for information), they can now rely on a corpus of confirmed appeals and compare and contrast the similarities and differences between them. In forensic linguistics, establishing the similarities between suspect and authentic texts is as important as establishing the differences.

After talking in more detail about current practices in author identification, in the case of police investigations, I will discuss how technology both advances and hinders our efforts to establish authorship beyond reasonable doubt. Ideas for further research and enquiry follow.

Some present day aspects of interest

While many avenues of investigation and research exist regarding forensic linguistics , and many more are made possible given the growing attention to digital programs capable of collecting and analyzing large bodies of data, I will focus on the analysis of electronic forms of communication, both diachronic and synchronic. Many good reasons exist to focus on these not only as loci of investigation but also as elements of further study to fine-tune our techniques. The fact that many communications that were once conducted orally and not recorded are now written and documented facilitates both the identification of features that are specific to individuals as well as further theory-building research. While certain more formal written genres of an academic, professional nature are built on the expectation of close approximation to a standard variety of language, the tweet, the text, and the social media post are much less restricted. In fact, these are genres where creativity and innovation count and where people are looking to highlight their individuality through features of spelling, use of slang, abbreviations, and other peculiarities. People tend to also feel freer to break rules of punctuation, use of apostrophes, and other standard features for the sake of facility and speed.

One of the linguistic changes brought about by the proliferation of text messaging, social-media posting, online chatting, and other oral-turned-to-written forms of communication is the oral-like nature of the varieties used. Not only are people less likely to abide by standard language rules, many times people will, on purpose, further highlight elements of their idiolect for the sake of self-expression and ease of typing. In that respect, Internet users became more apt at using self-generated contractions, abbreviations, substitutions, and other features that made their discourse unique. In no time, people were texting "BRB" for "Be right back," "U" or "u" for "you," "2" for "to," among so many others. The Internet did not invent the use of acronyms (David Crystal, 2008, p. 43, writes of the use of "IOU" being documented since 1618, but digital modes have certainly accelerated the employment of such acronyms).

The individualization of discourse in that sense was very fortuitous for forensic linguistics. The more standard language used in a text, the more difficult it is to try and identify the author of a text. On the other hand, if an analyst can identify a pattern in the variation and individualization of text creation, the better the chances of identifying an author. For example, if an author of texts systematically uses "C U L8er" for "See you later," or "talk 2U," for "talk to you," the easier it is to compare a suspect text to known texts by that person. The challenge of course comes in the form of free variation. While discourse can become more individualized in the Internet age, with less concern for standard English (or standard forms of languages in general), people can also be less concerned about keeping that individualization patterned. In that sense, a person can write "talk to U," in one text, "talk 2 you" in another, "talk2u" in a third, and "talk to u" in yet another.

Forensic linguists, therefore, develop analytical tools to measure the use of forms, frequency of features, syntax, regional and social variety markers, errors, and even such items as placement of punctuation (i.e., with or without spaces for example) and frequency of function words. While the outcome of the analysis is as dependent on the methodology of the researcher as it is on the features that happen to be present in the text, the literature corroborates the successful use of these techniques to both discard and confirm suspects in a number of legal cases.

For example, Olsson and Luchjenbroers (2014, pp. 173–176) relate a case that exemplifies the above. The analysis of texts sent through the phone of a missing person in an attempt to portray the situation as an intentional departure and life change, showed that the suspect had intentionally but unsuccessfully tried to reproduce the uniqueness of the known texts by using abbreviations, slang, and other features of a youth variety, and "kisses" ("xxxxxx") which nonetheless failed in terms of frequency, placement, and other specifics. In these situations, it was the presence of clear elements of people's idiolects, appearing unencumbered by the homogenization of standard discourse, that facilitated the solving of the crimes.

This switch, which at first meant an expansion of the possibilities of analysis, is now challenged by the very nature of documentation. For the sake of clarity, in this text, when I refer to synchronic communications, I mostly mean chats and texts, and by diachronic communication, I mean emails and social media posting—even though there are several other possibilities for each and despite the fact that what sometimes is intended to be read on the spot is not (and vice versa).

Since then, however, the advancement of text correctors, voice commands, and other developments in technology have started to make what were once some of the best sets of linguistic clues available, much more difficult to spot. If a person "speaks a text," which is then automatically transcribed, these markers of the idiolect are replaced by a standardized output by the program used. If a person verbally inputs "See you too" in a voice recognition app, it will not have "u" in its output. Nor will it have "U" or "2." It might make mistakes. For example, failing to cognize syntactic clues, it might have "to" as the output, but chances are these mistakes will be systematic rather than individualized. The system is also likely to get rid of abbreviations by replacing them with standard forms as the person types or speaks. Finally, many text editors now automatically offer suggestions for terms that could appear next in a sentence. As a result, discourse that in the Internet era was becoming more and more individualized is now being curtailed by the advancement of the very technology that made such high variation possible.

What the future may hold

The advancement of digital modes of analysis and further developments in computational linguistics and artificial intelligence are sure to bring innovation and precision to forensic linguistics. The more corpus of linguistic data we have, the better the predictive capacity of our tools will be as well. Teams of applied linguists and specialists in other areas are needed in all aspects of the enterprise, and increasingly interesting and challenging questions need to be asked by applied linguists in the pursuit of refined methods for author identification. Below are a few suggestions in that regard.

Questions for research:

1. When it comes to analyzing texting data, information gathered from phones in the early 2000s often reveals preferences of the texter that can help determine authorship. For example, U, u, you, ya, y can be studied so that a forensic linguist can establish the likelihood that they are in free variation or not in texts of known authorship and thus make claims about their use (or not) in contested texts. With improvements in automatic spell checking and the wide availability of smartphones, are these idiolectal choices becoming more restricted? Is text across authors becoming more uniform, and if it is, what are the implications for this kind of forensic analysis?
2. What different analyses of text can be made possible by corpus studies and new computer technologies? What are some areas of forensic linguistics that can be expanded through these methodologies?
3. How can linguists help revisit and reconstruct the idea of the idiolect so that it both encompasses the great variation within a person's language while still capturing the elements that make it unique? How can they test new models applying new findings to forensic linguistics?
4. What knowledge from world Englishes can inform forensic investigations?
5. What are some of the implications of changing text and word-processing technology for forensic linguistics?
6. Questions surrounding the idiolect usually result from the idiolect being defined too narrowly (refer to papers that limit it for example to voice characteristics or word choice (regional variation)). How can research be furthered to establish the elements most likely to be subconscious, so that even a person familiar with linguistics would be unable to manipulate them?

Notes

1 Zuiker, A. (2000–2015). *CSI: Crime scene investigation.* USA/Canada: Alliance Atlantis Communications, CBS Paramount Network Television, CBS Productions.
2 Davis, J. (2005). *Criminal Minds.* USA/Canada: Touchstone Television, Paramount Network Television, The Mark Gordon Company.

3 To read more about the case, please refer to www.pbs.org/speak/seatosea/american-varieties/DARE/profiling/ retrieved on December 14, 2017.
4 Yagoda, B. (2018, July 19). 'The suits,' 'lightbulb went off,' and 'tree lawn': Investigations of a language nerd, Lingua Franca, The Chronicle of Higher Education. Retrieved on August 25, 2018 from www.chronicle.com/blogs/linguafranca/2018/07/19/the-suits-light-bulb-went-off-and-tree-lawn-investigations-of-a-language-nerd/.

Works cited and further reading

Argamon, S., and Levitan, S. (2005). Measuring the usefulness of function words for authorship attribution. Retrieved on August 29, 2018 from http://citeseerx.ist.psu.edu/viewdoc/download?doi=10.1.1.71.6935&rep=rep1&type=pdf.

Ariani, M. G., Sajedi, F., and Sajedi, M. (2014). Forensic linguistics: A brief overview of the keyelements. 14th International Language, Literature and Stylistics Symposium. *Social and Behavioral Sciences 158*, 222–225.

Coulthard, M., and Johnson, A. (2007). *An introduction to forensic linguistics: Language in evidence*. London: Routledge.

Crystal, D. (2008). *Txtng: The gr8 db8*. Oxford: Oxford.

Macleod, N., and Grant, T. (2012). *Whose Tweet? Authorship analysis of micro-blogs and other short-form messages*. In: *Proceedings of the International Association of Forensic Linguists' tenth biennial conference*. Tomblin, Samuel; MacLeod, Nicci; Sousa-Silva, Rui and Coulthard, Malcolm (Eds.). Aston University, Birmingham, UK.

McMenamin, G. (2002). *Forensic linguistics: Advances in forensic stylistics*. Boca Raton, FL: CRC Press.

Olson, J. (2012). *Wordcrime*. London: Continuum.

Olsson, J., and Luchjenbroers, J. (2014) *Forensic linguistics*. London: Bloomsbury.

9

WORKING ON PEACE, DIPLOMACY, AND NEGOTIATION

THIS CHAPTER WILL DO THE FOLLOWING

1. Discuss the field of peace linguistics as a nascent branch of applied linguistics.
2. Revisit some of the relevant research on language and peace, especially in the last decade.
3. Describe the history of peace linguistics in the context of peace studies.
4. Describe the relationship between peace linguistics, diplomacy, and negotiation.
5. Propose a research agenda for the investigation of language and peace.
6. Provide ideas for students and scholars who would like to conduct research on the intersection of language and peace.

Introduction

From the way we talk to one another every day, to the talks that go on in international organizations and across governments around the world, words matter. Approaching a conversation from the perspective of cooperation as opposed to competition or an adversarial position will significantly influence the outcome. Yet, work at the intersection of language and peace is not often taken into consideration neither within linguistics nor between applied linguistics and other areas of knowledge when it comes to informing such fields as diplomacy and negotiation. What is more, such knowledge is not often used to improve communications at the individual level either.

In this chapter, I would like to discuss the viability of peace linguistics, a nascent branch of applied linguistics that dwells exactly at the intersection of language, society, and peace studies. My hope is to show avenues for research that could make a compelling case for further participation of applied linguistics in an interdisciplinary pursuit peace through language.

Peace linguistics in the context of sociolinguistics and applied linguistics

Peace linguistics and the fields of diplomacy and negotiation can benefit from a solid understanding of the insights from sociolinguistics and applied linguistics. After all, if we were able to establish best practices when it comes to the selection of linguistic and sociolinguistic elements before we engaged in the teaching and the pursuit of peace, we would stand much better chances of success. In the very least, applied linguistics research would be able to tell us just how much linguistic choices matter in this case. The opposite is also true: understanding how language can mediate peace processes and/or create goodwill at the individual and communal level can also provide insight for sociolinguistic research and new avenues for the application of linguistic knowledge in applied linguistics, a discipline I believe has stayed surprisingly silent in investigations of peace and its relation to language.

One would think the close connection between language and its capacity to generate peace and goodwill is intuitive: through language human beings can potentially seek agreement and common ground, explain differences and ask productive questions that can in time lead to consensus. Language can reveal people's biases, hopes, and fears, and can help individuals reframe conflict in productive ways. Through language, one can reframe obstacles so that they seem more like challenges than impediments. It is not a unilateral process; much less noble uses of language are available to all too. However, the more peace-seeking and peace-restoring uses of language can be emphasized and encouraged, especially by human institutions such as education, policy, and media. It is, nonetheless, incumbent upon us, to establish through research just how much, or how little, this intuition about the overt teachability of peace is right. To empirically investigate peace in relation to language is where I suggest applied linguistics could go next.

Why not peace?

It is not always easy to argue for peace, the counterintuitive nature of this statement notwithstanding. Peace, of all things, one would hope, should be a goal for everyone to have. The achievement of peace should be a forefront concern in our minds as we go about life, however challenging and work-intensive reaching that goal can be. Nevertheless, having been involved in linguistic peace research for several years now, I have experienced firsthand the skepticism of some and the arguments more favorable to the deconstruction of conflict than to the building of peace of others. The claims I have heard in face-to-face conversations and have read in articles and books include some acknowledgment that we live in a world full of conflict, that there is too much war going on to focus on peace, and that conflict is the natural state of human beings—all of which are, in my opinion arguments that would support more investigation of peace rather than less.

Furthermore, although it looks like it would be very productive for more researchers to embrace peace as a worthwhile subject for empirical investigation and theory building (I have heard this from many teachers and students who would like the same), it is the case that several counter voices express cynicism regarding the place of peace research in academia. More often than not, these same voices will then make arguments for more conflict-centric research agendas or view peace simply as the absence of war or conflict. The very nature of academia at times contributes to these dynamics: discursively speaking, academics are used to advancing knowledge through disagreement and argumentation, and to talk about peace is in a way the opposite of all of that. The infrequency of articles and books within applied linguistics and related disciplines discussing peace and language is noted by Curtis (2017, p. 24), who laments the lack of prominence of the topic and hopes "Peace Linguistics will catch on" given that, he continues, "if there is one thing that our bruised and battered world needs right now, it is less war and more peace." In sum, it is possible to acknowledge that conflict is a part of human experience and recognize, at the same time, that peace is a more desirable state.

The issue of conflict-centric versus peace-centric research presents itself to me as one of point of view: if you think your glass is half-full or half-empty, you will be right either way. Likewise, if one believes peace to be a state to be pursued and lived, and another that conflict is unavoidable, both will be right. However, their experience of life will be significantly different depending on which of these two points of view predominates and directs their investigations. If one constantly theorizes war and conflict, their research universe will present itself very differently from the universe of a researcher who is looking to systematize the nature and experience of peace. Neither one is wrong, but results, being question-dependent, will reflect the theoretical line of enquiry. Long ago, I chose peace as the lens through which I would seek to understand the human experience of language and the one by which I hope to effect positive change within my realm of action and communities of practice.

As a result, in the last decade, I have been an advocate for peace linguistics and to my knowledge, the third person to use the term, after Gomes de Matos (1996) and Crystal (1999). Taking it a step further, I conceptualized peace sociolinguistics (Friedrich, 2007b) to include not only those goals of peace linguistics (i.e., to study and understand the impact of a peace-mediated vocabulary, language structure, and discourse options and apply that understanding to everyday communications and education), but also to insert that understanding in a social milieu influenced by linguistic power; prejudice; attitudes toward language; and considerations of race, ethnicity, class, age, and disability status. To theorize and apply conceptual understandings of peace does not preclude an acknowledgment of the existence of conflict, the same way that to focus on health and well-being does not negate the existence of disease. In either case, however, depending on the focus, the prescription—or, in this case, observational conclusion—will be different.

While Curtis (2017) is justifiably preoccupied with the future of peace linguistics, there is reason to be optimistic. About a decade ago, I issued a request (Friedrich, 2007) for works that elaborated on the relationship between peace and language and utilized peace frameworks to advance an understanding of language and peace. While I do not, of course, claim that all of these works result from that request, in the following sections, after a brief history of peace linguistics and some other considerations, I highlight those articles and books that have focuses on the importance of peace in relation to language. Once again, I invite the reader to join the group of linguists and language specialists trying to understand and apply their knowledge of linguistic peace to the macro and micro level of their experience. I then describe and explain the relevance of the study of peace to other fields such as TESOL, negotiation, and diplomacy. Finally, I offer some suggestions for empirical research involving language and peace.

History of peace linguistics

When it comes to peace studies, peace linguistics is actually a surprisingly late addition to the core disciplines that contribute to what is a very interdisciplinary undertaking. The study of peace within this group of subject areas developed to a great extent as a response, given the large and world-changing conflicts of the twentieth century. While in my own research I prefer not to define peace as the absence of war, but rather as an independent, self-contained frame of mind in itself (a commonality among those who study peace rather than conflict resolution primarily), the genesis of peace studies did come about as an attempt at positive institutional building to create a culture that would be more amenable to dialogue and cooperation than to war. Conflict resolution (1950s), peace education (more prominently 1960s), peace psychology (1980s), and cross-cultural communication (1980s) had already had years of research attached to them when peace linguistics came along in the 1990s. Discussions had become fertile in the terrain of positive and negative peace (Galtung, 1969), the many meanings of peace (inner, global, individual), the difference between non-violence and peace, and the psychology of peace and war. Yet, when it comes to peace linguistics, little has, to date, been done to account for the linguistic aspect of all those phenomena.

In time, this absence started to be noted: not only do we need a better understanding of the above in relation to language, but new aspects of linguistic interest became more visible: we also had to further elaborate on the ramifications to and needs of different groups of individuals, including the linguistic rights of language minorities, people living with disabilities, those who have been disenfranchised by the widespread use of the Internet (including internet-specific phenomena such as flame wars and trolling), perception of peace linguistics across cultures, among so many other worthwhile pursuits.

As far as peace is concerned, many can be the interpretations of the word and the scope of investigation and action. In English, the term is encompassing enough to include considerations of "tranquility," "harmony," "inner peace," "peace among individuals," peace among nations," "the absence of war" (e.g., times of peace = no major war is happening = negative peace), "the building of strong institutions that bring peace and tranquility" (positive peace). The two latter forms are covered by and provide the basis for much of Galtung's (1964) theoretical work.

The term peace linguistics itself can be linked to the work of Brazilian linguist Francisco Gomes de Matos who not only is the first self-titled peace linguist but also who was one of the original proponents of the Universal Declaration of Linguistic Rights in 1984. The declaration was adopted at the World Conference on Linguistic Rights in 1996 in Barcelona.[1]

Already in the 1970s, Gomes de Matos had written a dictionary entry (1977) describing the term peace linguistics. He himself acknowledges that when in the 1990s, David Crystal used the expression in his own dictionary of terms (Crystal, 1999, pp. 254–255) the discipline gathered some momentum. At the time, Crystal explained peace linguistics as, "an approach which emerged in the 1990s among many linguists and language teachers in which linguistic principles, methods, findings and applications were seen as a means of promoting peace and human rights at a global level."

Besides working on linguistic human rights and his "pedagogy of positiveness," Gomes de Matos went on to publish many pedagogical works and to write rhymed, peace-inspired reflections. A decade ago (Friedrich, 2007b, pp. 74–75), I called attention to the elements of peace linguistics we could invest in. Referring to Galtung's (1964) famed framework, I argued that,

> one can imagine a positive peace through language, one that can be achieved by long-range respect for and maintenance of linguistic rights, the ecology of languages, cultural and linguistic diversity, and language education. Such a peace is of much interest in sociolinguistic studies because its elements speak directly of the survival of languages, the ways in which we use language, and our role in changing language relations through education.

In Friedrich (2007a, pp. 11–14), I gave a brief overview of the development of peace-related disciplines in the Western-world, which together provided a basis for the development of an interdisciplinary peace studies, and which I summarize and append here. In the 1950s, it was conflict resolution that took center stage. To this day, many university degrees, training programs, and educational courses exist that utilize conflict-resolution lenses. They can be used to instruct business people, healthcare professionals, diplomatic workers, teachers, counselors in the intricacies of conflict resolution, or to use more updated models and nomenclature, conflict transformation.

Prominent in the 1960s and throughout the 1970s, peace education, shifted the focus a bit from conflict as a starting point, to peace itself at the center of the endeavor. Peace education continues to advance into areas of environmental education, sustainability, and children's peace education. The next addition was peace psychology in the 1980s, in part as a response to the challenges posed by the fear of nuclear war and also the Cold War. Parallel to all this, fields such as cross-cultural communication and contrastive rhetoric developed, given the description of rhetorical patterns by Kaplan (1966), greater cross-cultural awareness made possible by such work as, for example, Hofstede (1984) and his cross-cultural dimensions, and later Connor (1996) who continued to investigate and describe aspects of contrastive rhetoric. Interestingly enough, these concepts were and are more often picked up and embraced by other disciplines (e.g., business, negotiation, and communication studies) than by applied linguistics, which has stayed mostly outside of the investigation of the application of peace studies concepts to language. TESOL has provided some wonderful examples of what language specialists can do with regards to peace and language, for example Arikan (2009) and Kruger (2012), but still these remain mostly as isolated efforts, usually picked up by peace education venues (both these articles were published by the *Journal of Peace Education*).

Peace linguistics as a nascent branch of applied linguistics

Peace linguistics is peace applied to language in the context of individual interactions, group communication, and worldwide, cross-cultural exchanges. To build an applied linguistics of peace, one must ask the question of how our understanding of the dynamics of language could potentially allow us to model, teach, advise, and create policy that would give individuals interested in fostering peace the necessary tools to undertake that task. At this point, it would be fortuitous and productive if applied linguistics started making statements, building frameworks, and discussing the place of peace studies within the discipline. As I explained in Chapter 1, applied linguistics has historically held close alliances with language acquisition, language teaching, and TESOL (as well as world Englishes), and it would be important for those related disciplines to conduct research that tests and validates the extent of the possibilities of peace linguistics at a more practical and fundamental level. For example, one could ask if the intentional teaching of peace vocabulary in educational environments results in greater active use of such a lexicon and if the use of the lexicon, in turn, results in less conflict. By the same token, one could seek to understand what, in terms of language acquisition, is at stake when a vocabulary of peace rather than one of conflict is emphasized. Finally, linguistics can combine peace linguistics, applied linguistics, and language planning to study the place of peace in education and policy.

Vocabulary considerations are just a start, but an important start

One of the big concerns in the work of Gomes de Matos (1996, 2012, 2016) is the avoidance of dehumanizing language—that which relies on metaphors of violence and other violent terms to make a point. In Friedrich and Gomes de Matos (2012), we provided many examples of how widespread the use of violent, dehumanizing language is: for example, expressions such as "battle of the sexes," "war of words," or "war on the middle class"—many of which have become somewhat invisible to us—put human beings in a position of conflict with one another and consequently of defensiveness. Dehumanizing language, Gomes de Matos postulates, should be replaced by language that includes *positivizers*, that is, words with the potential to generate positive responses and goodwill. From verbs that carry positive connotations (e.g., include, uplift, ameliorate, conciliate, cooperate) to changes in conversational strategies (fewer complaints, more explanations; less critique, more recommendations), Gomes de Matos (2016) sees in every word, syntax, and strategy choice an opportunity to foster more linguistic peace and more awareness that words matter.

Even from a practical point of view, let alone from a more humanitarian one, this approach makes sense: it has the potential to reduce conflict, cut down on negotiation times, bring about more fulfilling emotions, and a sense of accomplishment. Yet, just how much a change in vocabulary can shape the outcome of interactions should be a matter to be empirically verified by peace linguistics as soon as possible, so we can all move from the realm of possibility to the realm of empirical evidence and corroboration.

Gomes de Matos's work encourages us to arrive at any conversation with the goal of coming to an agreement and an understanding rather than winning an argument. That requires active listening, rather than just speaking, which is interesting from an applied linguistics and TESOL perspective because language education has, since the communicative-approach era, tended to emphasize speaking over listening. Once listening was even considered, along with reading, to be a "passive" skill. He also discourages pompous language, used simply to separate as is the case at times with academic discourse, and calls for the humanization of language professionals, teachers, speech therapists, and all professionals, who help us understand and use language more effectively and humanely.

Linguistic changes are indeed an important beginning, but if we take the matter of peace into sociolinguistic realms as well, many more possible areas of investigation become visible. For example, the matter of linguistic inclusion, the valuing and acceptance of different linguistic varieties, access to education in one's language, use of languages of wider communication not only to convey linguistic meaning but also to advance peace-fostering practices—those becomes extremely relevant to the undertaking. Peace linguistics refers to an approach that encompasses the uses of peaceful language, the use of language to procure peace, and the interaction of peace concerns with the realm of language and its sociolinguistic reality. Research could also seek to understand whether there are implications for research on gender, given that different genders tend to be acculturated differently to perform more collaborative or competitive rituals (Tannen 1990). This kind of research could be updated not only to include a consideration of where peace figures in the collaboration-competition continuum but also how new constructions of gender (i.e., less binary ones) affect and are affected by discussion of peace, acculturation, and linguistic ritualization. The ultimate question is, given that different groups of people are acculturated to interact with others more competitively or more collaboratively, is it possible to include a pedagogy of peace as a resource in their repertoire regardless of their favored communication rituals?

Linguistic violence

Although I prefer to write about peace as its own self-contained unit, one that is not necessarily derived from notions of war and conflict, it is sometimes unavoidable to acknowledge those elements that threaten peace. One such element is linguistic violence. In Friedrich (2007a, p. 10–11), I argued that linguistic violence is any linguistic and sociolinguistic act that violates one of the four basic needs of human beings (established by Galtung,1996) through language. Galtung's theory posits that our basic needs are survival, well-being, identity, and freedom and that instances of violence are "avoidable insults" to those basic needs. Keeping the parallel between linguistic and other forms of violence means that offending a person through *ad hominem attacks*, for example, would constitute linguistic violence, since that linguistic act violates one's sense of well-being. Likewise, denying a person's own sense of inclusion in a speech community (e.g., claiming someone is not really a speaker of English because they did not acquire it as a first language) would constitute linguistic violence because it is an attempt to violate their sense of identity. Under this broad definition, we can also add and include phenomena that have recently been reintroduced as part of our cultural repertoire. For example, "gaslighting," the linguistic act of trying to convince a person (verbally) that what they experience and feel has no bearing on reality, causes victims to question their own senses and understandings (and thus violate both their well-being and freedom). To the same category, it is possible to add the dissemination of false information, internet trolling, bullying (online and in "real life"), and flame wars because all of them, at the very least threaten the well-being of others.

In Friedrich and Diniz de Figueiredo (2016), we have also argued that we need a new linguistic theory to account for internet phenomena such as trolling because unlike other forms of linguistic violence, in many instances involving trolling, the individual creating these internet texts does not necessarily believe what they are communicating, nor is this form of "lying" motivated by what pragmatics would understand to be a self-serving, purposeful violation of one of Grice's (1975) maxims; that is, to avoid a violation of one particular maxim, the language user chooses to violate another (e.g., not tell the truth to avoid hurting someone's feelings). Instead, in the case of trolling, the individual in question simply wants to provoke a reaction by other internet users and resorts to linguistic violence in an attempt to do so. To my knowledge internet trolling has no antecedent outside of digital communications. Unlike bullying and dispensing *ad hominem* attacks, the expression "trolling"[2] only made an appearance with this meaning because of digital domains of language use. Should further investigations demonstrate that this is indeed true, it might be reason enough to start thinking up a theoretical framework to systematize and account for it. Peace linguistics could certainly help.

Research state of the art

Given research into the intersection of language and peace both in peace linguistics and in the related areas of peace education, peace psychology, and other aspects of peace studies, a picture of existing understandings—and further research needs—starts to emerge. At this point, it is still a very partial picture, and those of us engaged in this kind of research often lament that more emphasis and resources have not yet been placed in the endeavor (see, for example, Curtis, 2017 and Gavriely-Nuri, 2010, p. 566).

However, we have to continue and, it is to be hoped, persuade others of the importance of contributing language knowledge to peace studies, especially if we believe, and I certainly do, that our contribution is not marginal, but rather central to peace itself. Funk and Said (2010, p. 121), for example, explain how,

> In every language and culture, peace-related words take on distinctive meanings and overtones as a result of historical experiences, ongoing public conversations, and (in many if not most cases) associations with religious texts and traditions. Because this vocabulary supplies locally rooted understandings of what peace *is*, drawn from a cosmology or worldview with which people resonate, it is among the most basic of raw materials for peace building. [emphasis in the original]

Funk and Said's commentary takes place within the context of pointing out how important it is to localize peace, anchoring it in the understanding a people have of their own histories, stories, myths, and assumptions about peace and conflict. Likewise, he explains elsewhere (2010, p. 115) that it is vital to remember that many Western peacemakers operate from a more individualistic perspective with such values as "self-determination," "formal procedure," and "analytical problem-solving" at the forefront considerations. Those values of course will transfer more successfully to some societies but not to others; I would argue, in agreement with Funk and Said, that this transfer depends upon such elements as the degree of collectivism, views on leadership, level of hierarchical distance, among others (see also Hofstede, 1984).

Finally, Funk and Said also postulate that "While ideas about peace and conflict need not be locally rooted and completely indigenous to be of use to individuals and groups in any given context, it remains true that every cultural community has its own vernacular language for conflict and conflict resolution" (121) which means the role of language in peace building processes cannot be overstated. It is through language, in language, and because of language that we find new meanings for our experiences of conflict and our search for peace. To access how differently populations react even to the idea of peace, one must investigate the linguistic elements (analogies, metaphors, synonyms, imagery) used to talk about that experience or ideal.

In discussing the matter of peace psychology's greater attention to the "political" as well as the more military aspects of conflict, Gibson (2011, pp. 9–10) explains that less attention has been placed on the matter of language itself. He goes on to suggest that we need the kind of stance where "language becomes the object of study rather than the vehicle" (p. 10), a position that he believes is at odds with traditional cognitive psychology approaches to peace and conflict, but one that is necessary if we are to further understand this essential element (constitutive part, I would argue) of both. This difficulty within theory and common practice in cognitive psychology is much less of a problem in peace linguistics, since, as I explained earlier, linguists tend to recognize the three dimensions of language: vehicle (communication, education, cognition), language itself (theoretical linguistics, vocabulary, structure), and language as inserted in a socio-cultural milieu (applied linguistics, sociolinguistics, cross-cultural rhetoric). Gibson goes on to conclude that "[o]ne immediate priority for a critical discursive peace psychology should therefore be to interrogate how the language of peace is used" (p. 12).

It should not surprise linguists that oftentimes other disciplinary orientations take language for granted because although they rely on patterns of behavior and thought to understand and predict future occurrences in their own fields, many people outside of language studies do not think of language in this systematic way. A naive perception that "language just happens" is very common, in STEM, for example, and it often takes a degree of exposure to linguistic theory and to applied linguistic science for individuals in other disciplines to start to realize that language behavior, just like psychological patterns or social dynamics, presents variability but is also principled. At the same time, it is encouraging to see aspects of overlap between what a discursive peace psychology would do and the goals and accomplishments of a peace linguistics. In fact, I see no reason why we could not conflate the two into the same enterprise.

Gavriely-Nuri (2010, p. 566) calls attention to the importance of language in relation to peace by arguing that "the semantic vagueness surrounding the term peace" can transform the term "into a black box, or more precisely, into an attractive but empty box. This semantic void," she continues, "facilitates the loading of the concept with semantic, cultural and political cargoes that are sometimes bereft of the universal positive aura enveloping this concept."

On the other hand, I would posit, researchers have spent too much time trying to define peace in monolithic, universal ways that are perhaps unachievable (much like they have tried to decide if the natural state of humanity is one of conflict or one of peace) rather than, as Funk and Said (2010) propose, *localizing* peace. That is, to not be hollow, the concept of peace does not need to point exclusively to one universal construct. It can instead be explained in context, given the cultural understanding by the group and groups in question of peace and surrounding/auxiliary concepts. Much like it happens with such abstract but very important notions as pain, happiness, duty, responsibility, success and so many others, who utilizes the term *peace* and in what context they utilize it matters, and trying to impose exo-normative notions of it tends to generate less understanding instead of more.

Localizing peace, to use Funk and Said's expression one more time, is work-intensive because it means one cannot conduct research in one environment and then apply it uncritically everywhere. Yet, it means that once a significant advancement has been made in different environments, a follow up step can be to find the universals within those local patterns and abstract them from the diversity that should remain diverse. This is a way of thinking that is very familiar to linguists: we often study individual languages to arrive at universals—not all languages have verbs, but all languages have a way of expressing action, and not all languages have similarly constructed and positioned time expressions, but all languages have ways of expressing the passing of time, etc. Maybe an analogy is possible here: not all cultures understand peace or what would lead to it in the same way, but all cultures have an understanding of what peace in their context would mean.

Research in TESOL and peace

At the beginning of this book, I hinted at the close historical connection between applied linguistics, Second Language Acquisition (SLA) and TESOL, so it is appropriate to refer to the work that has been done to further the study of peace in those domains. The TESOL International Association, arguably the most important professional association for English language teachers in the world with over 12,000 members[3] has an interest group for those members who are drawn to issues of peace and social responsibility. The Social Responsibility Interest Section website (TESOLers for Social Responsibility, 2018) lists the following statement of purpose:

> TESOLers for Social Responsibility comprises TESOL members who are actively engaged in integrating language teaching with social responsibility, world citizenship, and an awareness of global issues such as peace, human rights, and the environment. The Interest Section aims to promote social responsibility within the TESOL profession and to advance

social equity, respect for differences, and multicultural understanding through education.

Three of the goals of the group speak directly to peace, namely to work toward the elimination of negative stereotypes that hinder the establishment of peace, organize training and workshops that introduce TESOLers to peace education, and create links to other organizations that promote peace themselves.

Kruger (2012, p. 17) argues that "language teachers should be at the forefront of promoting peace education." He goes on to acknowledge that currently, they "are playing only a peripheral role" when it comes to peace education. He suggests that concepts of peace education be introduced to the language curriculum. I believe we can do more than that by going back to the idea that language is not simply a vehicle but also the ideal content area from which peace can be approached.

The efficacy of teaching peace in the classroom is still, however, a matter of speculation. Kruger, whose point parallels what is one of the central claims of this book and of this chapter, mentions that peace needs to be empirically investigated so we can start addressing its role in different realms. In that respect, it would be advantageous to empirically research peace in the classroom not only as a vehicle of peace education, but also as a central linguistic area of study in the TESOL classroom. This linguistic focus, in turn, should go beyond the teaching of peace-related vocabulary (although that is also a part of it), and into the more sociolinguistic realm, in which the role of soft power and negotiation are intrinsically connected to success in interactions both at the micro and macro levels.

Peace linguistics, negotiation, and diplomacy

One of the sources of skepticism regarding peace linguistics is the assumption that it is naive to expect that individuals who make a living out of negotiating (be it in business, diplomacy, or other areas where one is a stakeholder in an arbitration- and conciliation-type of dynamics) will always behave and use language peacefully rather than fight hard to make their goals and needs heard and fulfilled. Peace-based approaches, one could claim, are naive in their lack of accountability for the force necessary to engage in negotiation. I believe, however, that such claims are misguided.

In her work, Biljana Scott (2016, p. 150 and 154) makes the point that, in diplomatic communications, force is not achieved through being disagreeable but rather "through assertion." Grace, on the other hand, is achieved "through attentiveness." Soft power, the kind that grace represents, I would add, remains linguistic and otherwise underexplored, in part because, in modern societies, soft power tends to be associated with the feminine and hard power with the masculine. The latter, in turn, is given more prominence and status, thus in many contexts grace is seen as weakness and thus not attempted.

In truth, there is great power in a soft, fluid kind of linguistic expression, where the focus is on collaboration, the good of the collective, and ultimately understanding. Note that we are not necessarily in the realm of language used by men and language used by women, but rather at the realm of characteristics associated with some abstract concept of masculinity and femininity. Each individual has the capacity to explore either aspect of communication, and different situations will likely call for more or less employment to strategies from each. While assertiveness is often reinterpreted as a masculine trait and grace a feminine one, in either case—choosing to be more assertive or more gracious—appeals to violence and disagreeableness are unnecessary. Graciousness does not beget disagreeableness but neither does true assertiveness. This is the reason why peace and diplomacy do not stand in contradiction but are instead completely aligned: peace can easily account for assertiveness and not simply attentiveness. They are both part and parcel of the same dynamics and can be used complimentarily in the pursuit of one's goals.

Empirical research has shown that societies associated with this abstract "feminine" often display not only a valuing of soft power but also great concern for its citizens' well-being: frequently in these environments, there is great attention to education, childcare, healthcare, and more balance (of roles, rights, responsibility, access) across genders. Hofstede (1984), whose work was a milestone in the understanding of cultural values and beliefs, concluded through empirical research that the list of the most feminine countries in the world includes Sweden, Norway, the Netherlands, and Denmark. These are environments where the understanding of the value of soft power in bringing about social well-being, security, and harmony has not been overlooked. Further empirical work should include other examinations of how in these societies soft power is reflected in language, and whether the classroom reflects those choices. Anecdotally, it is known that multilingualism and the study of multiple languages tends to be revered in those environments. The classroom reflects a balance between time to work and time to play. Creative pursuits are encouraged. Respect exists for knowledge obtained through the lenses of humanities and art. All of these elements should be researched alongside linguistic considerations in applied linguistics because they all point to variables that could potentially impact the outcome of interactions and negotiations that are peace-fostering.

The study and publication of work that combines language learning, diplomacy, and peace is, surprisingly in its infancy. In 2016, I edited what is, to my knowledge, the first book that presents diplomatic English as an area of research and practice (Friedrich, 2016). Many of the teaching-English materials used within diplomatic realms currently come from business English and business negotiation, which means that specific pragmatic and sociolinguistic aspects of interaction in that domain of use and within that community of practice might not get addressed. This is yet another area where applied linguistics can make a difference: the application of linguistic and sociolinguistic knowledge to this specialized branch of negotiation and diplomacy.

Given current research, what else can be done?

Gomes de Matos (2014, pp. 418–419, reproduced here with permission by the author) writes of two beliefs and four guidelines that can be applied to the study of linguistic peace. The beliefs are:

1. Life can be improved communicatively when language use is thought of—and implemented—as a peacebuilding force;
2. Life can be communicatively improved when language users are educated to learn to use languages peacefully for the good of persons, groups, Humankind.

To that, he adds four guidelines:

i. Language should have peacebuilding, peacesupporting, peacesustaining functions in human life;
ii. Languages should be taught/learned/used for human-improving, dignifying purposes;
iii. Language users/learners should learn how to interact and be interacted with in constructive, character-elevating ways;
iv. Language teachers should be educated to know how to help their students communicate in peaceful ways, with a focus on communicative peace as a deeper dimension of everyday communicative competence.

Questions and ideas for further research

I believe Gomes de Matos' guiding principles are a good end for this chapter and a good start for a section on what can be done to address the gap in applied linguistics research on peace. As the beliefs show, it is easy to intuit that better communication can be achieved if peace is included in instruction and taken into consideration. However, it is also important to ask if applied linguistics can figure out ways to confirm that belief both qualitatively and quantitatively. Thus, a variety of research projects can be designed to test that idea. For example:

1. If two otherwise identical university courses were offered to students with similar profiles, where one class is taught regularly and the other is overtly instructed to use more peaceful communications, would outcomes assessment turn out different for each class?
2. What would the attitude of English learners be to the instruction of a curriculum of peace linguistics to the general offering of their program?
3. What would a discourse analysis of essays of First Year Composition students, overtly taught about peace and language, reveal?
4. Would a group of business people be able to identify and change, where appropriate, elements of their boardroom negotiations after being instructed about peace linguistics? What would their attitude about those changes be?

5. What would the feedback of future diplomatic workers be if they were overtly taught about peace linguistics in an effort to facilitate their future interactions in the field?
6. What would a discourse and content analysis of ESL/EFL/world Englishes/IEL instructional materials reveal with regards to their peace-fostering potential?
7. What would an inventory of peace-enhancing and conflict-fostering content in different media (movies, TV series, recent bestseller books) reveal and how could the result influence our next steps in peace linguistics and peace education?
8. What could a survey of academics reveal regarding their openness to attitudes toward peace linguistics education (and peace education in general) at the university level?

Notes

1 The World Conference on Linguistic Rights, "Universal Declaration of Linguistic Rights," Barcelona Spain, June 1996.
2 The term can be found to have been used in the sense of "lure on as with a moving bait entice, allure" as early as the 1500s. Its internet-related use is a close approximation with words being used as bait. See https://www.etymonline.com/word/troll.
3 TESOL statistics. See www.tesol.org/about-tesol/membership/membership-statistics retrieved on 11/16/2017.

Works cited and further reading

Arikan, A. (2009). Environmental peace education in foreign language learners' English grammar lessons. *Journal of Peace Education*, *6*(1), 87–99.
Belmihoub, K. (2012). *A framework for the study of the spread of English in Algeria: A peaceful transition to a better linguistic environment* (MA Thesis). University of Toledo. Retrieved on September 28, 2017 from http://utdr.utoledo.edu/cgi/viewcontent.cgi?article=1285&context=theses-dissertations.
Belmihoub, K. (2015). English for peace in Algeria. *Reconsidering Development*, *4*(1), 35–50.
Cadman, K. (2008). From system to spirit: A personal story of changing priorities in teaching English as an additional language. *TESOL in Context*, *17*(2), 29–37.
Connor, U. (1996). *Contrastive rhetoric: Cross-cultural aspects of second language writing*. Cambridge: Cambridge University Press.
Crystal, D.(1999). *The Penguin dictionary of language*. London: Penguin Books.
Curtis, A. (2017). Whatever happened to peace (linguistics)? *The English Connection*, *21*(3), 23–24. Retrieved on September 28, 2017 from https://koreatesol.org/sites/default/files/pdf/Andy%20Curtis%20-%20TEC%20pp.%2023–24.pdf.
Friedrich, P. (2007a). *Language negotiation and peace: The use of English in conflict resolution*. London: Bloomsbury.
Friedrich, P. (2007b). English for peace: Toward a framework of peace sociolinguistics. *World Englishes*: *26*(1), 72–83.

Friedrich, P. (2012) Teaching language for peace. *The encyclopedia of applied linguistics*. New York: Wiley-Blackwell.

Friedrich, P. (2016, ed.). *English for diplomatic purposes*. London: Multilingual Matters.

Friedrich, P., and Gomes de Matos, F. (2012). Toward a nonkilling linguistics. In Friedrich, P. (Ed.) *Nonkilling linguistics: Practical applications*. Manoa: Center for Global Nonkilling.

Funk, N. C., and Said, A. A. (2010) Localizing peace: An agenda for sustainable peacebuilding. *Peace and Conflict Studies, 17*(1), Article 4. Retrieved on September 28, 2017 from http://nsuworks.nova.edu/cgi/viewcontent.cgi?article=1113&context=pcs

Galtung, J. (1969). Violence, peace, and peace research. *Journal of Peace Research, 6*, 167–191.

Galtung, J. (1996). *Peace by peaceful means: Peace and conflict, development and civilization*. London: Sage.

Gavriely-Nuri, D. (2010). The idiosyncratic language of Israeli 'peace': A cultural approach to critical discourse analysis (CCDA). *Discourse & Society, 21*(5), 565–585.

Gibson, S. (2011) Social psychology, war and peace: Towards a critical discursive peace psychology. *Social and Personality Psychology Compass, 5*(5), 239–250.

Gomes de Matos, F. (1996). *Pedagogia da positividade*. Recife: Editora da Universidade Federal de Pernambuco.

Gomes de Matos, F. (2012) *Nonkilling linguistics: practical applications*. Honolulu: Center for Global Nonkilling.

Gomes de Matos, F. (2014). Peace linguistics for language teachers. *D.E.L.T.A. 30*(2), 415–424.

Gomes de Matos, F. (2016). Pedagogy of Positiveness Applied to English for Diplomatic Purposes. In Friedrich, P. (Ed.) *English for diplomatic purposes*. London: Multilingual Matters.

Grice, H. P. (1975). Logic and conversation. In Cole, P. and Morgan, J. (Eds.), *Syntax and semantics 3: Speech acts* (pp. 41–58). New York, Academic Press.

Hashmi, A. M. (2014). The role of language in peace education. *Asian Journal of Multidisciplinary Studies. 2*(6), 76–81. Retrieved on September 28, 2017 on http://ajms.co.in/sites/ajms2015/index.php/ajms/article/viewFile/365/343.

Hofstede, Geert. (1984). *Culture's consequences: International differences in work-related values* (2nd ed.). Beverly Hills, CA: SAGE Publications.

Iloene, G. O., and Iloene, M. I. (2014). Applied peace linguistics and language therapy in conflict management and control. In Emezue, G. M. T., Kosch, I. and Kangel M. (Eds.), *Justice and human dignity in Africa*, (pp. 427–444). HPC Books.

Kaplan, R. B. (1966). Cultural thought patterns in inter-cultural education. *Language Learning, 18*, 1–20.

Kulkarni, D. V. (2017). *Sustainable peace in the twenty-first century: Bridging the gap from theory to practice*. Charlotte, NC: IAP.

Kruger, F. (2012). The role of TESOL in educating for peace. *Journal of Peace Education, 9*(1), 17–30.

Kruger, F. (2015). *Mapping peace and violence in the TESOL classroom*. (PhD Dissertation). University of Pretoria. Retrieved from https://repository.up.ac.za/dspace/bitstream/handle/2263/52936/Kruger_Mapping_2016.pdf?sequence=1.

LeBlanc, J. (2010). *How ESOL teachers become aware of communicative peace*. (MA Thesis). SIT Graduate Institute. Retrieved September 28, 2017 from http://digitalcollections.sit.edu/cgi/viewcontent.cgi?article=1498&context=ipp_collection.

Scott, B. Force and grace. (2016). In Friedrich, P. (Ed.), *English for diplomatic purposes* (pp. 149–172). London: Multilingual Matters.

Tannen, D. (1990). *You just don't understand: Man in women in conversation*. NY: Ballantine Books.

TESOLers for Social Responsibility. (2018). *The newsletter of the social responsibility interest section*, TESOL International Association. Retrieved on August 25, 2018 from http://newsmanager.commpartners.com/tesolsris/issues/2018–03–14/10.html.

10

APPLIED LINGUISTICS AND THE NEW LITERATURE

THIS CHAPTER WILL DO THE FOLLOWING

1. Discuss the emergence of a new literature in English(es).
2. Point to some of the features of that literature and its relation to digital modes.
3. Use the case of fan fiction as illustrative of new writing.
4. Argue for a better understanding of the linguistic and sociolinguistic features of these modes.
5. Describe and explain the different ways in which applied linguistics can engage with this new literature.
6. Provide ideas for students and scholars who would like to conduct applied linguistics research as it pertains to online writing and the new literature.

Introduction

If everyday conversations, classroom interactions, ESL text production, and learners' writings have long been of interest to applied linguists, new textual developments made possible by the digital age, and their respective and resulting online exchanges, have brought new possibilities for linguistic analysis, discovery, and (inter)action, many of which can be meaningful for applied linguistics. Not only have new means of communication been designed to make full use of digital capabilities, the speed of interaction and change has also been deeply affected by our digital era as have the formation and maintenance of new speech communities.

In this chapter, I will discuss changes in literary production in the twenty-first century and then focus on new literary forms made possible by the perceived democratization of media, stopping for quite a while on literature that is produced to be shared, whether professionally or in amateur form online. I discuss what the proliferation of such media might mean for language studies, not only in what the actual textual elements of the studies are concerned, but also the linguistic innovations and the rules of community interaction that such media allow. My goal is to inform the reader about these developments while suggesting new areas for linguistic investigation and research. While my focus is, in general, on these developments in the US and in English, I invite the reader to make inferences and to consider other loci of change where these developments might be important too as well as the many interlanguage possibilities that arise from these interactions.

Literary production now

There was a time, not very long ago, when a great deal of the literary production one could access (and would likely consider to be literature), was mediated by a standard process of submissions to literary magazines, newspapers, and publishing houses. Idealized was the relationship between author and editor, one in which there was a bidirectional correspondence that led to the polishing of a manuscript and its subsequent publication. It could be argued that this process was accessible to few (it still is), and outside of it, on their own, one would have a very hard time finding an audience. Access to writers was also very limited. A reader could write a letter praising a work but often, they did not hear back. If they did, it was hardly in a dialogic form. Writers were elusive beings, and between them and their readership was an institutional system that made communication difficult and access almost impossible. No wonder reading was, for the longest time deemed, together with listening, to be a passive skill.

While this kind of dynamics has not completely disappeared, it has come to exist alongside many other dynamics and possibilities of partnership, interaction, and feedback. These opportunities (listed on a range, starting on the more traditional side of publishing) include the hiring of a literary agent by aspiring writers (through an increasingly competitive process of querying and submission), who then negotiates publication with large publishing conglomerates. Contrary to what happens with academic works, it is generally not possible to write directly to large publishing houses to sell fiction and creative non-fiction without an agent. Authors have other options, though, such as submission of manuscripts to mid-size and small presses, often done directly (and electronically); the formation of beta-reader groups that do quite a bit of the work that once was done by editors; the possibility of self-publishing in electronic modes, the opportunity to write fan fiction, the chance of finding support through writer associations by genre or type of audience, the establishment of book clubs, etc. In the process, a whole new industry developed around writers, with services that include editorial help, book coaching, book cover design, e-book formatting, social media advertising, website design, outsourced public relations, among many other amenities (retreats, cruises for writers, merchandize design).

A much greater interface between written materials and other media also exists: for example, authors now often publish "deleted scenes," photos, book trailers, and other visual elements relating to their story on their websites. Writers are invited to take part in book club discussions (by joining these groups in person or through online live communication); and online launch parties for new books are now the rule rather than the exception, a phenomenon which makes sense if one considers how very few brick-and-mortar bookstores remain, and how expensive it can be to do a book signing in one of them. At vacation locations, readers photograph themselves with beloved books to share on social media. Fan-club gatherings happen in online environments, bringing together readers and writers from the most diverse locations to interact, many times in chat format. Book trailers advertise new releases, and increasingly audio books become a viable way to explore books: of linguistic interest, oftentimes, authors are given a chance to select the kind of reader they would like for their audiobook, including their accent.

These new speech communities and communities of practice offer ample possibility for linguistic and sociolinguistic expression and analysis. It can be argued that traditional publishing exerts a conservative, conventional, centripetal force (Bakhtin, 1981) on language. After all, editors in traditional publishing houses have a tendency to subscribe to much more prescriptive views and rules of language. In fact, it is not by chance that some of the most traditional literary journals continue to only accept snail mail submission and publish paper copies of their issues; it is a clear symbolic attempt to point at their exclusivity and traditional values. While every literary production can have the potential to expand the boundaries of language, once one is embedded in a large publishing conglomerate, it is almost inevitable that to keep work manageable and parallel to what is being done elsewhere in the company, they will apply what is standard in their practice to the work they are editing. Those authors publishing in such media will also, consciously or not, lean toward this kind of linguistic accommodation of the standard, knowing what the editorial process will entail and what it takes for a submission to be successful.

Enter the world of online publishing—with self-publishing, fan fiction, flash fiction, small-press printing and blog postings dominating certain areas of the digital universe—and the reality could be quite different. Gone could be the intermediaries between reader and writer and those parties more likely to curb down on linguistic creativity, innovation, and non-conformity to the standard. Often, in this new universe, there is little standing between writer and reader in terms of traditional institutional forces, although one could argue that more than a removal of these forces, what we are seeing is a change in who/what the power forces are. It could be claimed, for example, that powerful online retailers now exert quite a bit of the power that once belonged to publishing houses themselves, although their biases and bases for decision might be different. Yet, between writing and final published product, there are fewer steps and fewer intermediaries than before, and linguistic prescriptivism might be not a primary concern in these new environments, where feedback from the reader is also direct and intimately connected with sales. More important is the sense of being a member of the community, of belonging, and of interacting with like-minded individuals. These texts are, therefore, more malleable in terms of linguistic creativity and likely to exert a significant centrifugal force (Bakhtin, 1981).

This is not to say that everything is perfect, both linguistically and socially in the world of self-publishing and/or in a world less mediated by traditional institutional forces. Literary publishing has become a very complex, fast-paced endeavor, and writers are increasingly responsible for not only writing their stories but communicating with readers, participating in group activities (such as book clubs or writers' groups), advertising their creations, designing increasingly intricate campaigns, becoming a recognizable brand, and producing at a faster speed to continue to be competitive in the literary market. Just writing the former sentence, I realized how much things have changed: words such as "brand," "competitive," "product," and "market," which were traditionally much more associated with quintessential consumer goods, such as cars or electronics, are now commonly employed to describe features and dynamics of literary production. And while a more democratic access to works that would never been possible before now exists (notice the expansion in genres such as science fiction, fantasy, and romance that were traditionally considered to have less literary merit), the overwhelming output makes it difficult for one to make their work visible in digital spaces.

The numbers alone can be overwhelming. Science fiction, fantasy, and romance, the genres that were more commonly disregarded in traditional publishing, now help shape literary production both online and on paper. An astounding 90% of romance books sold are e-books while fantasy and science fiction do not lag very much behind at 75% (Author Earnings, online).[1] According to *Publishers' Weekly*,[2] in 2014 romance produced by traditional publishers sold more than 30 million books (where the total size of the traditional fiction market was about 131 million books). Chloe Kizer of Written Word Media[3] posits that small and mid-size publishing houses, independent publishing, and the in-house imprints of the largest internet retailer now account for over 50% of all the book sales in the US. Furthermore, professional writing now competes with amateur writing, done primarily to be shared freely, amended, and expanded by other readers. I will discuss the features of such an environment below. This pattern has clear implications for the use of language, language innovation, and the role of different stakeholders on controlling (or not) how and what people write and read. The expansion of interest in areas of applied linguistics seems like a normal extension of the interest already expressed by literary studies, which now has university researchers investigating the social role and literary characteristics of romance, science fiction, and fan fiction (or of their combination). The reader can refer, for example, to Bianchi and D'Arcangelo (2015) for an exploration of issues facing translation of historical romance and Tapper (2015), for an examination of the reasons why "[r]omantic fiction is the most popular and profitable genre in twenty-first century fiction publishing" (p. 249).

Fan fiction

It seems curious that in many social circles people complain that no one reads anymore. The fear that reading is losing its place is probably derived from a perception that videogames, movie streaming, and other forms of entertainment are taking over. The disappearance of traditional bookstores and a more limited reliance on physical books can also contribute to this view. Yet, one could argue, never before have as many people been involved in as many forms of literacy as they are now. Every day there are innumerous emails to write, posts in social media to contribute, blog entries to create. Writing is increasingly made public not only by professionals but by everyday people, and among the most popular forms of amateur writing is fan fiction.

It is easy to discard fan fiction as unfinished, unpolished writing. After all, it is not subjected to the usual channels of approval and control that professional writing is. It is produced by individuals with the most diverse backgrounds; levels of communicative competence; understandings of story, plot, character development, purpose, and audience. It is written both for self and for others. Much as it has happened throughout history, new forms of literary expression are often met with criticism and skepticism, many times by individuals who neglect to enquiry what the purpose of these forms might be.

What these preoccupations also mask is the reality that to learn to write one must, above all, write. Fan fiction offers an opportunity for a virtual writing lab, one that includes feedback from readers and co-creation. There will certainly be all levels of writing proficiency represented—but there is also engagement, rewriting, revision, commitment to multiliteracies and multimodality, and proofreading. In the very least, producing fan fiction is akin to learning to write (with writers in this case both strengthening their first language skills or using this kind of writing as part of the process of learning another language), the potential weaknesses (from a more prescriptive point of view) notwithstanding. These make the genre and the community that forms around it interesting subjects for enquiry and research.

We can arrive at what fan fiction is by what its creators do. According to Lindgren Leavenworth (2015, p. 40),

> Fanfic authors comment on and transform the canon through switched narrative perspectives, altered romantic combinations of characters, expansions of minor characters or scenes, or a play with the temporal boundaries in prequels and sequels.

The author highlights the multimodality of fan fiction environments, the emphasis on science fiction and fantasy (where stretching the boundaries of reality is already inherent to the genres), while also explaining that fan fiction is not a new phenomenon, given that its current incarnation dates back to at least the 1960s, when stories were "published in homemade fanzines" (p. 43). Historically speaking, forms of fan fiction can be well observed in other, earlier historical periods, from fans of Sherlock Holmes forming clubs to add to his adventures, to the many rewrites of Jane Austen novels (Burt, 2017).

Fanfiction bridges the worlds of cartoons, literature, anime, manga, movies, and music. In the process, according to Barnes (2015, p. 68), fanfiction develops as "a form of imaginary play that reflects both emotional engagement with and resistance to the source material." By that, we can abstract that engagement can come in such forms as filling in perceived gaps in the original stories with fanfic, expanding the stories beyond their original endings, or even building parallel universes that reproduce the themes and the dynamics of the original stories. On the other hand, resisting might entail changing an undesirable ending, modifying relationships, swapping the genders of characters, or making a secondary character into a protagonist, among other maneuvers. The second kind of process, the resisting one, may point to a desire to reaffirm one's identity or to mediate social relationships by making characters with less relative power have more or to signal at problematic aspects of original texts.

As for the popularity of the genre, Burt (2017) contends that,

> fanfic requires neither cultural capital nor much actual capital to make. You don't have to take a class, or move to the city, or find an angel, or find an agent; most of your readers may never know your offline name. For all these reasons, fanfic can give its creators a powerful sense of participatory equality.

It is this democratization of writing and of language use that makes fan fiction so interesting. Democratic engagement can also be among the chief reasons for its success. Unencumbered by the constraints of traditional modes of text production, fan fiction writers are free to imagine new worlds and the language that accompanies them. As Rebecca W. Black (2009a, p. 402) observes of the adolescents' fanfiction she writes about, "their online activities afforded them a great deal of creative agency as they took up, reconstituted, and then redistributed cultural, linguistic, symbolic, and ideological material to a broad audience." In the world of fan fiction, one does not have to accept the rules of universes created by others. They can create their own.

To grasp the scope and reach of fan fiction, one should look no further than the statistics of the most popular fan fiction archive on the Internet (fanfiction.net). With more than two million registered users, the site currently (May 2018) features in its 20 most popular fandom categories an aggregate of more than 2,623,000 stories.[4] In a month, the site can receive over 145,000,000 visits (April 2018).[5] Of linguistic interest, users of more than 30 languages are strongly represented on the site.

According to Black (2009b p. 690), "[p]articipation on the site extends beyond posting texts for entertainment, as fans engage in activities such as peer reviewing, collaborative writing, and exploring certain genres of writing." She goes on to further explain that discussing composition and themes addressed by this genre is also quite common. Black has concluded that participation in these communities can lead to improvement of "print literacy" competence (p. 691), "multimodal and technological literacy," and, as a result of the latter, development of "information literacy" (p. 693). These results seem to indicate that many users and contributors to fan fiction archives use the genre and the medium to spearhead their language learning and to develop skills that might otherwise depend on formal instruction, money spending, etc. Moreover, as Lehtonen (2015, p. 8) explains, "[f]an fiction sites are often viewed as safe, emancipatory spaces where participants can share their experiences as fans, experiment with their own writing in a supporting, interactive environment." Thus, participants explore issues of identity and membership that are pertinent to language studies as well. Arguably, one of the most significant pedagogical uses for fan fiction to be investigated by applied linguistics is its application in second-language learning and first and second-language writing practices.

Fan fiction and other modes of online writing thus have a possible, viable pedagogical dimension. Writing about the proliferation of such digital elements as blog posts, wikis, and chats and their relationship and incorporation to L2 learning, González-Lloret (2016, p. 135) suggests that,

> These tools are interesting because their interactive and dynamic nature allows teachers to harvest information, transform it and become part (with their students) of a collective intelligence. They provide countless sources of authentic input, both written and aural (e.g., blogs, podcasts, journals, fanfiction sites, forums where expert speakers interact), and allow for opportunities to produce output with a real audience.

Writing about the role of fan fiction crafting in Task-Based Language Teaching (TBLT), Sauro and Sundmark (2016) report that that their "[f]indings revealed that carefully sequenced collaborative fan fiction could facilitate analysis of a literary text, learners' use of creative writing techniques and language development, particularly at the level of lexis." I would add that in reading to then write, learners engage with the texts, the original and the derivative one, in more complex and meaningful ways than if they were to engage with each separately.

Politeness

Dial (2017, p. 3) argues that the concept of face (Goffman, 1955, p. 222) is very relevant in the context of fan fiction. The former posits that one's reputation and good standing in the community is what helps them attract readers and that the fact that most participants are anonymous (only know through aliases) makes it possible that they construct their public image or face with great care. She continues by explaining that "[m]any times, fanfiction authors use avoidance processes, which ensures that the authors stay away from topics that may threaten their face, or emphasize their own modesty so they are not discredited." Because interactions between writers and readers are so direct in this case and because feedback can be easily incorporated in new iterations of text or in subsequent chapters (and because the offer of other texts is so large), it seems writers are particularly aware of the importance of how to behave.

Fan fiction's individual fandoms provide a great example of how dynamic speech communities work. While for an outsider, all communities may look the same, and their specific jargon possible across communities, insiders identify one another by more subtle and specific linguistic uses within their community. Not only that, it appears that inside knowledge of the jargon of specific communities is a bigger predictor of success and acceptance in that community than writing or linguistic skill. Dial again (2017, p. 17) explains that,

> The only requirement for new members is that they desire to understand and properly use the communicative repertoire. As long as they demonstrate that they are making an effort (such as writing a story and using some form of fan jargon), they will usually receive support and encouragement.

What is even more striking in these communities, especially if one takes into consideration that flame wars and negative feedback are quite prevalent in online environments is that within fandoms there seems to be an unspoken agreement that politeness and saving face are predominant values. It is as if in creating a movement that in many respects stands outside of what standard prescriptive norms of writing, these fan fiction community members created new ones, some of which send us back to a preoccupation with being polite, reminiscent of yesteryear. Dial (2017, p. 22) explains it as follows: "The community seems to have a cultural norm that dictates that feedback should be positive and helpful." She explains that even stories that would by prescriptive standards be considered to have many errors receive such feedback as "I can't wait for the next chapter!" or "This is so good. Update soon!"

A final example also from Dial (2017, pp. 24–25) gives us insight into what happens when the social norms of the group are not observed. When the writer of a piece, which, according to prescriptive norms, had many grammatical mistakes, was met with impolite comments such as "This is the worst thing,I've ever read. [sic]" and "I can hardly understand what you wrote, ever try spell checking? [sic]," and decided to cancel the story after a few chapters, the original harsh reviewers rallied around the upset writer with words of apology and encouragement, such as "you [sic] don't have to erase this just re edit [sic] it. I'm truly sorry about what,I [sic] said the first time." It is interesting to observe that in every one of the instances that Dial offers of authentic language, the very critics were also using the kind of language that prescriptive grammarians would have pegged as errors.

It would be a good project for applied linguists to investigate what might be at the center of this behavior that is so intuitively different from many of the behaviors we find in social media and comment sections of other media as well as find out what parallel cases can be found in other communities in which particular attention to politeness might apply.

Linguistic creativity

I would like to offer a fictitious example of dialogue using terms and structures from fan fiction for illustrative purposes. It could go something like this:

A: Have you seen any stories about time travel lately?
B: There are many. I just read an AU crossover of *Harry Potter* and *Star Trek* that has time travel in it.
A: Any good?
B: Better than in the Sherlock fandom. It seems Harry and Hermione will get together in this one. I'm shipping them so hard.[6]
A: I know. Imagine your OTP. I think that's the same for Harry and Hermione.
B: That's not in the canon, but it should be!
A: Is it long?
B: Twoshot.
A: I should read it.

If you were a little lost, you were likely not alone. A facet of fanfiction that might be of great interest to applied linguists is its linguistic productivity (see Romano, 2016 for more terms). One very productive word is "canon" used in a spectrum that varies from the traditional use in literature (as in "the literary canon"); to a term to designate the original work, upon which fan fiction adaptations are built; to the original fan fiction work, upon which revisions by other fans are created. For example, someone might say, "This character is not in the canon."

Perhaps the most productive case in fanfiction, one that has since become common outside that speech community, as well as in youth language, is *shipping*. Derived from *relationship*, *shipping* refers to the sponsorship or endorsement of two characters' pairing. If one is wishing and hoping that two characters get together, they are "shipping the characters." *OTP* (i.e., one true pair) is a common acronym used to refer to the best pairing possible, a kind of perfect match of soulmates. The *fandom* is the community of fans itself; whereas the *fanon* is the set of details made up by the fans to add to the canon. Romano (2016) explains that sometimes details from the fanon make it back to the canon and influence further original stories. The recursive nature of this and other forms of new literature can be of great research interest because they add an important level of intertextuality and reader participation to the creation of fiction.

Another productive term in fan fiction is *fusion*, or *crossover*, both of which refer to the kind of narrative in which characters from one story are transposed to the setting/environment of another, creating an *AU* (alternate universe, another fan-fiction acronym). An example could be *Harry Potter* characters (Rowling, 1997 and after) transported to the interstellar environment of Star Trek (Paramount Pictures, 2002) as illustrated in the dialogue above.

Finally, there is a case of suffix creation pointed out by Dial (2017, p. 9) which also appears in the dialogue. The ending "-shot" indicates a story with however many chapters as the number that forms the root of the word. This oneshot (or one-shot) is a story told in one chapter, twoshot, in two and so on. It is important to make clear that in the example above, the terms I use are generic and likely to appear in communications across many fandoms. However, each particular community, writing about specific canonic works, will also have further specialized jargon, a knowledge of which will make one an insider to the group.

I hope this chapter makes clear that it is not just in lexical innovation that digital literature offers space for applied linguists to learn (though innovation features as a highlight). As speech communities form around these new kinds of literature, new rules of interaction are also created as seen above. The same way that this can be observed in any dynamic speech community, its members shape these rules and determine the boundaries of their reach, but these boundaries are also often changing. Not much in linguistics has been written yet about these dynamics although they offer ample possibilities for linguistic research.

Tasks for applied linguists

Given the possibilities and the gap in research in areas relating to the exploration of new literatures by applied linguistics, I suggest the following areas of foci and the following questions:

1. Investigate linguistic innovation in those multimodal environments: what linguistic practices are common in what digital environments? Who is included and who is excluded by these practices? What does innovation look like? How does the concept of multimodality apply in these contexts?
2. Investigate forms of interaction, membership, rules of politeness, the role of grammar and prescriptivism, in these environments. How do members of different speech communities signal politeness, opposition/resistance, solidarity? How are prescriptive grammar values represented and opposed? What might be the origins of specific rules in given communities? When do they start to change? What do these rules mean to new and existing members of these communities?
3. Discuss notions of authorship, relationship between language and literature competence. Who counts as an author? What kinds of linguistic and extra-linguistic competence do these new authors bring to language? What are the

institutional, linguistic, and societal forces that help shape self-perceptions of authorship?

4. Discuss the ethics of online research given that authentic language output in accompanying commentaries are easily accessible and searchable. What are our ethical obligations when we conduct studies, not only small-scale discourse and content analysis, but also corpus studies and computational analysis that looks at authentic language in writer communities?

Notes

1 http://authorearnings.com/report/january-2018-report-us-online-book-sales-q2-q4-2017/, retrieved on May 23, 2018.
2 www.publishersweekly.com/pw/by-topic/industry-news/bookselling/article/65387-the-hot-and-cold-categories-of-2014.html, retrieved on May 23, 2018.
3 www.writtenwordmedia.com/2017/01/04/top-ten-trends-in-publishing-every-author-needs-to-know-in-2017/, retrieved May 23, 2018.
4 https://en.wikipedia.org/wiki/FanFiction.Net, retrieved on May 29, 2018.
5 www.similarweb.com/website/fanfiction.net#overview, retrieved on May 29, 2018.
6 Sherlock is of course a reference to Sir Arthur Conan Doyle's famous Sherlock Homes and Harry and Hermione are beloved J. K. Rowling's *Harry Potter* characters.

References and further reading

Bakhtin, M. M. (1981). Discourse in the novel. In Holquist, M. (Ed.), *The dialogic imagination: Four essays by M. M. Bakhtin*. Emerson, C., and Holquist, M. (Trans.). Austin: University of Texas Press.

Barnes, J. L. (2015). Fanfiction as imaginary play: What fan-written stories can tell us about the cognitive science of fiction. *Poetics, 48*, 69–82.

Bianchi, D., and D'Arcangelo, A. (2015). Translating history or romance? Historical romantic fiction and its translation in a globalised market. *Linguistics and Literature Studies 3*(5), 248–253.

Black, R.W. (2009a). Online fan fiction, global identities, and imagination. *Research in the Teaching of English, 43*(4), 397–425.

Black, R.W. (2009b) English-Language learners, fan communities, and 21st-century skills. *Journal of Adolescent & Adult Literacy, 52*(8), 688–697.

Burt, S. (2017). The promise and potential of fan fiction. *The New Yorker*, August 23, 2017, retrieved on May 22, 2018.

Dial, A. (2017). *Speech events in online fan fiction*. (Honors thesis). Arizona State University.

Goffman E. (1955). On face-work: an analysis of ritual elements in social interaction. Psychiatry: *Journal for the Study of Interpersonal Processes* 18, 213–231.

González-Lloret, M. (2016). Technology-mediated L2 teaching. *ELIA*, 16, 133–138.

Lehtonen, S. (2015). Writing oneself into someone else's story: Experiments with identity and speculative life writing in *Twilight* Fan Fiction. *Fafnir – Nordic Journal of Science Fiction and Fantasy Research*, *2*(2), 7–18.

Leppänen, S. (2007). Youth language in media contexts, insight into the functions of English in Finland. *World Englishes, 26*(2), 149–169.

Leppänen, S. (2008). Cybergirls in trouble? Fan fiction as a discursive space for interrogating gender and sexuality. In Caldas-Coulthard, C. R., and Iedema, R. (Eds.). *Identity trouble: Critical discourse and contested dentities*. Basingstoke: Palgrave Macmillan.

Lindgren Leavenworth, M. (2015). The paratext of fan fiction. *Narrative, 23*(1), 40–60.
Milli, Smitha and Bamman, David (2016). *Beyond canonical texts: A computational analysis of fan fiction.* Proceedings of the 2016 Conference on Empirical Methods in Natural Language processing, Austin, TX, the US. *Association of Computational Linguistics*: 2048–2053.
Paramount Pictures. (2002). *Star Trek, the next generation.* Season 7. US: Paramount Pictures.
Romano, A. (2016). Canon, fanon, shipping and more: A glossary of the tricky terminology that makes up fan culture. *Vox*, June 7, 2016. Retrieved on May 29, 2018 from www.vox.com/2016/6/7/11858680/fandom-glossary-fanfiction-explained.
Rowling, J. K. (1997). *Harry Potter and the Sorcerer's Stone.* London: Bloomsbury.
Sauro, S. and Sundmark, B. (2016) Report from Middle-Earth: Fan fiction tasks in the EFL classroom. *ELT Journal, 70*(4), 414–423. Retrieved on May 22, 2018 from https://doi.org/10.1093/elt/ccv075.
Tapper, O. (2015). Romance and innovation in twenty-first century publishing. *Publishing Research Quarterly, 30*(2), 249–259.

11

TEACHING LINGUISTICS TO SPEECH-LANGUAGE SCIENTISTS AND THERAPISTS

With Kendra Beeley[1]

> **THIS CHAPTER WILL DO THE FOLLOWING**
>
> 1. Discuss the connection between linguistics and speech sciences and the rationale for programmatic decisions involving linguistics.
> 2. Make a case for a more significant presence of linguistics in the education of speech science professionals.
> 3. Present a possible annotated curriculum and activities for a linguistics course for speech therapy/pathology/science majors.
> 4. Discuss the features of such an offering.
> 5. Provide ideas for further curricular developments.
> 6. Provide ideas for students, scholars, and instructors who would like to work at the intersection of these disciplines.

Speech science, pathology, and therapy

This chapter will be a bit different from the ones that preceded it although it also builds a bridge between knowledge of applied linguistic and other fields of (applied) knowledge. While much of this book is about research in linguistics and its application in the real world, this one is more about curriculum development in an area where linguistics can have significant impact when informed by applied research (not that developing educational materials in not a real-word application). More specifically, it provides an example of curricular items and a plan for a course for students preparing to become speech therapists, speech scientists, and those who work within a discipline that became known as speech pathology. While we find the latter term problematic in many respects because it is an unnecessarily negative (and somewhat ableist) way to frame the different ways speech development and production may occur, it is a term with currency in the profession and therefore it will appear occasionally in this chapter alongside the other two. Most of the time, the three (speech science, pathology, and therapy) are used interchangeably here (though we acknowledge that, in other contexts, they may be used differently). As linguists, however, we have the same reservation to "pathology" that we have to terms such as "abnormal psychology." These constructions, depending on how they are framed, tend to result in very distinctive approaches to difference and diversity themselves (i.e., they often involve a deficit perspective), and applied linguists tend to be more descriptive than judgmental/prescriptive about phenomena related to language and their concrete manifestations when people use language.

As a result, the course we propose here should offer an opportunity for future speech therapists to question the place of prescriptive ideas about language in the context of applied linguistic knowledge. It is easy to see the "norm" playing a big role in speech treatment traditionally speaking. That is, a notion of what the "correct" production of language entails is likely the strongest linguistic influence considered by speech pathologists. Yet, without a more relative notion of what success means and what interventions are really necessary or even adequate, the picture is incomplete. Treatment that affects one's interaction with the world necessitates a consideration of what the social reality in one's slice of that world is. It is hoped that the inclusion of more overt linguistic knowledge in curricular offerings can help speech therapists in training achieve the necessary balance to better serve their clients.

Who speech therapists/pathologists are

Speech-language pathologists are professionals licensed and able to diagnose and treat patients from birth to later years through a wide variety of methods and techniques in an effort to help affect and ameliorate their clients' life conditions if these clients are living with speech/neurological disorders/conditions or have received diagnoses that include among others the following: traumatic brain injury, autism, aphasia, stuttering, developmental language disorders, and phonological disorders (this is not an exhaustive list).

While linguists and applied linguists, of course, do not clinically treat individuals living with these disorders and conditions, the linguistic knowledge they possess may serve as important background information and may be a crucial part of the education of speech pathologists/therapists. In fact, certain areas of linguistics are already covered by their graduate programs, but they tend to be punctual theoretical subdisciplines such as phonetics and the anatomy of speech, and not involve the more socially engaged counterparts. We, therefore, in this chapter, explore the many ways in which linguistic (and applied linguistics) knowledge can help inform these professionals by describing a potential graduate course on linguistics for speech pathology graduate students. Please also refer to the chapter on disability studies for ways in which linguists can help humanize phenomena that for a long time were perceived and systematized almost exclusively from a medical/diagnostic, clinical perspective, including the search for better terms and accompanying frames of mind and of study as we mentioned above.

Even more importantly, this chapter has as one of its secondary goals to have the reader consider what their own linguistic expertise could contribute to areas of speech science in particular and to the increasingly large body of disciplines with which linguistics intersects and whose problems are interdisciplinary in nature. By presenting curricular items pertinent to this interdisciplinary endeavor and discussing existing research that can infuse courses with materials for reflection, we hope to also provide tenets of what a graduate course in linguistics could offer when geared toward non-linguists. We will present activities that can accompany the teaching materials and will conclude with ideas for further research, practice, and pedagogy. We invite the reader to extrapolate the suggestions offered and think about what curricula in forensic linguistics, peace linguistics, computational linguistics and all other real-word disciplines presented in this book could potentially look like given what we discuss in this chapter.

Where speech therapists work

The work environment of speech therapists is varied. Professionals can be found, for example, in schools, where their job focuses on academic success, from preschool to high school, in all public, private, and charter educational institutions. They may also work for educational institutions focusing on the education of a particular population, such as students presenting with hearing or visual impairment. Speech therapists also work in medical environments such as clinics and hospitals, where they can provide their expertise in inpatient and outpatient settings to adult or pediatric populations. Finally, speech pathologists can practice independently and offer home visits and support to a variety of clients with many different needs.

Requirements for certification and licensing in the US are quite demanding and include a Master of Science degree in Communication Sciences and Disorders or Speech-Language Pathology, 400 clinical hours of practice, a 3-month full-time externship, successful completion of the national PRAXIS exam, a nine-month fellowship, the obtaining and maintenance of a national certification as well as state license. The curriculum for the required degrees have several necessary requirements.

Suggestions offered in this chapter could be delivered through elective linguistics courses or embedded in the curriculum as required study areas allow. Specifically, target students could be in their second year of their clinical Master's in Communication Sciences and Disorders or Speech-Language Pathology when some understanding of language dynamics might already have been afforded by other disciplinary offerings. It is important to note that knowledge of linguistics is highly variable for these students given that they come from completing Bachelor's degrees in a variety of areas. In general, linguistic content in other program courses focuses on phonological disorders, child language disorders, neurological disorders, and stuttering.

Aims and goals of the course

This idea of the course annotated here is to offer an introduction to linguistics and applied linguistics for the use of graduate students in speech-language pathology and communication sciences and disorders. While we are calling this an introduction, there is no reason not to invest is a more in-depth exploration of these topics, given that the audience is that of graduate students and that in the future they will be working with language. Topics addressed in the course include, but are not limited to, phonology, syntax, language and culture, sociolinguistics, and clinical linguistics and their intersection and application to speech sciences. Building on this theoretical base, students will then work with sets of studies that address various purposes (e.g., to develop theory; to improve therapeutic practice; to understand how language behaves) and analyze case studies using linguistics tools and frameworks.

Among course outcomes are understanding and using key linguistic terminology to describe language, describing and utilizing research papers in speech pathology with the language of linguistics emphasis, analyzing and applying recent language and linguistics research in the field of speech-language pathology, and making connections between speech science and applied linguistics. The rationale for pursuing these outcomes is that in general clinical masters do not include as much reading or writing research as more scholarly counterparts do but that, if these are added to a course of study, students will learn how to research clinical methods in a linguistic context to add to their repertoire and thus enhance their practice. This in turn allows students to learn how to distinguish between sound and questionable research. Additionally, they might learn to self-monitor their practice and discern when and how to apply research to their practice.

Instructional strategy

To meet the goals stated above, this course will involve a variety of instructional strategies. Information can be presented primarily through assigned readings but also presentations, workshops, lectures, and discussions. The readings are to be discussed in class to highlight and clarify important concepts. Students will respond to discussion questions and analyze cases and problems so they can apply the course concepts. These activities will occur in individual, small group and whole class work, informal discussions and formal presentations.

Components of the course

An emphasis on discussions to support the new skill of reading and processing academic research is also an asset here. New linguistic concepts grounded immediately into the speech therapy context to demonstrate relevance of linguistics to their clinical practice is part of the teaching strategy too. Additional important components of the formulation of the course include the following:

1. Explaining basic concepts in linguistics and the relationship between different subareas of linguistics: since this was done in the introduction of this book, we will not explain it here again, but depending on need this overview can be as simple as describing disciplines such as phonetics, phonology, morphology, sociolinguistics, pragmatics, etc., or can be expanded to include broader discussions of the place of each discipline in relation to applied linguistics or to what I am calling "applied linguistics in the real world" in this book.
2. Teaching the fundamentals of these disciplines in modules: of course, this will be a very simplified instruction, but programs will likely cover some of the most important theoretical areas as part of their speech science and speech pathology content. So here it is the connections and the application that matter.
3. Using research texts and a course book to further the students' understandings of these connections and application to speech therapy. The more the texts present problem-solving through a partnership with and understanding of linguistics, the better.
4. Providing many opportunities for questioning guided by a goal of allowing students to engage in critical thinking. Examples of questions include, "Are the concepts of receptive and productive skills still relevant for speech therapy if so why?" or "How can the concepts of competence and performance be framed in your discipline so you can better address the challenges of your practice?"
5. Reinforcing knowledge through continual opportunities for systematization, narration, journaling, and assessment. Assignments can be short and direct but should be distributed through the course at regular intervals.

Annotated research content

The reading list

In the following, we provide examples of research papers that could be used for discussion of linguistic topics in this course and present ideas for utilizing them in class and in assignments as well as the kind of linguistic material that could be highlighted through them.

The idea is to add a component of critical research reading, one that the students could model and then pursue throughout their careers. As sciences develop and further expand, keeping practices current and inclusive could depend on further reading and implementation of techniques. These materials are of course examples, and many other texts could fulfill the purposes of this course element. The discussing can be enriched by the addition of texts that are interdisciplinary and bring in feminist, disability studies, and sociolinguistic perspectives among others.

Study text # 1

Duque, C. and Lashewicz, B. (2018). Reframing Less Conventional Speech to Disrupt Conventions of "Compulsory Fluency": A conversation analysis approach. *Disability Studies Quarterly, 38*(2).

This might be a unique way to inaugurate the discussion on literature relevant to speech sciences, but we believe it is a very important one. Since this book is a work on connections across disciplines, to start with an article that brings together not only applied linguistics and speech therapy but also disability studies seems like a great place to start. Duque and Lashewicz (2018) discuss the precariousness of models of communication that depend upon what they call "compulsory fluency," which they define as "conventions for what constitutes competent speech." More importantly still, the article problematizes traditional views of what fluency and communication are and how they are socially constructed. In that sense, fluency of the compulsory kind "is standardized and idealized and imposed on all speakers including those whose speech is less conventional." The authors go further and explain the following:

> We are troubled by the ways a remediation model of practice contributes to viewing and treating people who have less conventional speech—namely, people with developmental disabilities and acquired impairments—as inadequate.

This article, as well as the view it espouses, can help speech therapists and linguists become further aware and discuss whether it is possible to practice a speech therapy that is not based on a deficit model and that instead takes into consideration individual differences in everything from communication styles, to desired outcomes, to disability status in respectful ways. By calling attention to the ways speakers, all of us, both comply with and resist conventional discourses about what fluency and successful communication mean, the authors open the door to an applied linguistics (and consequently a speech science) that once again takes its cues from the real world and the real-world needs of users of language in all their diversity.

It is to be hoped that by starting the seminar-like discussions with this text, we can establish a mindfulness that can then permeate the reading of all other texts, no matter how different and purely "technical" they turn out to be.

Study text # 2

Law, J., Garrett, Z., and Nye, C. (2004). The efficacy of treatment for children with developmental speech and language delay/disorder: A meta-analysis. *Journal of Speech, Language, and Hearing Research (H.W. Wilson – EDUC)*, *47*(4), 924.

In this research article, the authors conducted a meta-analysis of "interventions for children" presenting with "developmental speech and language delays/disorders." The researchers wanted to find out the efficacy of interventions on phonological/vocabulary production difficulties, as well as challenges facing syntax and receptive language. Analyses of a series of articles indicated that speech therapy had a greater chance of success on phonological/vocabulary items, for example, than on syntax. At the same time, not much information was available which could point to evidence of effectiveness of speech intervention on the so-called receptive skills. What is more, whether the interventions were performed by parents who had been trained by professionals or by professionals themselves, the results were not significantly different. An item that was significant was the duration of treatment, being that longer treatments had better outcomes than shorter ones, which seems somewhat predictable given what we know of language acquisition and development of skills in general.

Several important discussions can be conducted with the speech therapists in training through this article. First of all, the nature of vocabulary acquisition, of phonological knowledge, of syntax, as well as productive and receptive skills (and whether they should be referenced by such names) can be a part of the conversation. Then the methods used in the studies gathered can be discussed. Finally, speculation of the reasons why trained parents obtained similar results from those of speech pathologists can follow.

Study text # 3

Spencer, E. J., Schuele, C. M., Guillot, K. M., and Lee, M. W. (2008). Phonemic awareness skill of speech-language pathologists and other educators. *Language, Speech, and Hearing Services in Schools*, *39*(4), 512–520.

Spencer et al. (2008) contribute to an understanding of the role of phonemic awareness for literacy development especially starting at kindergarten. This greater inclusion of the link between recognition of sounds in relation to spelling then calls for specialized knowledge by those who teach these young learners, especially in the case of children who need more help with literacy skills. The authors point out that when research is conducted, it becomes clear that there are gaps in the phonological and linguistic knowledge base of educators who will be performing these important teaching roles. To measure the extent of knowledge/gaps in knowledge, the researchers looked at a group of speech-language pathologists, kindergarten teachers, first-grade teachers, and reading teachers to compare and contrast their phonemic-awareness skills.

Results indicate that the knowledge/awareness of reading and special education teachers was comparable to that of first-grade and kindergarten educators. Speech pathologists were significantly more proficient than others when it came to word segmentation, yet even their accuracy was relatively low, in some tasks being at 54%. Actual performance was also not as good as expected (which for our purposes would be a great reason for more inclusion of applied linguistics content to their education). Given the results, the authors suggest that increasing the phonological awareness applied to performance of all these educators is crucial. Instructional materials should follow so as to offer these educators the necessary support. Finally, greater alliance between speech therapists and teachers is suggested.

We, as linguists can use readings such as this as a springboard to discussions about the place of linguistic knowledge, not only phonological knowledge in the education of teachers and speech therapists. Not only is it possible that the curriculum of speech-science graduate programs is not inclusive enough of linguistic information, the same may be happening to the curriculum for teacher certification programs, as it clearly already happens to, for example, most English degrees in the US, which unless they contain a linguistics track (i.e., all of those more generalist degrees) focus very little on linguistic awareness.

Articles such as this would allow for interesting discussions about the linguistic skills necessary for the successful performance of speech-language therapy.

Study text # 4

Nelson, R., and Ball, M. J. (2003). Models of phonology in the education of speech-language pathologists. *Clinical Linguistics & Phonetics*, *17*(4–5), 403–409.

In this article, the authors discuss knowledge of phonology (theoretical and by different schools of thought) by those who teach future speech therapists. They introduce a short questionnaire that asks instructors to indicate both the number of courses they have taken on the subject as well as the theoretical approaches they are familiar with. It should be noted that sometimes these approaches on the surface may sound similar while they are leading, in practice, to very different forms of intervention, and one of the goals here was to try and establish whether instructors were aware of these differences. Results indicate that that only a few of the approaches presented ("phonemic, distinctive features, and processes") are the ones that make it to the classroom in many cases. While in many instances the number of actual phonology courses present in the education of these instructors was low, it is unclear whether they might have acquired their knowledge through literature and/or conferences. I must add that the researchers seem to not have included less direct but equally important sources of phonetics and phonology knowledge besides courses in applied linguistics, namely, courses in historical linguistics, and, in the case of English, old, middle, and modern English.

Nevertheless, this short article offers a good opportunity for instructors and students to discuss linguistic knowledge and establish, perhaps through their own custom-made diagnostic questionnaire areas of linguistics that they might want to explore in courses for speech-therapy students. These questionnaires can approach applied linguistics, sociolinguistics, and other areas in the same way done here for phonology.

Study text # 5

Bryant, L., Spencer, E., and Ferguson, A. (2017) Clinical use of linguistic discourse analysis for the assessment of language in aphasia, *Aphasiology, 31*(10), 1105–1126.

The use of discourse analysis in clinical environments offers the addition of an important tool for understanding what might be going on with a client's language production.

However, Bryant et al. (2017, p. 1108–1109) have argued that there is a disconnect between that notion and what actually goes on in practice: their look at the literature indicates that systematic use of discourse analysis in clinical setting is somewhat rare. On the other hand, they explain, "most speech pathologists implemented interventions that targeted discourse skills," with the Aphasia Pathways Best Practice Statements by the Clinical Centre for Research Excellence (CCRE) in Aphasia Rehabilitation formally recommending that interventions on patients living with aphasia include discourse interventions.

Setting out to discover just how much discourse analysis practitioners were actually using this form of linguistic analysis and what their attitudes were toward this form of this linguistic analysis, the authors created and administered a questionnaire that focuses, among other things, on frequency and methods, preparation and use of discourse samples, and analysis on the discourse itself. Amongst the participants, 60% indicated that they used discourse analysis at least some of the time. Those who did not overwhelmingly cited lack of time as a primary reason not to use it. Recording and transcribing were not used by the majority of the participants. It also became clear that understanding of what discourse analysis entails varied a lot among participants.

Reading this article would allow speech-therapy graduate students to become further acquainted (or first aware of if they weren't already) with discourse analysis and its possible use in clinical settings. It would also allow the instructor to focus on linguistic knowledge on aphasia which can complement clinical knowledge. Supplemental articles could focus on specific schools of those within discourse analysis and the importance of applied linguistics and sociolinguistics knowledge when it comes to situating clinical phenomena, such as aphasia, into a social context.

Note: an important element of the selection of texts is making sure they have a critical dimension to them. That is, the intersection of linguistics and speech sciences is at its best when it not only presents technical knowledge of language and language development but when questions regarding the social, political, economic, attitudinal, and affective dimensions of language arise.

Annotated examples of activities and assessment

In the following, we provide examples of quiz, midterm-exam questions, group-presentation prompts, and journal entries that would be aligned with what a course such as this one would teach. We comment on aspects of the rationale for inclusion at the end of the section. Note that these would constitute the major foci of assessment as well.

Linguistic terms quiz

Draw a line between each word and its correct definition. Expand the definition after that, using your own understanding of the disciplines.

Pragmatics	The branch of linguistics that studies words and their form and relationship to other words.
Morphology	The study of the use of language in context, taking into account turn taking, politeness, etc.
Phonology	The study of sounds and of the sound systems of languages.
Semantics	The study of internal rules that support the way words are combined to form sentences.
Syntax	The study of the meaning of words and how humans decode such meaning.

Finish the sentence with a short definition.

Language is the

____.

Linguistics is the

____.

The connection between linguistics and speech science is that

____.

Discourse is

____.

Discourse analysis is

____.

Compare and contrast the following terms:

Phonetics and phonology:

____.

Morphemes and words:

____.

Semantics and pragmatics:

____.

Applied linguistics and sociolinguistics:

____.

Discourse analysis and content analysis:

____.

Note: This quiz aims to provide an opportunity for students to showcase their knowledge of key linguistic terminology. The focus on definitions and contrast between terms that could be confused or conflated is later supplemented by work done on journal entries, which is more interpretative and narrative and thus presents greater opportunity for critical thinking and application of concepts.

Midterm

1. What is Evidence-based Practice and how does it relate to linguistic oriented research in speech-language pathology?
2. Describe how you would explain these linguistic terms in each scenario.
   a. Explain pragmatics to a parent of an autistic child.
   b. Explain pragmatics to a new 7th grade science teacher.
   c. Explain syntax to the spouse of a new patient with aphasia.
   d. Explain syntax to a new patient with aphasia.
3. Why is phonemic awareness important for educators and speech-language pathologists to have? What types of therapy does the therapist need to have well developed phonemic awareness?
4. Name five morphemes learned/acquired by typically developing children by age three.
5. Explain the difference between a phoneme and an allophone and the implication of such knowledge for speech therapy.
6. Explain the relationship between the concept of semantic features and language acquisition.
7. Choose three of the following terms to define: Agent, Action, Object, Location, Entity, Possessor, Possession, Attributive and Demonstrative.
8. Write child utterances for the following structures: Agent + Object, Possessor + Posession, Action + Location.
9. Write a syntax tree for the following sentence: The dog is sleeping.
10. Explain what the possible application for the information in questions 8 and 9 could be.

Note: A number of the questions require some theoretical knowledge of linguistics; the idea here is building a bridge between that knowledge and applied linguistics or better concepts of linguistics applied to the practice of speech therapy. The questions proposed for the mid-term aim to provide an opportunity for students to apply their knowledge to several areas of speech sciences and to cause students to think about the context-specific adaptations that they would have to make to communicate this technical information to stakeholders and to help different clients with different challenges and linguistic goals.

Group presentations

Prepare a conference-style presentation in which you focus on one aspect of the intersection between applied linguistics and speech therapy. Below you will find examples of topics and the coverage they could receive in these presentations. Group work will be assessed on the basis of its success in presenting a relevant topic in an interdisciplinary manner and on making useful connections between theory and practice.

Examples:

1. Compare and contrast the application of linguistic theory across different graduate programs in speech pathology that you have researched. What differences do you find? What aspects tend to stay the same?
2. Present a panoramic view of linguistics and applied linguistics and discuss where you believe speech sciences fit in that model.
3. Create a short treatment plan for a linguistic challenge you have identified. Explain the profile of an imaginary client who could benefit from that plan. Explain how the linguistic knowledge you have acquired would inform that plan and make sure to include social elements that would inform your plan.
4. Present an account of current controversies in speech therapy (e.g., an area in which specialists disagree on the best course of action).

Note: this kind of group presentation would work best if assigned for the end of the term, this way the students could present a plan or an idea based on the holistic knowledge of linguistics they have acquired throughout the course.

Journal entry

Write a journal entry in which you reflect on the significance of a concept or theory for your practice of speech therapy (about three double-spaced pages long). This reflection should be supported by evidence presented in the research materials you have read and should also have significance for phenomena in the real world.

Some directions for your journal entry could be:

1. Describe a concept, explain why it is important for speech therapy, indicate how you would make use of it in the real world.
2. Present a research finding, discuss why it is problematic, indicate other strategies for research in that area.
3. Present a fallacy about language, explain why you consider it a fallacy, and rework it accordingly.
4. Identify language in a technical paper in speech science that could be considered to be prescriptive, or ableist, or problematic in other ways and explain what language, concepts, and ideas you might use instead.

Note: journal entries are opportunities for students to systematize knowledge they have acquired. While students can use outside references to support their arguments and ideas, the focus on the entry is on the student's own reasoning and insight, on their thought processes, and on what information they kept thinking back to after class.

Final considerations

In this chapter, we attempted to provide a few ideas of items and the rationale for their use in a graduate course on linguistics geared toward future speech therapists/pathologists. We have clearly only scratched the surface, but the idea is to get us thinking more and more about areas of knowledge that are connected to linguistic knowledge but that not always involve as much applied-linguistic background as they could do. Below, the reader will find ideas of research questions that would help facilitate this interaction further.

Questions and ideas for further research

1. What are some of the attitudes toward language commonly held by speech therapists and how do they influence practice?
2. In a needs analysis, what are some of the areas of linguistics knowledge that speech therapists do not commonly study but which would benefit their practice? What are some of the repercussions of having phonological knowledge be the primary form of linguistic knowledge in most programs?
3. What would alternative curricular offerings in a speech-therapy look like?
4. What is the role of applied linguistics in speech-therapy programs?
5. Conversely, what can the knowledge in speech sciences contribute to applied linguistics?

Note

1 A number of materials and ideas presented here, as well as foundations of the text come from an applied project undertaken by Kendra Beeley as part of the requirements for a Master of Arts degree in Linguistics. Beeley is also a coauthor of the chapter.

Works cited and recommended reading

Bellon-Harn, M. L., and Garrett, M. T. (2008). VISION: A model of cultural responsiveness for speech-language pathologists working in family partnerships. *Communication Disorders Quarterly, 29*(3), 141–148.

Blood, G. W., Mamett, C., Gordon, R., and Blood, I. M. (2010). Written language disorders:Speech-language pathologists' training, knowledge, and confidence. *Language, Speech, and Hearing Services in Schools, 41*(4), 416–428.

Bryant, L., Spencer, E., and Ferguson, A. (2017) Clinical use of linguistic discourse analysis for the assessment of language in aphasia. *Aphasiology, 31*(10), 1105–1126.

Caesar, L. G. (2013). Providing early intervention services to diverse populations: Are speech-language pathologists prepared? (original study) (report) (author abstract). *Infants & Young Children, 26*(2), 126.

Carragher, M., Sage, K., and Conroy, P. (2015). Outcomes of treatment targeting syntax production in people with broca's-type aphasia: Evidence from psycholinguistic assessment tasks and everyday conversation. *International Journal of Language & Communication Disorders, 50*(3), 322–336.

Duque, C., and Lashewicz, B. (2018). Reframing less conventional speech to disrupt conventions of "compulsory fluency": A conversation analysis approach. *Disability Studies Quarterly, 38*(2). Retrieved on July 23, 2018 from http://dsq-sds.org/article/view/5821/4901.

Ebbels, S. H., van der Lely, Heather K. J, and Dockrell, J. E. (2007). Intervention for verb argument structure in children with persistent SLI: A randomized control trial. *Journal of Speech, Language, and Hearing Research, 50*(5), 1330–1349.

Fava, E. (2002). *Clinical linguistics: Theory and applications in speech pathology and therapy.* Philadelphia: John Benjamins.

Girolametto, L., Weitzman, E., and Greenberg, J. (2012). Facilitating emergent literacy: Efficacy of a model that partners speech-language pathologists and educators. *American Journal of Speech-Language Pathology/American Speech-Language-Hearing Association, 21*(1), 47–63. doi:10.1044/1058–0360(2011/11–0002).

Grodzinsky, Y. (2000). The neurology of syntax: Language use without broca's area. *Behavioral and Brain Sciences, 23*(1), 1–21.

Herbert, R., Gregory, E., and Best, W. (2014). Syntactic versus lexical therapy for anomia in acquired aphasia: Differential effects on narrative and conversation. *International Journal of Language & Communication Disorders, 49*(2), 162–173.

Kimble, C. (2013). Speech-language pathologists' comfort levels in English language learner service delivery. *Communication Disorders Quarterly, 35*(1), 21–27.

Law, J., Garrett, Z., and Nye, C. (2004). The efficacy of treatment for children with developmental speech and language delay/disorder: A meta-analysis. *Journal of Speech, Language, and Hearing Research (H.W. Wilson – EDUC), 47*(4), 924.

Marinellie, S. A. (2004). Complex syntax used by school-age children with specific language impairment (SLI) in child–adult conversation. *Journal of Communication Disorders, 37*(6), 517–533.

McAllister, J., and Miller, J. E., (2013). *Introductory linguistics for speech and languagetherapy practice.* Malden, Mass; Chichester, West Sussex: Wiley-Blackwell.

McLeod, S., Verdon, S., Bowen, C., and International Expert Panel on Multilingual Children's Speech. (2013). International aspirations for speech-language pathologists' practice with multilingual children with speech sound disorders: Development of a position paper. *Journal of Communication Disorders, 46*(4), 375. doi:10.1016/j.jcomdis.2013.04.003

Mortimer, J., and Rvachew, S. (2010). A longitudinal investigation of morpho-syntax in children with speech sound disorders. *Journal of Communication Disorders, 43*(1), 61–76. doi:10.1016/j.jcomdis.2009.10.001.

Nelson, R., and Ball, M. J. (2003). Models of phonology in the education of speech-language pathologists. *Clinical Linguistics & Phonetics, 17*(4–5), 403–409.

Rvachew, S., Nowak, M., and Cloutier, G. (2004). Effect of phonemic perception training on the speech production and phonological awareness skills of children with expressive phonological delay. *American Journal of Speech-Language Pathology, 13*(3), 250–263.

Spencer, E. J., Schuele, C. M., Guillot, K. M., and Lee, M. W. (2008). Phonemic awareness skill of speech-language pathologists and other educators. *Language, Speech, and Hearing Services in Schools, 39*(4), 512–520.

Snow, P. C., Sanger, D. D., Childers, C., Pankonin, C., and Wright, S. (2013). Response to intervention in secondary settings: Speech-language pathologists' perspectives. *International Journal of Speech-Language Pathology, 15*, 463–70.

Van Kleeck, A. (2014). Distinguishing between casual talk and academic talk beginning in the preschool years: An important consideration for speech-language pathologists. *American Journal of Speech-Language Pathology/American Speech-Language-Hearing Association, 23*(4), 724.

Webster, D., Dyson, L., and Herbert, R. (2012). Effects of syntactic cueing therapy on picture naming and connected speech in acquired aphasia. *Neuropsychological Rehabilitation, 22*(4), 609–625.

Williams, C. J., and McLeod, S. (2012). Speech-language pathologists' assessment and intervention practices with multilingual children. *International Journal of Speech-Language Pathology, 14*(3), 292–305.

Zwitserlood, R., Wijnen, F., Weerdenburg, M., and Verhoeven, L. (2015). 'MetaTaal': Enhancing complex syntax in children with specific language impairment—A metalinguistic and multimodal approach. *International Journal of Language & Communication Disorders, 50*(3), 273–297.

12

APPLIED LINGUISTICS, WORLD ENGLISHES, AND THE "MULTI" IN THE STUDY OF WRITING

THIS CHAPTER WILL DO THE FOLLOWING

1. Discuss the connection between applied linguistics, world Englishes, rhetorical knowledge, and the idea of "multi" in its various incarnations.
2. Discuss the intersection of world Englishes as an embodiment of the "multi" and its role in the teaching of writing.
3. Discuss the features of a world Englishes pedagogy when applied to writing.
4. Provide ideas for further curricular developments.
5. Provide ideas for students, scholars, and instructors who would like to work at the intersection of these disciplines.

Introduction

The first world Englishes (WE) project I ever conducted was a survey with language learners. The year was 1997, and I wanted to know more about Brazilian students' attitudes toward the varieties of English they were being exposed to in the classroom and whether there was indeed a multiplicity of varieties that were being addressed in that context. At the time, I hoped results could help the institution in question make pedagogical decisions about materials, curriculum, etc. Some of the results, I hoped, would be applied to the teaching of writing, which had in many ways become secondary to the teaching of speaking. The investigation resulted in an article (Friedrich, 2000), published in *World Englishes*. It is to this day one of the most cited pieces of my works (I also periodically receive requests for the research instrument I designed and used). This continued interest in issues of language attitude shows how much linguists believe attitudes impact everything regarding language—from selection of instructional varieties to students' motivation to learn. It also demonstrated that while in theory we would like to think that students were learning through a multi-variety perspective, in practice American and British English were the two large-scale varieties that were making a significant appearance in the classroom.

Quite sometime later, I edited the volume *Teaching Academic Writing*, for which I contributed a chapter (Friedrich, 2008) on action research in the classroom and student journals. Students who read texts by second-language writers wrote down their thoughts on language, cultural orientation, and linguistic membership as part of the project, sharing the insights they gained from exposure to Englishes and cultures other than their own. This was done in the context of a cross-cultural writing (English) course at a large university in the Southwest of the US. The larger goal of putting together the edited volume was to provide a guide to those teachers of composition who might not have extensive preparation opportunities before being assigned university courses about academic writing. Issues of the "multi" in its various incarnations were a recurrent theme in the book and in my chapter, they were paired with the idea of membership depending on languages and varieties one knew.

Since then, I have written several books, articles, and chapters often using different methodologies and arguments, but I often go back, in my classroom practice as well as in my research designs, to relying on surveys, interviews, and journals to both teach and get research information. One of my concerns is to always gather information on diverse perspectives and figure out if individuals from a variety of backgrounds and profiles are having their needs addressed. The view of people in the real world about the place of different language forms has thus become an integral part of my theorizing, and it should not be any different if I want to practice an applied linguistics that results from observation and contact with the world.

In this chapter, I would like to share some of the insights on the "multi" that I gained from conducting such research projects (and others) and discuss how the combination of surveys/interviews and an understanding of the kinds of literacies and linguistic expression being demanded of students by an increasingly complex communication system intersect with WE classroom research as well as with applied linguistics topics. This chapter also benefits from the work that several scholars have conducted at the intersection of language and multi-perspectives, multi-skills and multiliteracies. I will argue for the complementarity of the WE paradigm and, in this illustrative case, research on several aspects of the "multi," such as multilingualism and multiliteracies, with a special focus on composition, and, at the end, offer thoughts on research-design processes for conducting research that involves perceptions and attitudes toward variety and diversity. I believe this is an appropriate way to finish a book that in so many ways argues for the multiplicity of manners in which applied linguistics can be further engaged in the real world. This chapter is recursive in that it further brings together disciplines that were written about in other chapters, this time not only in collaboration with applied linguistics but also with each other.

The particular texts I will be using to illustrate the possibilities of WE research in the composition classroom rely both on theoretical discussions and empirical research. They are varied in terms of their disciplinary allegiances and textual design. Their pairing is not necessarily intuitive at first sight, but by the end of this chapter, the relevance of their incorporation—it is to be hoped—should be clear. By the same token, rather than a prescription, I attempt to offer readers a few (less linear) reflections on aspects of those pieces of research that I learned along the way while conducting WE and applied linguistics scholarship. In the sections that follow, I will try to interlace elements of the concepts of plurality, diversity, and hybridity arguing that they are not self-exclusive.

Applied linguistics and the composition classroom

Applied linguists tend to make wonderful writing and composition instructors, composition being a discipline that benefits greatly from a diverse faculty body with a variety of subject orientations. I hope I have successfully demonstrated in the chapter about the new literature that linguistics knowledge and awareness is paramount when it comes to identifying and furthering the goals of writing activities that are embedded in the societies they are written in and for. While the misconception exists that linguists would necessarily focus on grammar and structure when teaching composition to the detriment of more socially engaged rhetorical practices, instructors with a good understanding of linguistics demonstrate every day that the reality is quite different: not only do linguists engage with rhetorical grammar (as opposed to decontextualized grammar—see Kolln and Gray, 2012) they also engage with different varieties of English, issues of power and representation, deep structure of texts, rhetorical and cross-cultural patterns, among so many other aspects of writing.

By the same token, WE scholarship—which has contributed greatly to an understanding of the written word, from its engagement with postcolonial literatures to its advocacy for multiple varieties in the classroom—is at an interesting historical moment. This is a perfect time to reflect on methodology and on its interaction with other linguistic and education phenomena. On the one hand, calls exist for researchers to thoroughly understand and appreciate the particulars of the paradigm and its history (and remain in that paradigm) to better engage with world Englishes (Berns, 2017). On the other, it is clear that WE has become an influential field beyond its own paradigm, often referred to and used to provide a framework in studies and a pedagogy that goes even beyond Englishes themselves. In that respect, WE is like an adolescent discovering its own identity so that it can grow into a mature adult. The process is not always simple or easy, but reflection at this crossroads is necessary if the discipline is to thrive and provide applicable knowledge for years to come. In either case, attention to the details of the paradigm, as well as an understanding of methodological tools, is crucial.

Kubota (2014, p. 3) writes of a "multi/plural turn in applied linguistics," one that has very strong implications for WE and related disciplines. She goes on to aptly describe two orientations within that "multi" view: one pluralist and one hybrid, which are crucial to the discussion carried out here. About the former, she explains the following:

> The pluralist orientation focuses on using and learning multiple languages or varieties of a language in social and educational contexts. Frameworks such as WE, traditional foreign language pedagogies, and immersion or maintenance bilingual education are pluralist in the sense that they challenge previous linguistic norms—Anglocentric native speakerness or monolingualism—and embrace linguistic pluralism and multilingual competence.

On the other hand, she explains, the hybrid orientation,

> regards multilingual linguistic practices as products of language users' multiple repertoires that are employed in a contingent and flexible manner rather than an aggregate use of languages that are separated along structural boundaries.

She continues by suggesting that world Englishes frameworks, as well as concepts such as code-switching, belong to the pluralist orientation and that English as a Lingua Franca (ELF) and translanguaging belong to the hybrid orientation. Kubota's is arguably the clearest explanation of why some scholars have considered these to be opposing views, and why some in the hybridity end of the spectrum have, I believe unfairly, claimed that the alleged perception of boundaries within the pluralist view signifies a retrograde move, almost like a new monolingual/native speaker paradigm, concerned with not accepting the alleged greater fluidity of the hybrid paradigm.

In my view, nothing could be further from the truth. World Englishes scholars, many of whom work with sociolinguistic concepts such as code-switching, recognize the existence of nation states in their practice because that construction impacts the lives of those living in the "real world," outside of our academic-linguistic discussions. Everyday people utilize those social concepts too and are socially judged on the bases of them. By the same token, these scholars acknowledge the construct of distinct languages because people who are not "in the know" regarding our discussions, communicate in those terms. I do not believe that many within the pluralist orientation would claim that the borders between these constructions are not porous and changing all the time or that there is not great fluidity of form that transcends geographical, time, and language lines: this is the very *raison d'etre* of a discipline such as world Englishes. Yet, they appreciate that when acting and interacting in the world, people are asked questions about those constructions, or about "languages" they speak, about linguistic attitudes they encounter depending on the languages and varieties others perceive them to be using. They also signal membership through reliance on the concept of different languages. It would not work for a language student to arrive at a language institute and say, "I'm here to access all of my linguistic repertoire" (which they would in certain terms do, however unaware); for practical purposes, they would have to state, "I'm here to learn German" or "I would like to have conversation classes in English." By the same token, an Argentine in New York, upon seeing a potential compatriot might approach them in English and ask "Do you speak Spanish?" which does not mean such an abstract concept as "Spanish" can in reality be pinned down to a limited number of linguistic elements in common: there is a tacit agreement that the "codes" these individuals share are similar enough to be acknowledged as such. These are shortcuts to a complex reality of multilingualism and multiliteracy which is increasingly the reality of all of our lives, to a greater or smaller degree, but which is also punctuated by references to "modern" concrete concepts.

In sum, the two views, pluralist and hybrid, seem to have too much in common for the problematization that arises when scholars try to separate them. Concepts such as world Englishes and code-mixing/switching already have a lot of space for what has become known as ELF, translanguaging, and codemeshing. There is nothing in those former abstractions that says language boundaries are anything but human constructions and systematizations to facilitate what our brain likes to do, which is to categorize to learn. Some of these confabulations end up seemingly creating a problem that does not exist for the sake of solving it, whereas there are crucial, real problems in the world—problems of access, linguistic prejudice, lack of literacies—to be addressed.

In the meantime, one of Kubota's most enlightened commentaries is an important critique of the direction our discussion of hybridity/pluralism has taken in its disregard for ideas of monolingualism and related concepts in the real world. She writes,

> Hybridity and related notions are neither neutral nor apolitical; they involve contextual and relational arrangements of power. Without addressing power and ideology, advocacy of multi/plural approaches and hybridity in language use can become complicit with domination and will fail to solve real problems. Furthermore, when our intellectual engagement becomes entrenched in the popularity of the multi/plural turn, we may lose sight of the persistent demand for monolingualism and linguistic purism in various locations as well as Anglocentrism and English-only ideologies in many non-English–dominant neoliberal societies.
>
> *(p. 9)*

About a decade ago, I had a real-world lesson on that very idea. I was giving a keynote address in Brazil, my country of birth, speaking of how important it was to be a language teacher and how we should all be very proud of the varieties we used, whatever they were. After the well-received talk, there was a reception, during which a local teacher very politely but also very astutely pointed out to me that it was easy for me to say that, given that I spoke "such nice American English" (a variety much prized in Brazil). That meaningful insight taught me something that is well represented in Kubota's (2014, p. 8) discussion and that we should all be mindful of, namely that "[p]ostcolonial theory, which favors Eurocentric textual analysis and European theorists but overlooks social, economic, and political struggles experienced by the underprivileged, creates a privileged location." In my eagerness to stand in solidarity with those teachers, I had failed to recognize my own position of linguistic privilege and the privileged location from which I was speaking.

Multiliteracies pedagogy

A pedagogy then for a "multi" writing classroom has to recognize the contributions of pluralistic and hybrid views while not disregarding the many pressures in the real world that cause writers to be in a position of tension between their diverse ideals and the institutional forces of monolingualism and standardization that still exist (and maybe always will).

The changes the world has been faced with in the twenty-first century were foreshadowed by the visionary work of the New London Group, whose conclusions—derived from the conversation during a week-long gathering in 1994—are described in, for example, Cazden, Cope, Fairclough, Gee, Kalantzis, and Kress (1996), and in several related publications. In this article, readers will find the basis of the Group's work on multiliteracies and the relation between those concepts, citizenship, and critical thinking. Three important issues are discussed here: the relationship between changing social dynamics and the need for multiliteracies, the advantages of a multiliteracies approach over traditional ones, and an appreciation of how multiliteracies relate to access.

The Group makes the argument that changes in how we make meaning at present—through not only written and oral texts but also the integration of video, audio, and other forms of interconnected and combined communication—necessitate a theory and a practice that is equally multimodal, multi-genre and consequently multi-literate.

A description is offered of how in a world where the public and private, the global and the local, the diverse and the specific are always at play, traditional ways of knowing and learning might rely on a sense of separation that does not exist in practice in our interactions. The authors explain that "[e]ffective citizenship and productive work now require that we interact effectively using multiple languages, multiple Englishes, and communication patterns that more frequently cross cultural, community, and national boundaries" (p. 64).

A conversation follows, centered on the ideas that there are two goals to literacy and how multiliteracies help students reach them both: the first refers to the creation of access to the ever-changing language of work, community, and power itself and the second relates to how one engages critically with these elements to forge their own "social futures" (p. 60).

That seminal article contains a theoretical discussion and therefore the elements outlined here do not lend themselves to a consideration of the questions, methods, and results of an empirical study. However, the farsighted nature of the work and the fact that it brings together social elements (i.e., the design of social futures), literacy ones, as well as an appreciation of world Englishes makes it necessary reading for a variety of professionals interested in education and language studies and those who would like to conduct classroom research, especially when it comes to students understanding and incorporating the elements of literacy that will make them succeed and be the actors of their own futures.

The implications and the reach of the work are noteworthy. It has become practically impossible to talk about literacy without using its plural form "literacies" and more specifically "multiliteracies" much like an awareness of the diversity and variety within English makes it difficult to refer to it as anything other than its plural form "Englishes," and more specifically "world Englishes."

A quote from work by two original members of the New London Group (Cope and Kalantzis, 2009) makes a case for the multiplicity of Englishes that need to be taken into consideration if the classroom is to fulfill its role of preparing students for dynamic interactions with users of different varieties. They write:

> For all the signs that English was becoming a world language, it was also diverging into multiple Englishes. Whereas traditional literacy curriculum was taught to a singular standard (grammar, the literary canon, standard national forms of the language), the everyday experience of meaning making was increasingly one of negotiating discourse differences. A pedagogy of Multiliteracies would need to address this as a fundamental aspect of contemporary teaching and learning.
>
> *(pp. 165–166)*

As it is clear from this quote, an understanding of language as necessarily dynamic and diverse is part of the core beliefs of both world Englishes and a pedagogy of multiliteracies. Thus, in this chapter, I suggest that we conduct WE classroom research (action research, diagnostic research, as well as traditional empirical research) in the writing classroom to try and find out if this goal of making students aware of the need of addressing multiple Englishes and the tenuous line between them is indeed being reached. World Englishes provides an ideal paradigm in which the concept of "multi" is in operation at all times. World Englishes is multi-Englishes and multi-varieties (also within the same person, where the idiolect is realized in a dynamic multilect form). World Englishes is multi-domain (e.g., family, employment, education) and multi-function (e.g., imaginative, regulative), multi-circle (inner, outer, expanding and increasingly the three together in digital communications, a realm that is also very important within a pedagogy of multiliteracies). Therefore, I believe the two orientations, WE and multiliteracies, to be in tandem and when combined, provide a great site for world Englishes and applied linguistics scholarship and learning.

The concept of multiliteracies, as postulated by the New London Group, involves two main aspects of the "multi"—a plurality of communication channels and/or media, and the plurality represented by linguistic and cultural diversity (Cope and Kalantzis, 2000). Even at a time when multimedia and multimodal communications were not yet what they are today, the Group already had the insight that "new communication media are reshaping the way we use language" (6) and an awareness that the successful teaching of literacy would involve a dynamic model that took into account meaning that was linguistic, audio, visual, spatial, gestural, and/or multimodal, that is, a combination of any of the five (as opposed to a purely linguistic form of literacy). Members of the New London Group (again, Cope and Kalantzis, 2000) were also aware of the multiplicity in Englishes, as evidenced by the following reflection:

> At the same time as it is becoming a *lingua mundi*, a world language, and a *lingua franca*, a common language of global commerce, media and politics, English is also breaking into multiple and increasingly differentiated Englishes.
>
> *(p. 6)*

Notice that the use of *lingua franca* by the Group is akin to that of most world Englishes scholars and different from the use by most EFL proponents (more about this later in this chapter; see also Chapter 7 on corpus linguistics). Given these commonalities, it seems intuitive to expect that elements of a pedagogy of multiliteracies make their way into the WE classroom, especially in classes that focus on writing. These can be environments where a pedagogy that recognizes aspects of the "multi" is practiced and where a combined methodology of survey and journal-entry analysis could provide valuable insight.

This in not to say that using surveys and journals is an approach that works universally. If the goal of the research project were to learn whether students had indeed developed multiliteracies skills, it would be best to investigate by applying pre- and post-instruction instruments which would address the actual use of Englishes in a variety of communities and media. It would be advisable that the instrument address oral and written modes of communication, as well as the intersection between the written word and visual texts. Finally, it would be advisable to design an instrument able to measure students' understanding of the dynamic and ever-changing nature of language by offering real lifelike situations of communication that were multimodal in their own natures and ask students to perform linguistic tasks within those modes and media. For that kind of research, analysis of surveys and journal entries might not be the best method.

Pluralization in the composition classroom

Changing understandings of the role of different varieties of English among members of different speech communities necessitate a reflection on issues of prescriptivism in such environments as academic writing and thus require a consideration and possible incorporation of features of varieties other than a "standard" one in academic texts. Canagarajah (2006) wonders what the "textual and pedagogical spaces are for world Englishes in academic writing" (p. 586) as well as how diversity in English varieties can be accommodated in academic writing. He argues that given the communicative needs of students who are producing purposive texts in a variety of media across traditional linguistic divides, a classroom model in academic writing based on a monolithic set of "native" norms will not do. He posits that students, instead, "should strive for competence in a repertoire of codes and discourses" (p. 592). In this paradigm, errors, rules, and strategies acquire new meanings, with the first seen as a stage of linguistic development and the second being replaced by the third as a better path to "negotiate the norms relevant in diverse contexts"(p. 593).

Canagarajah further suggests codemeshing, the conflation of codes rather than a hierarchizing of them in the classroom. The author claims that vernacular expressions from different Englishes when used in a combination of codes will signal to multicultural, multilinguistic students that these forms belong in academic writing too. He points to traditions in many non-Western communities of being multilingual and multimodal (p. 600). Multilingual writers can affect voice and identity representation in their texts by including WE variation. In the same way, discussing grammatical choices "without prejudice or preconception" (p. 609) yields positive results and builds students' sense of agency.

Canagarajah argues that there is still a hierarchy of Englishes in the composition classroom, with certain varieties, which he calls Metropolitan Englishes (ME)—and we could assume that to mean "traditional" standard dialects—taking the most prestigious positions. Therefore, in this context, world Englishes will often be considered appropriate for more informal uses but will not usually be the variety for more formal ones. He discusses the possibility of intermingling different varieties by encouraging students to write early drafts in WE and using editing strategies to approximate ME in final versions (a practice advanced by Elbow, 2004), thus working toward the acceptance of multiple varieties while also making accommodations for the social and educational demands that currently hold ME as the model for academic production. He, however, narrates having had difficulty convincing students who use WE varieties to not carry them into latter drafts. His attempted solution to the problem is the use of *codemeshing*, the merging of different codes within the same text.

While this is a mindful alternative, and its merit is the inclusion of different Englishes and—as one would hope—their further integration in academic society, this is not a path without difficulty for many of the reasons that Kubota (2014) points out. For as long as there are gatekeepers of academic norm, there will likely be one variety, or a cluster of related varieties, which is considered standard for academic purposes in a given academic context. The same goes for further ventures into the publishing world, where agents, editors, and publishers have the authority to select texts written in the varieties they find pertinent and where not everyone (in fact, potentially very few) is versed in the sociolinguistics of multiple Englishes. While this is not reason enough to succumb to being mono-dialectal, it is enough to cause us to have to consider strategies that mediate such tensions and give the students the best chance to navigate this highly institutionalized environment while also having enough space for self-expression, pride in their varieties, and a sense of belonging to different speech communities.

Additionally, this view of the linguistic situation of WE takes for granted that other students, those whose varieties while not fully ME present similarities to those academic models, are not making genre-specific adaptations. That is, even if ME-approximating informal varieties are not, in terms of a continuum, as far from the academically endorsed varieties as some WE varieties are, students are still having to negotiate the place and the degree of use of home varieties and out-of-classroom varieties, which strengthens the argument for negotiation and strategic decision-making regarding when and where to include variations from a prescribed norm for all students.

Finally, it is important to consider intelligibility. While WE varieties develop organically, differently, and legitimately to address the communicative and affective needs of the communities they serve, when it comes to wider communication and communication across varieties, we are also negotiating understanding and nuances of meaning that can complicate the matter of language choice. There is no easy solution in this case, but with thought-out strategies we can go a long way in helping students figure out the best balance between autonomy/self-expression and standardization for communicative purposes when they craft their texts.

English as an academic language

Bolton and Kuteeva (2012) set out to investigate the use of English for academic purposes in a Swedish university. The idea was to provide students and academic staff with a questionnaire regarding some aspects of English use in academic settings in the country. The researchers collected 668 academic-staff responses and 4,524 students replies which aimed to illuminate how the use of English varies between the undergraduate and graduate level, what some of the patterns of use of English across different areas are and what some of the student and staff attitudes toward the use of English in education in Sweden could be.

Questionnaires were filled out by students and academic staff. The questionnaires were made available online and contained 41 questions for students and 59 questions for staff. Seventy-five percent of the students reported Swedish as their first language. A balance of female and male respondents that was proportional to the makeup of the student body as a whole was achieved. Researchers highlight the limitations of self-reported data.

General results indicate that respondents consider English to be a pragmatic choice in the sciences and best described as an additional language in the humanities. In the sciences, many lectures are given in English while in the humanities more seminars use English as the medium. Students made note of what they considered to be poor English-language skills of some of the academic staff while the staff indicated not having a lot of difficulty with English. Use of English was more pronounced in the graduate level as compared to the undergraduate level. Students feel confused when it came to taking examinations in Swedish in cases where the language of instruction was English When asked whether or not English was a threat to Swedish, students were divided. Staff disagreed with the premise that English was a disadvantage as a medium of instruction at the university. In the end, English is considered a lingua franca of education.

The results of the questionnaires reveal the complexities that surround the choice of a language of instruction and the competing demands to use a language that helps students be a part of an international community while at the same time remaining accessible to their population and considering the existing and potential language skills of the faculty. They also point to some inconsistencies regarding individuals seeing English as a likely threat to Swedish but at the same time wanting that it be part of their educational and professional lives.

Results of the survey highlight the importance of discussing medium of instruction and the possible ramifications of these choices. They also indicate that analyses of the macro-level and the micro-level can reveal tensions that need to be addressed on a recurrent basis.

One of the interesting aspects of the inclusion of this study here is that, when taken into consideration together with Canagarajah's article above, it points to several tensions relating to the use of English in academic environments, given the present-day diversity of Englishes and other languages in those milieus. That is, while Canagarajah suggests that students be encouraged to codemesh elements of different varieties within their academic English use—which is healthy if one is considering linguistic identity and other affective elements of language use—such a choice is made more complex by the realization that English tends to be used as an academic lingua franca, one that needs a certain degree of coincidence to be understood across speech-community boundaries. In this respect, the use of English itself already brings complexities to academic environments, such as preparedness of the student body and academic staff, transitions and switching between English and Swedish, and attitudes toward English in the macro and micro-level (which do not always coincide). If one adds, the potential inclusion of students' idiolectal variation, the complexity is even greater.

While one of the downsides of many forms of prescriptivism is the curbing down of individual expression and the potential for a hierarchizing of varieties (which can and does lead to linguistic prejudice in many situations), another more pragmatic function exists: that of working toward a code that is, in general, intelligible to a great number of people.

With our keeping that in mind, it might be important to consider the different uses of students' varieties in academic environments with a view of both valuing those varieties and at the same time allowing students to expand their existing repertoire so that they can make pragmatic decisions based on the context of use. Ultimately, we want to prepare students for an encounter with prescriptivism and with several gatekeepers who might know nothing about different Englishes and their functions. We can, at the same time, reaffirm to students that all varieties actively used by speech communities are functional, internally rule-governed, and grammatically viable.

Linguistic ecology and the classroom

Siemund, Schulz, and Schweinberger (2014) set out to establish the individual linguistic ecology of Singaporean university students through a language-background questionnaire. Interviews were held with 300 university/polytechnic students who helped provide a clearer picture of language use in the country. This is a complex environment, with English and Chinese existing in a continuum, which in the first case ranges from a more "standard" variety to Singlish (a creole) and in the second has Mandarin (an official language) alongside different dialects of Chinese. The situation of Malay is not much different. Yet, these dynamics exist against the backdrop of governmental attempts to curb linguistic diversity. The researchers wanted to find out what languages are part of the linguistic background of students in these university and polytechnic environments, what some differences are in the use of multiple languages at university and polytechnic and university environments, what attitudes students hold toward Singlish and other languages, and what the future may hold for languages in Singapore.

To answer these questions, the researchers created a structured questionnaire that reflected the 15 most-used questions in language background questionnaires and added questions about language used in different situations. In the end, the questions pointed to a general linguistic background profile, a language use description, educational and socio-economic background, and a language attitude profile. The most significant section of the questionnaire referred to language use and included information on whom students use particular languages with.

Results showed that university and polytechnic students are mostly bilingual or trilingual, with a significant portion also using four languages. Monolingualism is rare. The most common combination is English and a mother tongue. According to the authors, "Singapore is developing into a multilingual society of mainly bilingual speakers" (p. 357). The research also established that for these populations, bilingualism is the most common pattern for university students while trilingualism is the most common among polytechnic students. Proficiency in Malay is also more common among polytechnic students. The number of languages used correlates with self-perceptions about linguistic ability: the more languages a student uses the higher they rank their linguistic ability.

Finally, the authors predict a rise in the status of Mandarin Chinese that can in the future come to match that of English. They also predict that Singlish will continue to be a "solidarity language" given how Singaporeans look at it favorably and derive a sense of identity from it.

While this study offers a glimpse at a specialized, particular population of Singaporean students, the results lead us to some interesting questions about the use of English around the world and its dynamics in academic settings. First of all, English has retained the status of a language of education even in environments where several competing languages are present. The fact that polytechnic students tend to use the most languages might indicate their awareness of the more pragmatic aspects of English use, one that we cannot, as researchers, forget when we speak of motivations for language learners and the role of academic writing in English.

Despite the worldwide dynamics of English, it is important to investigate local ecologies so that pedagogical decisions can be made on the basis of the specific needs of local communities.

The articles discussed here would not necessarily and intuitively be brought together in many reviews. They cover very broad themes and various facets of language use in the classroom and of conducting research with and relevant to students. However, the reason why I wanted to bring them together is to highlight the incredible complexity and multilayered linguistic experience that students now have in our *glocalized* (Robertson, 1995), multi-literate, multimodal, and fragmented experience of English and other languages. This is a reality that causes us to have to rethink traditional ways of seeing learning, language use, partitions such as native language and second language, concepts such as proficiency and the very future of world Englishes and other languages.

These complexities likely also cause us to revisit the viability (or not) of traditional forms of learning, those designed with twentieth-century concrete and patterned modes of interaction and work. As we advance further into the twenty-first century, we witness more and more learning environments that break the barriers, both physical and abstract, of classroom walls (many more have expansive spaces with a variety of sitting and standing arrangements) and walls between disciplines and learning modes.

The case of Singaporean students evidences how rich and varied the ecology of languages in certain parts of the world can be, and to a great degree this complex, layered situation is the norm rather than the exception.

Two of the articles highlighted here focus on pragmatism and the practical uses of Englishes in the world, and two others focus on the "multi": a plurality of experiences with language, modes of learning, and hybrid texts, whose very makeup needs to be negotiated given practical considerations. Those practical considerations, in turn, are never too far removed from attitudes toward different languages and issues of identity, which have to then be at the forefront of our consideration when we design curriculum and conduct classroom research.

Given all of these complexities, the global and the local, the general language dynamics and the specific contexts of learning, our pedagogical and research practices need to be constantly revisited and further understood. In the next two sections, after a brief conclusion, I offer a sample questionnaire to start the conversation with the students and then commentary on works that can offer pedagogical and research tools to move this project forward.

Conclusion

Guided by a compelling research question, I would like to next consider the kinds of items that could potentially shed light onto the attitudes and perceptions (and even just general awareness) students might hold (or not) regarding different varieties of English and multiliteracies in a classroom research project as well as pedagogical/methodological questions and expectations instructors might have. This can be done more informally, to help shape curriculum, or more formally, as part of a larger classroom research project. For example, regarding interest in multiliteracies and WE, I might pursue the question, "What kind of understanding of the concepts 'multiliteracies,' 'applied linguistics,' and 'world Englishes' do students possess?" To start addressing that question, I might use the following questionnaire:

a. Which of the following is more important when you try to successfully communicate across Englishes? (choose two)
   ( ) Knowing grammar
   ( ) Practicing strategies for when I don't know exactly what to say
   ( ) Having clear pronunciation
   ( ) Knowing linguistic conventions
   ( ) Having good comprehension skills
   ( ) Two or more of the above (Which? ______________________________)
   ( ) All of the above
b. If I was having trouble with a particular situation of communication, I believe my instructor in this class would recommend that I (choose one)
   ( ) Focus on the language itself
   ( ) Focus on the nonverbal communication (e.g., body language, facial expression)
   ( ) Focus on the context of communication
   ( ) Focus on a few of the above (Which? ______________________________)
   ( ) Focus on a combination of all of the above

c. When it comes to varieties of English in the classroom, I believe I am being exposed to (choose one)
( ) One variety (Which? ______________________________)
( ) Up to three varieties (for example, ______________________)
( ) Several varieties (for example, ________________________)
( ) What are varieties?
( ) I don't know which

d. I would consider myself to be multi-literate if I could (choose as many as you like)
( ) Communicate across varieties of language and using different media
( ) Understand different literary genres
( ) "Read" visual texts alongside written ones
( ) Engage with digital texts
( ) Other ______________________________
( ) All of the above
( ) Some of the above

e. What kinds of tasks and activities do you believe have helped you develop multiliteracies and an awareness of other Englishes?
____
____

f. How much awareness of multiliteracies do you believe your classmates have? (choose one)
( ) I believe they know the word but not necessarily what it entails
( ) I believe they know a bit about it but there is a lot to learn
( ) I believe they think they know a lot, but I don't think it is true
( ) I believe most people in the digital age know about it well
( ) I believe they don't know about it at all
( ) Other ______________________________

g. How could the concept of multiliteracies help a person navigate different Englishes?
____
____

h. When you think of linguistics what are some of the first associations that come to mind? Select the two primary ones.
( ) Grammar and language mistakes
( ) Rules about language
( ) Knowing many languages
( ) Understanding why, how and who uses language(s)
( ) I don't really think about it
( ) Other ______________________________

i. How important it is for you to be multilingual? (choose one)
( ) Somewhat important
( ) Very important
( ) Not important at all
( ) I never thought about that
Why? ______________________________

j. Which of the following more closely describes your view of English native-speaker accents? (choose one)

( ) If I had a native-English accent, I would have better opportunities
( ) I prefer to have my accent because it is my own
( ) Native-English accents represent better status
( ) Native-English accents are just like any other accent
( ) I have a native-English accent and I don't think much about it
( ) I have a native-English accent and believe there are benefits to that
( ) Other: ______________________________

Some of these questions can also be the subject of student journals (refer to Chapter 11 for information on using journals). I usually aim for two to three pages in which the student is free to explore the connection and applicability of classroom contexts to their own lives or to the world at large. Journal entries in this case focus more on the students' reflection than on the incorporation of ideas from the established literature. Of course, it goes without saying that in the case of journals used for research purposes (as well as everything else), ethical treatment of the subjects as well as the material is a must. That includes seeking informed consent for research use and utilization of the texts only for the intended purposes.

Some ideas of questions for journal tasks include:

1. What surprised you the most about the discussions on multiliteracies, linguistics, and world Englishes?
2. Select one aspect of multiliteracies work and discuss its relevance in the real world.
3. What are some of the most interesting aspects of world Englishes and what have you learned from studying them?
4. What are some controversies regarding the selection of varieties and how do they impact a pedagogy of multiliteracies?
5. What are some realms of language use where you believe people are still expected to conform to native-speakers norms?
6. What aspect of the "multi" is the most interesting to you? Provide real-life examples that support your point of view.
7. What do pluralist and hybrid views of language diversity have in common? How can that combination be used to empower students and users of language?

How to address WE and the multi: A few resources on methodology

The resources and approaches to addressing WE are as varied as the elements of the paradigm itself. In order to start incorporating this and other aspects of applied linguistics to a composition classroom, the following resources can be counted on. Any decisions on research methodology needs to take into consideration the many moving parts that are in operation within the paradigm and the many areas of study (TESOL, applied linguistics, sociolinguistics, language planning) that inform it.

In Berns's (2013) summary and discussion of research methods in WE, we find information on WE scholars and their works, and we learn about different approaches to WE studies, which include "the sociology of language" (p. 4), "critical linguistics" (p. 4), and "English studies" (p. 2) among others.

A review of pedagogical reasons for using journal writing in classroom-based activities (which can include research) can be found in Hettich (1990). Although this is an almost thirty-year-old text, its reading allows us to revisit the goals of journal writing to see if it is still fulfilling its promise, and, in case it is not, consider ways of updating the practice (e.g., though vlogs, blogs, and other forms of electronic memory-keeping, which, once again, speak to several aspects of the "multi").

In Friedrich (2000), I conducted a survey of perceptions of Brazilian learners of English regarding both the pragmatic reasons for studying and the attitudes they held toward different varieties and functions. It became clear at the time that the students did not have much awareness of world Englishes beyond American and British varieties. It would be interesting to revisit the topic in that particular context as well as establish new research in other places to see if our virtual lives have contributed to a change in perspective. The text should also help readers decide if using surveys with students is right for their research.

In Matsuda and Friedrich (2012), we set out to discuss the intricacies of selecting an instructional variety of English and to suggest which approach might work best in different environments. Classroom research can be a part of the process of understanding what instructional models students need and of creating an environment where, beyond an instructional variety, students are exposed to a number of different Englishes regularly.

Percillier and Paulin (2017) compiled a corpus of literary works through which they study localized features of English and the reasons (e.g., symbolic) for their incorporation. Access to texts displaying features of different Englishes can be a starting point for a discussion with students about the place of their own varieties in the texts that they compose in academia and beyond.

In Friedrich and Matsuda (2010), we made an effort to demonstrate how important it is to study different paradigms and frameworks and to understand the construction of different concepts in these sometimes parallel but not merged orientations. More specifically, the ELF paradigm differs significantly from WE historical development although in recent years, authors oftentimes blend concepts and terms as if the development of the theoretical orientations was not that important. I urge anyone who would like to engage in WE research to understand the paradigm first. Of course, new developments and new ideas, some of which might question existing assumptions are sure to come: that is part of the dynamics through which a field moves forward, and I am an advocate for interdisciplinary approaches. Nevertheless, those challenges and innovations should come after a careful rather than a cursory consideration of what came before. Please look to the references below for further titles on ELF.

Finally, Bolton (2005) is a seminal work on the central issues in world Englishes and should inform researchers interested in advancing classroom research, as well as other forms of WE investigations. The article contains information on major developments and trends in WE in the preceding 25 years, and therefore should be considered by those interested in understanding how to move the discipline forward with solid research, based on sound methodology.

Questions and ideas for further research

1. What do side-by-side analyses of world Englishes and English as a lingua franca scholarship reveal about their nature and compatibility?
2. What are some other aspects of the "multi" that need research attention at the moment?
3. What would a syllabus and other materials for a world-Englishes based composition classroom look like?
4. How have instructors and researchers reconciled the need for pedagogies that emphasize the "multi" while acknowledging the pressures of so-called standard varieties?
5. What does a critical-applied-linguistics analysis of the "typical" university composition classroom in a particular environment (a country, a region, a city, an institution) reveal?
6. What other resources are available for instructions for further incorporating these pedagogies and research methodologies to classroom practice and forms of action and diagnostic research?

Works cited and further reading

Berns, M. (2009). English as a lingua franca and English in Europe. *World Englishes, 28*(2), 192–199.

Berns, M. (2013). Research methods in WE. In Chapelle, C. A. (Ed.). *The Encyclopedia of Applied Linguistics*. Hoboken: Blackwell Publishing.

Berns, M. (2017). The WE family tree: Views on its vitality and viability, Panel presented at the *IAWE International Conference*. Syracuse, NY. July 1, 2017.

Bolin, A., and Khramitsova, I. (2005). Using student journals to stimulate authentic learning: Balancing Bloom's cognitive and affective domains. *Teaching of Psychology, 32*(3), 154–159.

Bolton, K. (2005). Where WE stands: Approaches, issues and debate in world Englishes. *World Englishes, 24*(1), 69–83.

Bolton, K., and Kuteeva, M. (2012) English as an academic language at a Swedish university: Parallel language use and the 'threat' of English. *Journal of Multilingual and Multicultural Development, 33*(5), 429–447.

Canagarajah, A. S. (2006). The place of world Englishes in composition: Pluralization continued. *College Composition and Communication, 57*(4), 586–610.

Canagarajah, S. (2007). The ecology of global English. *International Multilingual Research Journal, 1*(2), 89–100.

Cazden, C., Cope, B., Fairclough, N., Gee, J., Kalantzis, M., and Kress, G. 1996. A pedagogy of multiliteracies: Designing social futures. *Harvard Educational Review, 66*(1), 60–92.

Cope, B., and Kalantzis, M. (2000). Introduction: Multiliteracies—the beginning of a new idea. In The New London Group, *Multiliteracies: Literacy learning and the design of social futures.* New York: Routledge.

Cope, B., and Kalantzis, M. (2009). "Multiliteracies:" New literacies, new learning. *Pedagogies: An International Journal. 4*(3), 164–195.

Davies, A. (2008). We are not quite sure what ELF is. *Language Assessment Quarterly. 5*(4), 360–364.

Elbow, P. (2004) Should Students Write in Non-mainstream Varieties of English? Using orality to reframe the question. Paper Presented at the CCCC Convention. San Antonio, March, 25.

Friedrich, P. (2000). English in Brazil: Functions and attitudes. *World Englishes, 19*(2), 215–223.

Friedrich, P. (2008). 'I want to be part of the club': Raising awareness of bilingualism and second language writing among monolingual users of English. In Friedrich, P. (Ed.), *Teaching academic writing* (pp. 177–191). London: Bloomsbury Publishing.

Friedrich, P. (2016 ed.). *English for diplomatic purposes.* Bristol: Multilingual Matters.

Friedrich, P., and Diniz de Figueiredo, E. H. (2016). *The sociolinguistics of digital Englishes.* London: Routledge.

Friedrich, P., and Matsuda A. (2010). When five words are not enough: A conceptual and terminological discussion of English as a lingua franca. *International Multilingual Research Journal, 4*(1), 20–30.

Hamid, O. (2014). World Englishes in international proficiency tests, *33*(2), 263–277.

Hettich, P. (1990). Journal writing: Old fare or nouvelle cuisine? *Teaching of Psychology, 17*(1), 36–39.

Hino, N. (2012). Endonormative models of EIL for the expanding circle. In Matsuda, A. *Principles and practices of teaching English as an international language* (pp. 28–43). Bristol: Multilingual Matters.

Jenkins, J. (2007). *English as a lingua franca: Attitude and identity.* Oxford: Oxford University Press.

Kachru, B. (1992). World Englishes: Approaches, issues and resources. *Language Teaching, 25*(1), 1–14.

Kolln, M., and Gray, L. S. (2012). *Rhetorical grammar: Grammatical choices, rhetorical effects.* NY: Pearson.

Kubota, R. (2014). The multi/plural turn, postcolonial theory, and neoliberal multiculturalism: Complicities and implications for applied linguistics. *Applied Linguistics, 2014,* 1–22.

Liddicoat, A. J., and Taylor-Leech, K. (2014). Micro language planning formultilingual education: Agency in local contexts. *Current Issues in Language Planning, 15*(3), 237–244.

Matsuda, A., and Friedrich, P. (2012). Selecting an instructional variety for an EIL curriculum. In Matsuda, A. (Ed.), *Principles and practices of teaching English as an international language* (pp. 17–29). Bristol: Multilingual Matters.

Percillier, M, and Paulin, C (2017). A corpus-based investigation of world Englishes in literature. *World Englishes, 36*(1), 127–147.

Robertson, R. (1995). Glocalization: Time-space and homogeneity-heterogeneity. In Featherstone, M., Lash, S., and Robertson, R. (Eds.), *Global Modernities* (pp. 25–44). London: Sage Publications.

Seidlhofer, B. (2005). English as a lingua franca. *ELT Journal, 59*(4), 339–341.

Siemund, P., Schulz, M. E., and Schweinberger, M. (2014). Studying the linguistic ecology of Singapore: A comparison of college and university students. *World Englishes, 33*(3), 340–362.

INDEX